AN AUTOETHNOGRAPHY ON THE REASONS FOR MIXING

IDENTITIES

by

Cecilia Leal-Covey

Copyright 2015

A Dissertation Presented in Partial Fulfillment

of the Requirements for the Degree

Doctor of Education in Educational Leadership

University of Phoenix

Copyright Statement

This copy of the dissertation has been supplied on condition that anyone who consults it is understood to recognize that its copyright rests with its author and that no quotation from the dissertation and no information derived from it may be published without the author's prior consent.

Notes from author

For better online readability, the author removed the personal photographs used in Photovoice and the data collected from the dissertation. For more information about the photographs and data collected, feel free to contact the author at drlealcovey@gmail.com

ABSTRACT

The purpose of this study was to explore why some people with multiple cultures might turn into cultural chameleons to fit in or to adjust to a different culture. I explored my cultural experiences compared to the academic literature on disability, gender, and ethnicity. The study included qualitative analytic autoethnography inquiry, the Labovian life story interview, and photovoice, and the intersectionality, multiple cultural identities, and social categorization theories as combined framework. The study was an approach to illustrate my personal perspective and to provide a process to document my findings. The findings revealed 14 themes from the data and analysis of the Labovian life story, photovoice, complete-member researcher, and the commitment to theoretical analysis using NVivo10 software. Some of the findings revealed were burnout, doubt, trapped, vulnerable, boxed, betrayed, deceived, invisible, resist, and voiceless. The findings made significant contributions to the literature and revealed that mixing behaviors might develop based on the motives of contingency created by cognitive ambiguity across the powers of cultural difference. It also added to the growing literatures of cultural chameleon behavior, intersectionality, multicultural identities, disability, gender, ethnicity, and racial and ethnic minority as whole groups. I shared my cultural experiences, hoping readers could understand the reasons some people with multiple cultures might turn into cultural chameleons to fit in or to adjust to a different culture.

DEDICATION

To my husband Russell, to my father Jose, to my brothers Daniel and Jose, to my sister-in-law Sherry, to my cousin Mercedes, and to my friends and relatives, whose endless encouragement, support, and persistence provided me the determination needed to continue my journey. Your trust in me never failed. Thanks for being there for me, for being my family. Especially to my mother Rosa, who is watching me from somewhere next to God, for pushing me to emigrate to find the great soul inside of me and my go-getter persona. Gracias "Jefa!" Thanks also to Misty, Bootsie, Oliverto, Pepe, Annabelle, and Remy, my kids (dogs), for listening to me and for your unconditional love. Finally, I dedicate this dissertation to people with multiple cultures who turn into cultural chameleons to protect their inner self to follow a chosen pathway.

ACKNOWLEDGMENTS

First, thank you God for providing me with who I am and with the things I can or cannot do. Thanks for letting me be an inspiration to myself and for allowing my representation of multiple cultures to understand more than my eyes can perceive. I am blessed, thank you. I have not achieved this objective alone. Several people supported, led, challenged, reassured, pushed, and encouraged me through this journey; please forgive me if I missed someone. I thank my dissertation chair, Dr. Burkhalter, for her extraordinary patience, understanding, guidance, inspiration, and scholarly discipline and for helping me to discover this silent untraditional study called autoethnography. Thank you.

I thank my dissertation committee members, Dr. Green (1979-2014), Dr. Shaheen, and Dr. Ramos, for their patience and unconditional support. I thank the Department of Employment, Training, and Rehabilitation in Reno, Nevada, because it indirectly made my education possible. The Department of Employment, Training, and Rehabilitation has been a strong support for me, and I know it will always be. Finally, I thank the Land of Opportunity for showing me that ¡*Sí se puede!* and for allowing me to be a citizen of the United States of America, positively turning my life around. Thank you. I also want to thank Mexico for letting me be an Orgullo Hispano in America and to the Distrito Federal for inspiring me to become an Orgullo Chilango ¡Orale!

TABLE OF CONTENTS

LIST OF TABLES

LIST OF FIGURES

Chapter 1

Introduction

The most common definition of mixing identities is a behavior demonstrated by somebody who is dishonest, has low self-esteem, or perhaps has a mental health issue (Ungvari, Mullen, & Sandor, 2000). Less common definitions included mixing identities as a method to navigate cultural context, to cope with acculturation, as a multiple-self problem, identity demands, an expected norm behavior, or tension caused by dynamics between individuality and fitting in (Bazerman, Tenbrunsel, & Wade-Benzoni, 1998; Kreiner, Hollensbe, & Sheep, 2006; Lau, Yuen, & Chan, 2005; Saayman & Crafford, 2011; Torres & Rollock, 2009). These definitions also included the negative consequences of mixing identities as encountering conflicts within generations, obligations with families, social tensions, workforce identities, and inner contradictions of personal desires versus what should be done (Bazerman et al., 1998; Ekstedt & Fagerberg, 2005; Kreiner et al., 2006; Saayman & Crafford, 2011; Torres & Rollock, 2009; Tyrrell, 2010; see also Gardner, Gabriel, & Lee, 1999). Conscious of the common fallacy, of the different definitions, and of the possible consequences, I reflected within the study on my personal behavior of mixing identities. This qualitative analytic autoethnography involved determining if multicultural people are at greater risk of mixing identities.

A substantial amount of research on cultures and identities indicated the risk of mixing identities could stem from social influences, the acculturation process, doubts during cultural interactions, or pressures from multicultural environments (Barreto, Ellemers, Spears, & Shahinper, 2003; Chiao et al., 2010; Downie, Mageau, Koestner, & Liodden, 2006; Kiely, 2004; Mezzich, Ruiperez, Yoon, Liu, & Zapata-Vega, 2009; see also Gardner et al., 1999). Some other concerns that increase the risk of mixing identities included stereotyping, prejudice, rejecting social categorizations, willingness to relate to a categorized group, internalization, and the treatment received (Barreto & Ellemers, 2003; Bodenhausen, 2010). Border identity (Khosravi, 2007), social identities intersection, professional and social roles, or dominance patterns might be other influencers as well (Bodenhausen, 2010; Ngunjiri, Hernandez, & Heewon, 2010; Vivero & Jenkins, 1999). Emotional distress, illnesses, stress, depression, cultural shock, burnout, and acculturative stress were problems associated with mixing identities (Hayes, Chun-Kennedy, Edens, & Locke, 2011; Lau et al., 2005; Mezzich et al., 2009; Stamm, Stamm, Hudnall, & Higson-Smith, 2004).

I relate to the risk of mixing identities. I have experienced the effects of negotiating identities to fit in or to adjust to different cultures as a multicultural woman with disabilities who has lived in the United States since 1989. This study involved exploring the concept of mixing identities as a behavior some multicultural people who represent many social classifications might adopt to fit in or to adjust to different cultures. Understanding the notion of adopting a behavior might be a step toward shifting and preventing the mistaken common definition of mixing identities.

Researcher Positionality and Motivation

To understand the motives why I pursued the topic of mixing identities for my dissertation, I needed to share some events in my multicultural life as a person with multiple cultures or multiple social classifications. My subjective experience as an individual with multiple cultures primarily initiated my interest in the reasons people with multiple cultures might turn into cultural chameleons, later related to its systematic and social scopes. My personal life experiences also molded my philosophy regarding why some people with multiple cultures might experience the need to mix identities during social interactions. This dissertation provided several opportunities to move from my internal experience to outward expression and worked to take readers inside themselves and ultimately out again. The test for this autoethnography was to evoke in readers the feeling that the shared experiences were authentic, believable, and possible (Denzin, 2013).

Background of the Problem

People have many cultures and are surrounded by different cultures. I am not any different. I am a multicultural person symbolizing several social classifications, but I struggle trying to explain that I am continually striving to fit in or to adjust to one or more cultures. As an immigrant woman who uses a wheelchair, I often encounter cultural interactions in which my physical disability, my ethnicity, or my gender becomes my only attribute as a person. I have met people who are resistant to the idea that mixing identities could be a behavior used to fit in or to adjust to different cultures.

As a person representing multiple cultures, I identify as a strong woman who stands on her own ground, who advocates for equality and human rights, and who supports communities in need. Although I am strongly aware of my individual beliefs, I am also aware that I struggle to fit in or adjust to different cultures. For many years, I questioned whether I mixed my identities, but I did not find any answers. After I became familiar with

2

the "cultural chameleon" (Briley, Morris, & Simonson, 2005, p. 351; Downie et al., 2006, p. 530) concept as a behavior for adjusting to and fitting in different cultures, I answered my own question. I was not sure what influenced me to behave as a cultural chameleon, but I had more questions, including why it was important to confirm whether I behaved as a cultural chameleon.

The answer was significant for several reasons. First, it was important because multicultural communities should be aware of and understand that cultural chameleon behavior could result from cultural tensions (Stamm et al., 2004). Second, it was important because understanding that mixing identities do not indicate a mental health disturbance might change some perceptions of behaviors in multicultural communities (see Hong, Morris, Chiu, & Benet-Martínez, 2000). Third, it was important because according to numerous scholars, people with multiple cultural identities could empathize with several and different cultures based on their shared identity knowledge (see Benet-Martínez & Haritatos, 2005; Hurd, 2012; Hong et al., 2000). Fourth, it was important because several scholars discussed that facing internalized struggles, pressures, problems with identities at work, and self-denials of personal needs could be adverse concerns of mixed identities (Bazerman et al., 1998; Kreiner et al., 2006; Lau et al., 2005; Saayman & Crafford, 2011; Torres & Rollock, 2009).

Finally, it was important because during my doctoral program, I discovered the cultural chameleon as a method to manage social interactions. People who do not have access to this evidence might find this autoethnography informative and revealing. I also perceived that in exploring my cultural experiences, I would be better able to understand the people around me as well as myself. People are different and have several socially developed identities (Hong et al., 2000; Linder, 2011).

The study included a combination of the theories of intersectionality, multiple cultural identities, and social categorizations as a guide to understand cultural chameleon behavior. I explored this topic from the perspective of an adult woman with a physical disability who emigrated from Mexico to the United States in 1989. Chapter 1 contains the statement of the problem and the purpose of the study. The chapter includes a discussion on the significance of the study, including its importance to leadership; the nature and scope of the study; the research questions; the theoretical frameworks; and the study assumptions, limitations, and delimitations. The chapter also includes practical definitions of the unusual or unfamiliar terms used throughout this study and a summary.

Statement of the Problem

A review of a substantial body of research revealed an increase in the number of people negotiating multiple cultures and indicated such negotiation causes conflicts and stress for multicultural people (Adam, Shirako, & Maddux, 2010; Constantine, 2002; Downie et al., 2006; Lynam & Cowley, 2007; Rodríguez-García, 2010). Investigating racism, sexism, ageism, and other forms of prejudice, exploring ethnic and racial minorities as whole groups; and researching immigration issues have generated more interest among researchers (Bodenhausen, 2010; Mich & Keillor, 2011; Milner, 2007; Qin, 2011; Rodríguez-García, 2010; Speicher, 2010). These studies were valuable in understanding multicultural concerns, but left unexplored individual perceptions on behaving during social situations. Little research exists regarding why some multicultural people might turn into cultural chameleons (Downie et al., 2006; Ungvari et al., 2000). This qualitative analytic autoethnography involved exploring and connecting my cultural experiences to the larger academic literature on disability, ethnicity, and gender, as multiple social classifications, to explore the factors influencing cultural chameleon behavior.

Purpose of the Study

The purpose of the study was to explore why some multicultural people might turn into cultural chameleons to fit in or to adjust to a different culture. The qualitative analytic autoethnography involved exploring the intersection of disability, ethnicity, and gender to understand cultural chameleon behavior that some multicultural people might adopt as a method to respond to conflict and stresses while adjusting to a different culture. Previous research on the behaviors of multicultural people indicated social influences and pressures by multicultural environments might influence a mixing identities behavior. The review of literature revealed a gap in studies discussing conflict and stresses as some of the reasons multicultural people might turn into cultural chameleons (Chiao et al., 2010; Downie et al., 2006; Kiely, 2004; Mezzich et al., 2009).

The research method for the study was the qualitative method, and analytic autoethnography was the research design. An autoethnography is a form of qualitative research combining autobiographic and ethnographic methods with roots in anthropology extending to some humanities, health, and social sciences. The research design might use auto-interviewing, auto-ethnography, and critical event approach to eliciting self-perceived worldview. The concepts of auto (self) and ethno (culture) define autoethnography, which

4

implies to writing about the self and its relationship to culture. According to numerous scholars, autoethnography includes the process of researching, writing to self-reference, and studying cultural situations. The process requires alternating between experiencing and examining a vulnerable self to observe and reveal the experience's broader context (Adams & Jones, 2011; Allen-Collinson, 2013; Badley, 2014; Berlak, 2005; Bochner, 2012; Boufoy-Bastick, 2004; Chang, 2008; Cohen, 2010; Denshire, 2014; Denzin, 2014; Ellis, 2004, 2007, 2008; Ellis & Bochner, 2000; Fassett & Warren, 2007; Hamilton, Smith, & Worthington, 2008; Kahl, 2011; Smith-Sullivan, 2008; Spry, 2001; Wall, 2006, 2008; Warren, 2009).

The qualitative research method enables researchers to achieve a deeper and more significant awareness to understand unfamiliar behaviors. Including how people perceive ideas, how they process information, how they make decisions, and how they process their lives (Badley, 2014; Barbour, 2008; Denshire, 2014; Ellis, 1991; Pohlert, 2008; Sin, 2010; Warren, 2009; see also Boufoy-Bastick, 2004). Denzin (2013) discussed, "Qualitative research is about making the world visible in ways that implement social justice goals" (p. 392). Analytic autoethnography as a research design permits the self and the writer to explain and to analyze personal cultural experiences to provoke positive change (Allbon, 2012; Anderson, 2006; Badley, 2014; Boufoy-Bastick, 2004; Denzin, 2003, 2014; Ellis, 1991, 2004; Ellis & Bochner, 2000; Giampietro, 2008; Pompper, 2010; Sambrook, Jones, & Doloriert, 2014; Spry, 2001; Warren, 2009).

Significance of the Study

Before deciding on the topic, I shared my idea with two people who self-identify as multicultural, and one replied, "A cultural chameleon is a mask! Are you saying that people have the right to have only one identity?" (J. Leal, personal communication, October 22, 2012). After discussing her future spouse's job responsibility of temporarily residing abroad, the second person stated, "I need to mentally prepare to live there" (M. Meilleur, personal communication, November 5, 2012), although she described cultural chameleon behavior as a form of denying personal identity. These two different perspectives combined with my experience trying to explain my need to mix identities when fitting in or adjusting to different cultures, motivated me to continue my idea for the study. The autoethnography involved exploring why some multicultural people might turn into cultural chameleons.

My qualitative analytic autoethnography might be significant to various professionals in different theoretical fields. Scholars researching the factors that affect the psychological

5

well-being, adaptation, coping skills, and acculturation of immigrants might find this study valuable. Hayes et al. (2011) noted a need for further research on silent identities, personal expression, and negotiation of identities to improve services to multicultural people. Hernandez (2009) recommended more research on the immigration experience among diverse people, and Rees and Pease (2007) indicated the need for further study on changes of identity and the impact of cultural change.

This qualitative analytic autoethnography might also be useful to scholars investigating different cross-cultural intersections, cross-cultural and social psychology on cultural identities, and acculturation (Alexander, 2014; S. Chen, Benet-Martínez, & Harris Bond, 2008; Cox, Vanden Berghe, Dewaele, & Vincke, 2010; Frank, Redstone Akresh, & Bo, 2010; Gómez, Huici, Seyle, & Swann, 2009). Scholars researching the theory of intersectionality might find this study useful because I used this theory as part of a lens to understand cultural chameleon behavior. In the research, I supported scholars' recommendations on how a multicultural person might conceptualize and enact social identities (Downie et al., 2006; Hurd, 2012).

Researchers also showed an interest in some of the struggles encountered by multicultural people. The scholars were from the health and social service culture, survivors of violence, the disability culture, and the judicial system culture disciplines (Cramer & Plummer, 2009; Schneider, 2011; Trahan, 2011). The autoethnography generated awareness and understanding to cultural chameleon behavior.

Significance of the Study to Knowledge

Chang (2007) indicated autoethnography as an excellent tool for researchers to understand themselves and others. Chang discussed autoethnography as appropriate to her teaching of multicultural education, a feeling required to prepare students to become cross-culturally sensitive and efficient educators for learners of diverse cultural backgrounds. Dyson (2007) discussed autoethnography as an empowering tool for educators and Shibata (2012) for school counselors.

Doloriert and Sambrook (2012) argued that autoethnography offers a lens to understand better organization and management within higher education organizations. An autoethnography, according to Doloriert and Sambrook, could provide opportunities for people or organizations, learners and supervisors with different or similar experiences to develop a co-constructed autoethnography together (Ellis, 2007). The autoethnography might help to create and open an explorative space to investigate the culture of self, labor, and the interactions within the higher education organization.

Numerous scholars have used autoethnography as the methodology for the degree of doctor of education, doctor of philosophy in curriculum and instruction, or doctor of education in educational leadership (Cutforth, 2013; Jackman, 2009; Mercadel-Butler, 2007; Quinn, 2009; Tuura, 2012; see also Foster, McAllister, & O'Brien, 2006). Several autoethnographers wrote narratives about their experiences as teachers, and some addressed within their autoethnography the problems of education in the United States (Duarte, 2007; Mercadel-Butler, 2007; Pelias, 2000; Stinson, 2010; Tuura, 2012). Struthers (2012) explored the value of an analytic autoethnography as a valid instructive approach for the nursing profession, and Gardner and Lane (2010) to develop teaching and nursing practice.

Autoethnography could contribute to educational research, particularly within research based on the experiences of people with multiple cultures. Hamdan (2012) discussed that the field of education could use personal experiences in different themes related to teaching to increase knowledge. Narratives and first-person interpretations could provide experiences for other people as an educational element. Hamdan also noted autoethnography within research is useful for demonstrating, clarifying, and relating personal events to identity, exploring unusual readings, and analyzing traditions about unfamiliar territory.

Kahl (2011) argued "the need for a critical approach to study communication pedagogy" (p. 1927). Kahl indicated that many instructors do not understand the influence their teaching methods have on their learners including fostering authority and suppression. According to Kahl, many teachers do not examine the power within their classrooms resulting in overlooking hegemony.

Berlak (2005) also argued the issue and asked:

How is it possible for many white students and students of color to be present in a university classroom where they read about, see videos documenting, and engage in activities that demonstrate the pervasive and ubiquitous realities and effects of institutional and personal racism, and yet fail to become engaged with racism at a deep emotional and analytical level? (p. 123)

Numerous scholars indicated that a quantitative method to study education might not examine, within the classroom, the possible roles that racism, gender, social classifications.

Social and economic inequities, white privilege, differences, injustice, and lived experience represent (Berlak, 2005; Fassett & Warren, 2007; Kahl, 2011; Pelias, 2000). Struthers (2012) indicated that using an autoethnographic narrative involving self-understanding and analytic reflexivity offered contribution to learning by increasing reflective practices. Pelias (2000), Berlak (2005), Kahl (2011), and Fassett and Warren (2007) discussed that using an autoethnography to explore critical communication in teaching might encourage instructors to reflect on their teaching and learning. Shibata (2012) argued an autoethnography as tool to understand the process during a counseling session and the need to provide macro and micro counseling with language learners.

Analytical autoethnography might help researchers to develop educational elements. Analytical autoethnography might be a pragmatic scholarship for instructors and a tool to become aware of their possible hidden prejudices and authoritarian teaching (Berlak, 2005; Fassett & Warren, 2007; Kahl, 2011). The awareness develops because by using an autoethnography the instructor gives a name and critically reflects on the problem, and does something to find solutions or to create change (Kahl, 2001; Pelias, 2000). An analytical autoethnography might also help to explain, explore, and analyze the possible reasons some learners with multiple cultures might feel experiencing oppression (Hurd, 2012). Badley (2014) wrote about autoethnography related to her academic life:

> Surely, too, we privileged (?) academics can help empower the powerless to
> write their own scrappy stories in order to alert the world about their anguish
> and their plight and even seek to change their world bit by bit. And even the
> privileged few are entitled to write their own *sort of life*-stories. (p. 982)

Significance of the Study to Leadership

The research study might be significant to leadership, as it could illustrate self-leadership as a major method for empowerment, for leading oneself through complex cultural situations, and as inner motivation to persist against adversity during multicultural interactions (Furtner, Rauthmann, & Sachse, 2010; Houghton & Yoho, 2005; Manz, 1986). The qualitative analytic autoethnography might also be valuable for scholars studying self-leadership as a tool to help multicultural people during their interactions with multiple cultures (Nelson, Zaccaro, & Herman, 2010). According to most of the literature on leadership, researchers have paid less attention to the self-leadership aspect than to the employment and organizational environments (Curral & Marques-Quinteiro, 2009; Houghton

& Yoho, 2005; Manz, 1986). Many scholars have recommended exploring self-leadership as an important element of leader and follower. Including how people perceive self-leadership across cultural situations (Alves et al., 2006; D'Intino, Goldsby, Houghton, & Neck, 2007).

Educational leaders might use an autoethnographic method to encourage teachers and students to engage in interpersonal communication, exposing any authoritarian practices in their learning environments such a classroom (Berlak, 2005; Fassett & Warren, 2007; Kahl, 2011). The revelation using an autoethnography might provide a clear idea of how students might sense living under the control of critical authority (Pelias, 2000). According to Engstrom (2008), an autoethnography, as a method of research and training, might help improving intercultural training programs. An autoethnography provides a language that could help making sense of fragmented cultural experiences or "cultural ruptures" (Engstrom, 2008, p. 17).

Educational leaders might benefit from an autoethnographic method. Engstrom (2008) argued that in a teaching and learning environment an autoethnography requires five principles to focus the writing: (1) reflecting critically upon biases the instructor might bring to a classroom or to a teaching and learning environment; (2) examining the influence a teacher has on learners; (3) evaluating the part ethics play in one's writing; (4) conversing the effect that the writing has on oneself and on learners; and (5) reflecting on one's general learning about authority through their interactions with students (Engstrom, 2008; Kahl, 2011).

The acts of reflexibility, required by an autoethnography, might help the transformational goal of critical communication pedagogy (Engstrom, 2008). Reflexibility distinguishes autoethnography from a traditional teaching method because autoethnography requires to consider how past actions could affect future events (Kahl, 2011). Hurd (2012) noted an autoethnography could help to display the multifaceted contradiction between what a person desires to be and what a person is obliged to be.

Nature and Scope of the Study

The purpose of the study was to explore why some multicultural people might turn into cultural chameleons to fit in or to adjust to a different culture. The qualitative analytic autoethnography involved exploring the intersection of disability, ethnicity, and gender to understand cultural chameleon behavior that some multicultural people might adopt as a method to respond to conflict and stresses while adjusting to a different culture. Barbour

(2008) noted qualitative research helps researchers to understand inconsistent behaviors, to study circumstances, and to provide explanations. The qualitative analytic autoethnography involved exploring why some multicultural people might turn into cultural chameleons. The approach facilitated the creation of themes drawn from my cultural experiences and from the academic literature on disability, ethnicity, and gender.

Although Barbour (2008) discussed other research approaches, such as qualitative ethnography that includes interviews, focus group discussions, and the analysis of documents, qualitative analytic autoethnography was appropriate for exploring cultural chameleon behavior because other methods could confirm relationships but would omit important intersectionality factors. Historical research on multiracial individuals, for instance, focused on specific age groups, racial or ethnic groups, or biracial backgrounds (Pohlert, 2008). The exclusive use of interviews might have uncovered similar experiences while ignoring the dynamic of culture intersection. Applying quantitative research might have identified statistically significant links between variables and associations, as well as the distribution and strength of associations (Barbour, 2008). Exploring cultural experiences, examining personal perceptions, and adopting illogical behaviors to understand cultural chameleon behavior favored a qualitative analytic autoethnography that employed my experiences with different cultures compared to the academic literature on disability, ethnicity, and gender.

The qualitative analytic autoethnography involved using my story to represent the nature and scope of the study. The self-centered study involved an investigation and a participant. The study was not just a story to tell, a memoir, a biography, or an autobiography; it was my cultural experiences supported by research (Anderson, 2006; Burnier, 2006; Ngunjiri et al., 2010; Pompper, 2010; see also Chase, 2005). The foundations for this qualitative analytic autoethnography were my multicultural experiences as a woman in a wheelchair and as an emigrant from Mexico and my connection to a cultural chameleon. The study served as an opportunity to present an autoethnography that entailed a procedure and an outcome, valuable records, and self-observation to support my cultural experiences and involved using first-person voice to reflect my personal story (Denzin & Lincoln, 2002; Ellis, Adams, & Bochner, 2011; Lewis-Beck, Bryman, & Futing, 2004; McIlveen, 2008; see also Chase, 2005).

My autoethnography was about my personal culture experiences. The qualitative analytic autoethnography involved an exploration to understand others and myself by examining my actions and perceptions during my cultural interactions (Adams & Jones, 2011; Allen-Collinson, 2013; Anderson, 2006; Badley, 2014; Berlak, 2005; Atkinson, 2006; Bochner, 2012; Boufoy-Bastick, 2004; Burnier, 2006; Chang, 2007, 2008; Denshire, 2014; Denzin, 2003, 2013, 2014; Ellis, 2004, 2007; Ellis & Bochner, 2000; Fassett & Warren, 2007; Hamilton et al., 2008; Kahl, 2011; Pompper, 2010; Sambrook et al., 2014; Smith-Sullivan, 2008; Spry, 2001; Wall, 2006, 2008; Warren, 2009).

The research study included the issues of power, subordination, and control I encountered while fitting in or adjusting to a different culture. The study also contained how cultural interactions affected me as a person with multiple cultural identities known as social classifications. The study included intersectionality, multiple cultural identities, and social categorizations combined theories. The combination of theories served as a lens to investigate the intersection of disability, ethnicity, and gender coinciding as unexplored factors influencing me to behave as a cultural chameleon. The combination also served to explore and communicate how self-leadership skills guided my life's trajectory as an inner strategy for social interactions.

Biography, autobiography, or autoethnography. Autoethnography is ethnographical and autobiographical. The ethnographical element indicates that autoethnography uses ethnographic research and concerns with the cultural association between self and others within society. The use of ethnographic research method distinguishes autoethnography from autobiography, memoir, journal, and other narrative works (Boufoy-Bastick, 2004; Chang, 2007, 2008; Denshire, 2014; Denzin, 2013, 2014; Ngunjiri et al., 2010; Reed-Danahay, 2009; see also Atkinson, 2006; Badley, 2014; Coffey, 1999; Pensoneau-Conway & Toyosaki, 2011; Warren, 2009).

The autoethnographic method reaches around the self and culture to combine theme and research. The combination develops a place where multiple and shifting identities expose to offer understanding related to culture and society. A place where the author cultural and social lived experience is essential, and where the writing challenges the perception of insider and outsider related to a social system and control (Atkinson, 2006; Boufoy-Bastick, 2004; Chang, 2007, 2008; Denshire, 2014; Denzin, 2003, 2013, 2014; see also Coffey, 1999; Cohen, 2010; Pearson, 2010; Reed-Danahay, 2009; Tedlock, 2005; Warren, 2009).

Autoethnography is not the kind of autobiography in which the author as hero or heroine is neither constrained nor assisted in life by economic, social, or cultural position; autoethnography is also not a form of writing ethnography that erases the anthropologist and his or her encounters with research participants. It is a form of writing, a method for life writing and for social analysis, which depends upon an ethnographer's capacities for observation and sensibilities of empathy, reflexivity, and critique. (Reed-Danahay, 2009, p. 43)

Couser (2005) noted that an autoethnography includes three distinct senses: native anthropology, ethnographic autobiography, and autobiographical ethnography. The sense of native anthropology the author is a member of the theme's community. The ethnographic autobiography the author is the main subject, and autobiographic ethnography the author is an anthropologist.

Reed-Danahay (2009) argued that an autoethnography could also include "the work of people without anthropological training or people in other fields like literature who write with an ethnographic sensibility about their own cultural milieu" (Reed-Danahay, 2009, p. 31). An autoethnography could include not only an ethnographer's autobiographical narratives and the ethnography's process and events, but could also indicate what an anthropologist does when doing ethnography in their own society (i.e., native anthropologist; Reed-Danahay, 2009; see also Cohen, 2010).

Biographical writings indicate that life has a documented goal, for example, a person was born on this day and died on this day and between those years the person lived an exceptional life. Autobiographies include sincerity, subjective, historical, and fictional truths, where readers assume the author is telling his or her life's subjective truth. A historical truth relates to an account of present experimental data about an event or experience. The event relates to the writer's life as the reader wants to hear it. Fictional is when people argued that the truth is fiction; it is not real (Denzin, 2014; see also Pensoneau-Conway & Toyosaki, 2011).

Denzin (2014) indicated the scholars Shapiro, Pascal, and Renza contended autobiography as an imaginative set of experiences imposing a distortion of the truth. The statements in an autobiographic are perceived as a mix of fiction and nonfiction. An autobiography and biography present fictions about the assumed selves, experiences, events, and meanings.

The problem, these types of works experience, is getting the person into the text, bringing the person alive and making him or her believable (Denzin, 2014). Denzin agreed with Elbaz indicating that an "autobiography is fiction and fiction is autobiography, *both are narrative arrangements of reality*" (Denzin, 2014, p. 14). The autobiographical and biographical forms are partial fictitious creations and are fictional accounts with different degrees of truth about lives assumed real. Distinguishing the true in the autobiographic and biographic is difficult, for if an author could make up evidences about his or his life, nobody is to know what is true or false.

Denzin (2014) discussed biographies, as well as autoethnographies, are narrative expressions of life experiences with certain assumed conventions. These conventions helped defining the autoethnographic method as an approach to study human experiences, but existed since the creation of the (auto) biographical method. The conventions were:

(1) the existence of others; (2) the influence and importance of race, gender, and class; (3) family beginnings; (4) turning points; (5) know and knowing authors and observers; (6) objective life markers; (7) real persons with real lives; (8) turning- point experiences; and (9) truthful statements distinguished from fictions. (Denzin, 2014, p. 7)

An autoethnography allowed revealing the intersectionality and interlocking characteristics of my multiple cultures as a woman with a physical disability who emigrated from Mexico to the United States. The study allowed me to explore the academic literature on intersectionality, interlocking privileges and oppression, mixed behaviors, and social classification. Including multiple cultural identities characteristics, disability, ethnicity, gender, and the self from another viewpoint. The literature exploration enabled me to inspect and disclose a sincerer meaning and the influences of my cultural life experiences and society (Anderson, 2006; Chang, 2008; Reed-Danahay, 2009; Wall, 2008; see also Boufoy-Bastick, 2004).

Limitations of autoethnography. As does any research study, an autoethnography has some limitations. This study approach involved other field factors influencing the writer, including investing a substantial amount of time conducting research, neglecting daily life activities and family obligations, or progressing into personal fascination (Anderson, 2006).

Additional limitations were the disinterest of scientists and practitioners on my personal experiences. Writing an autoethnography involved many internal and external challenges, which made the process difficult (Denshire, 2014; Doloriert & Sambrook, 2012; Smith-Sullivan, 2008; Wall, 2008; see also Holt, 2003). Other limitations of an autoethnography are the inclusion of only one analysis and the inability to generalize (McIlveen, 2008). Wall (2008) noted identity and self-understanding could lead to some anxiety problems, and Hamilton et al. (2008) noted challenges related to the autoethnographer's situatedeness could develop.

Anderson's (2006) discussion was relevant to my personal narrative because I understood the need to maintain distance from other factors that could divert my attention. My advocacy and activist beliefs could have interfered as powerful fields that could influence my investigation when validating academic data. I was aware that my position as the writer was to share my cultural experiences, although my advocacy, activism, and beliefs played a strong role in my cultural experiences.

I understood the limitations of a qualitative analytic autoethnography, including the way I represented myself. Other limitations included possible isolation from my family or other people when reflecting and writing my study. Collecting my personal data could have been a limitation, depending on my memory or my ability to recall the events that encouraged me to share my story. I used Zotero online software to collect and store the researched literature and items selected from the Internet as documents, websites, and reports. I also used NVivo10 qualitative research software to store and code the data that conveyed a clear recollection of lived events.

I was aware of the limitation discussed by McIlveen (2008) relating to an autoethnography as a study that is not generalizable. My objective for sharing my story was to explore and discover my self-truth. I was more interested in raising awareness and reaching out to multicultural people than in generalizing the results of my study.

Conscious of the possible limitations discussed by Anderson (2006) associated with family obligations and activities, I took some precautions to avoid disturbing my time and my obligations to my family. The precautions included time management, taking time off, and attending fun games and activities with my family. I also used self-care plan management to process strong and negative emotions that emerged during the narration of my experiences interacting with different cultures.

According to Arvidsson, Bergman, Arvidsson, Fridlund, and Tops (2011), self-care involves internal and external conversations to recognize and satisfy signals from the body. Jenerette and Murdaugh (2008) indicated assertiveness skills, self-efficacy, coping strategies, social support, and communication are essential resources for self-care management. The self-care management used for this analytic autoethnography included journaling as a technique for inner conversation to understand my body signaling stress, tiredness, or any other possible need for coping. External communication to share my feelings, thoughts, and concerns included a mental health professional and my family doctor, who were available for support if strong emotions or health concerns developed.

Research Questions

This research study included my cultural experiences as a woman with a physical disability and immigrant as intersecting factors influencing cultural chameleon behavior. My experiences might have coincided with the experiences of women, other people using a wheelchair, or immigrants. Such coincidence does not indicate that my multicultural representation granted me the power or authority to generalize my cultural experiences. I realized that using an autoethnography I would have the opportunity to "…seeking to give notice to those who may otherwise not be allowed to tell their story or who are denied a voice to speak" (Denzin, 2014, p. 5; see also Yassour-Borochowitz, 2012) including myself. The focus of this dissertation was strictly exploratory.

Reflecting on my cultural experiences related to the reasons some multicultural people might turn into cultural chameleons led me to my research questions. The study involved exploring one central question and two secondary questions:

R1: What influences people with multiple cultures to turn into cultural chameleons?

R2: How do I behave as a cultural chameleon when my physical disability, my ethnicity, or my gender becomes my only attribute as a person?

R3: How and when do I perceive the need to behave as a cultural chameleon?

To answer these three research questions, I explored cultural chameleon behavior and investigated the reasons behind it. I explored the influences forcing or encouraging some people with multiple cultures to behave as cultural chameleons. The first research question was a central question focusing on disability, gender, and ethnicity domains.

The second question guided the investigation of the factors influencing my behavior as a cultural chameleon. This question led me to research the social and scientific

15

phenomena that create and reify ethnic minorities' classifications that might induce a multicultural person to behave as cultural chameleon. The third question guided the exploration of situations or environments in which I felt the need to mix identities. The question facilitated exploring whether I mix identities when I find myself discriminated against, demeaned, marginalized, rejected, hurt, or disempowered based on my disability, ethnicity, or gender. I illustrated my experiences interacting with different cultures by exploring how I mix identities and why I think it necessary to become a cultural chameleon in some social interactions.

There was also a need to recognize my role in this analytic autoethnography's process. According to numerous scholars, the challenge with the phenomenology methodology is for researchers to exclude bias, conjectures, or presuppositions to obtain the essence of the meaning. The process involved self-reflection, consciousness and looking at the data free of prejudgment, presupposition, and assumptions to describe the phenomena the way they are (Chang, 2007, 2008; Ellis, 1999; Ellis et al., 2008; Engstrom, 2008; Kahl, 2011; Pearson, 2012; Pichon, 2013; see also Chase, 2005; Hughes, Pennington, & Makris, 2012). I recognized that my background and my cultural experiences shaped my interpretation of the responses to the research questions and that I was compelled to understand and to fill a gap in the literature.

Autoethnographers typically write autoethnography in first person voice. The voice includes background details, conversations, emotions, self-awareness, and the stories affected by culture, history, and social construct (Chase, 2005; Dethloff, 2005; Ellis & Bochner, 2000). According to Dethloff (2005), "Self-study provides one significant aspect of the truth that too often is lost" (p. 59). Numerous scholars indicated that writing autoethnography allows readers to comprehend of a particular culture by drawing from the shared experience. The understanding develops because autoethnography links the personal to the cultural (Chang, 2007, 2008; Denshire, 2014; Dethloff, 2005; Dutta; 2014; Ellis, 1999; Fox, 2014; Geertz, 1988; Spry, 2001; Reed-Danahay, 2009).

An autoethnography could be a mix of art exemplification, scientific analysis, self-narration, and ethnography. Some forms could be evocative or analytical, depending on the style and how the autoethnographer writes and conveys the story (Ngunjiri et al., 2010; see Anderson, 2006). The self-disclosure or self-exposure, when writing about oneself, illustrates personal vulnerability. The autoethnographer shares pains, hurt, sorrows, lost, heartbreaks, fears, and other emotions lived as they struggle through experienced situations (Chase, 2005; Ngunjiri et al., 2010; Spry, 2001).

Spry (2001) wrote, "Autoethnographic performance is the convergence of the 'autobiography impulse' and the 'ethnographic moment' represented through movement and critical self-reflexive discourse in performance, articulating the intersections of peoples and culture through the innersanctions of the always migratory identity" (p. 706). Building a shared ground between the qualitative analytic autoethnography I used Geertz (1988) concept of "Being There… Being Here" (p. 144) as a connection between my past and shared cultural experiences in a different perspective. Geertz noted this concept as an inspired structure of "the Written At and the Written About" (1988, p. 144; Fox, 2014; Spry, 2001; see also Barth, 2002; Chase, 2005; Coffey, 1999; Freeman, 2014).

The purpose of the study was to explore why some multicultural people might turn into cultural chameleons to fit in or to adjust to a different culture. The qualitative analytic autoethnography involved exploring the intersection of disability, ethnicity, and gender to understand cultural chameleon behavior that some multicultural people might adopt as a method to respond to conflict and stresses while adjusting to a different culture. I was not seeking self-validation through others who might experience similar experiences to mine. I was seeking to challenge the homogenous singular conceptualization of mixing behaviors. Recognizing and giving a name to a method to respond to conflict and stresses while adjusting to a different culture when considering disability, gender, and ethnicity.

Theoretical Framework

The purpose of the study was to explore why some multicultural people might turn into cultural chameleons to fit in or to adjust to a different culture. The qualitative analytic autoethnography involved exploring the intersection of disability, ethnicity, and gender to understand cultural chameleon behavior that some multicultural people might adopt as a method to respond to conflict and stresses while adjusting to a different culture. For the study, I considered McDonald, Keys, and Balcazar (2007) methodological approach that applied intersectionality theory and multiple interlocking privilege and oppression. I also considered Deaux and Martin (2003) interpersonal networks and social categories conceptual framework. I reflected on Hong et al. (2000), Downie et al. (2006), Gavilán (2010), and Vivero and Jenkins (1999) concepts of multiple cultural identities (or multicultural identity) as different lenses to understand cultural chameleon behavior. I also considered Bowleg

(2012), Collins (1990), and Young's (1990) concept of oppression and multiple levels of domination. The approach provided the means of exposing how disability, gender, and ethnicity intersect, overlap, and reinforce one another within the experiences of multicultural people symbolizing several social classifications.

Enhancing intersectionality with multiple cultural identities and the interpersonal networks and social categories conceptual as framework for this analytic autoethnography enabled sharing my cultural experiences. The method enabled the readers to grasp how turning into a cultural chameleon is not an isolated and segregated experience. The method also allowed readers to realize how disability, gender, and ethnicity studies must incorporate intersectionality, multiple cultural identities, and interpersonal networks and social categories into their frameworks. In other words, the reader could see how social classifications reinforce and clash with one another, and generate distinct systems of disadvantage for people who represent multiple cultures (Alexander, 2014; Best, Edelman, Krieger, & Eliason, 2011; Bowleg, 2012; Case & Hunter, 2012; Hurd, 2012; McDonald et al., 2007).

McDonald et al. (2007) advocated a more inclusive framework. A framework that shifts away from additive analysis, toward realizing how disability, race, ethnicity, and gender intersect and interlock in everyday lives. Including in social interactions, and relationships. McDonald's et al. study outcomes implied the need for additional exploration into human diversity and self-society interactions in the context of oppression and social action. The scholars also indicated the intersections of multiple identities influence behavior in different ways.

Numerous scholars recognized the need for a more comprehensive framework when exploring multiple identities, behaviors, and the concept of oppression (e.g., Essed, 2010; Hendrix, Jackson, & Warren, 2003; Hurd, 2012; Platero, 2008; Rigoni, 2012; Young, 1990; see also Levy & Plucker, 2003). Essed (2010), argued that racism works back and forth and hinders with gender and other systems of oppression. Essed stated, "…intertwining systems of domination are expressed and experience in everyday life" (p. 1).

Rigoni (2012) discussed the manifestation of power and subordination. For example, class and gender, race and gender, class and sexual preferences, sexual preferences and gender, race and sexual preferences, and so forth. Platero (2008) investigated the limited notion of equality related to sexuality, gender, ethnicity, age, and class. Numerous other scholars explored the experiences of people with multiple social classifications and the

18

effects (Brooks & Redlin, 2009; Case & Hunter, 2012; Elu & Loubert, 2013; Frost, 2011; see also Hurd, 2012; James & Wu, 2006; LaPierre & Hill, 2013; Levy & Plucker, 2003; Ojeda & Bergstresser, 2008; Pearson, 2012; Pérez Huber, 2010; Warner & Brown, 2010).

Bowleg (2012) indicated "Complex multidimensional issues such as entrenched health disparities and social inequality among people from multiple historically oppressed and marginalized populations beg novel and complex multidimensional approaches" (p. 1272). Deaux and Martin (2003), Downie et al. (2006) revealed the need for a framework to advance the understanding of the differences on how a person with multiple cultures conceives and endorses those identities. Vivero and Jenkins (1999) explained the complications of code switching as leading to emotional and social misperception. If internalized, as Vivero and Jenkins explained, might result in self-blame and shame, and in the inability to express emotions verbally (i.e., alexithymia).

Hong et al. (2000) proposed a constructivist approach to study the effects of multiple cultural identities on people. The approach could help people understand that a culture is not the same within a defined population related to demographics, geographic, national, or ethnic selves. Hong et al. indicated that people use culture to navigate social domains as shared knowledge, and it is not a static massive object. According to Hong et al., people with multiple cultural identities are efficient enough to empathize with different cultures based on their shared identity knowledge.

Gavilán (2010) indicated to understand a person with multiple cultures, mainly his or her identity, as essential because each person is part of society's foundation. Gavilán also explained that misunderstanding the collective life within different cultures, in many cases, implicate the risk of unchaining cultural conflicts. Collins (1990) and Young (1990) demonstrated the need for a framework to identify personal and group experiences on multiple levels in order to understand oppression, rather than lessening oppression. Young's five faces of oppression as marginalization, powerlessness, exploitation, cultural domination, and violence allow readers to sense the various forms that oppression operates. Young also acknowledges the necessity to stop reducing and addressing different forms of oppression separately such as classism, heterosexism, ageism, racism, sexism, and ableism.

Numerous scholars recognized that social change could not evolve if the struggle for defeating racism while ignoring heterosexism, ageism, ableism, sexism, and classism continues (Bodenhausen, 2010; Collins, 1990; McGibbon & McPherson, 2011; Young,

1990). Bodenhausen (2010) recognized that a social change could not evolve if the struggle for defeating racism while ignoring heterosexism, ageism, ableism, sexism, and classism continues. The scholar explained that the complexity of social identity within the person overpowers social psychological research. Bodenhausen also indicated " …there are still many issues to be empirically investigated concerning the ways whereby different self-aspects influence how identifications arise, particularly in diverse group settings that afford many distinct opportunities for categorization the self and others" (p. 12).

Bodenhausen (2010) discussed that the complexity of social identity within the person overpowers social psychological research. The scholar also indicated " …there are still many issues to be empirically investigated concerning the ways whereby different self-aspects influence how identifications arise, particularly in diverse group settings that afford many distinct opportunities for categorization the self and others" (p. 12). Consequently, incorporating rather than adding perspectives could be theoretically and methodologically necessary to understand the differences in attitudes toward people with multiple cultures.

McDonald et al. (2007) recognized that adding a framework could be problematic. The approach order that layers race, ethnicity, gender, and disability rather than seeing how these domains work together altogether could be difficult to understand. This is because the systems of social classification interrelate creating "…domination and subordination as determined by the intersections of race, class, gender (RGC) and other relevant socially constructed identities and locations" (Barnett, 2007, para. 5). Every person owns a position in different systems of social classifications. Some people, such as women, might be a member of an oppressed group and, at the same time, a member of a group that oppresses others (see Browne & Misra, 2003; Shen & Dumani, 2013).

Deaux and Martin (2003) noted the need for a model integrating the concepts of interpersonal networks and social categories of identity context to understand a more inclusive identity process. Deaux and Martin argued one framework could help understanding that people use some group identities to describe themselves. Categories of identity might overlap, and categorical context could be a motivation forcing for negotiation and change of identity. Including that, a person selects the social category she or he wants to claim, or other people might assign categories meanly when visual indications are evident.

As the systems of classification link together, there is a considerable distinction within groups including to distinction between groups with respect to the distribution of economic, political, and social power (Berg, 2010). One would expect, for example, that a white woman using a wheelchair would have different social experiences than a Black woman using a wheelchair, who is in a less powerful position on *both* the race and gender classification ladders (Rohmer & Louvet, 2009; see also Browne & Misra, 2003; Ransford & Miller, 1983). The influence resulting from the domination and subordination alters personal views and life opportunities differently than would the effect of any single form of social classification (see Barnett, 2007; Browne & Misra, 2003; Demos & Lemelle, 2006; Ovadia, 2001).

Intersectionality and interlocking theories as a lens. The intersectionality theory referred to the concept of linking other factors related to identity (Bowleg, 2012; E. Cole, 2009; Cramer & Plummer, 2009; McDonald et al., 2007). The theory recognizes the struggles caused by the intersection of systems of oppression, acknowledges that people have multiple cultures, and recognizes people might experience control and marginalization (Cramer & Plummer, 2009; Linder, 2011; Shen & Dumani, 2013; Trahan, 2011; see also Salazar & Abrams, 2005). Intersectionality also has options for discussing multiple cultures, exploring silent identities, and studying cultures as intersectional (Bowleg, 2012; E. Cole, 2009; Linder, 2011; McDonald et al., 2007; see also Alexander, 2014). Some of those options for discussion include a common language for exploration, a form to conceptualize and analyze discrepancies and social inequities, and an academic lens for understanding unique or unexpected conclusions (Bowleg, 2012).

Söder (2009) summarized intersectionality as a perspective adopted by scholars to understand society and the intersection of different factors experienced by marginalized groups. Strolovitch (2006) discussed intersectional marginalization as the intersection of inequalities, unfairness, and lack of power or stigmatization. Strolovitch also described intersectionality as an approach reaveling that disadvantages are active and uneven, and define, shape, reinforce, and operate in combination with social categorizations. Intersectionality could help scholars to demonstrate how gender, ethnicity, and class are fused social classifications that form the conditions of marginalized groups, in addition to indicating who are the powerful and the powerless, the oppressors and the oppressed (Söder, 2009; see also Flynn, 2012). Although identity does not discuss power or oppression, it recognizes that each person belongs to numerous categories, and those categories build the person's identity (McGibbon & McPherson, 2011; Moriizumi, 2011; Söder, 2009; see also Crisp & Hewstone, 2001; Salazar & Abrams, 2005).

Brown (2012) contended gender and race intersectionality has received more attention than class, disability, ability, age, sexuality, and religion. The inequality of such attention raises several concerns about the magnitude and the type of intersection that researchers have considered and the possible consequences for not including other identity characteristics (Benet-Martínez & Haritatos, 2005; Brown, 2012; Hae Yeon & Ferree, 2010; see also Alexander, 2014). Rule and Modipa (2012), for instance, examined disability, gender, race, class, and other geographies as intersecting factors affecting a person's life. Söder (2009) argued that scholars included gender, class, and ethnicity as central elements when relating to disability, age, and sexual orientation, but missed to include disability as an essential factor in understanding how the intersection could form the life of a person with disabilities.

Exploring only social categorizations does not inform others about the experiences some people with multiple deprived cultures might experience (Best et al., 2011; Hurd, 2012; Linder, 2011; Shen & Dumani, 2013; see also Crisp & Hewstone, 2001; Salazar & Abrams, 2005). Intersectionality assists in exploring multicultural people's experiences by recognizing marginalization based on gender, ethnicity, and disability, while also exploring the ways people with multiple cultures might experience oppression, powerlessness, unfairness, and inequalities (Brown, 2012; Hae Yeon & Ferree, 2010; Shen & Dumani, 2013; Söder, 2009; see also Alexander, 2014; Salazar & Abrams, 2005). Intersectionality also permits the analysis of intersecting factors related to gender, ethnicity, and disability emerging within those social classifications when brought together (Best et al., 2011; Bowleg, 2012; Hae Yeon & Ferree, 2010).

Ovadia (2001) acknowledged:

Intersection theorists point out that individuals are *simultaneously* situated within the systems of race, gender, and class identity and to consider any one of these systems of difference without including the others may lead to incomplete, or possible incorrect, conclusions about similarities and differences within and among groups. Therefore, the integration of the ideas behind intersection theory may provide an important extension to the existing models in values research. (p. 342)

Interlocking identities refers to how people form themselves through contacting with other people. It also recognizes that multiple identities or social classifications create identity; that identity's aspects are separate yet joined and realizes the more identities the person has, the harder is to liberate the obstacle. It also recognizes that power differentials associate with different facets of identity, which bases on systemic process or matrix of domination. Intersectionality assists understanding the complexity of identities at an individual level, and interlocking identities supports seeing how relationships between people, at a systemic level, shape individuals' identities (Collins, 1990; Hendrix et al., 2003; McKenzie, 2011; Salazar & Abrams, 2005; see also Williams, 2005).

Multiple levels of domination. Bowleg (2012) described how oppressions in society operate simultaneously intersecting in multifaceted forms. For example, the social classifications of race, ethnicity, gender, sexual orientation, and class intersect at the micro level of the person's experience. At the macro level, social structural level, the intersection reflects multiple interlocking systems of privilege and oppression as racism, sexism, and heterosexism (as well as other aspects of identity). Bowleg also explained that viewing each oppressive element as additive rather than interlocking fail to emphasize the significance of power and privilege.

Identities, sometimes discussed to as identity symbols, intersect to multifaceted oppression. The identity symbols might include different traits of identity denoting social location (e.g., age, culture, disability, ethnicity, gender, and spirituality). The identity symbols that might determine access to the social and material necessities in life (E. Cole, 2009; McGibbon & McPherson, 2011). The interlocking systems of oppression, according to Bahm and Forchuk (2009), lacks research including how stigma affects the physical and mental health of people with multiple social classifications. Interlocking oppression referred to how characteristics of oppression manifest on a systemic level, how the oppressive systems intertwined, are inter-reliant, and co-establish one another within society. Oppression's systems develop in and through one another (Collins, 1990; McKenzie, 2011; Williams, 2005).

The metaphor of a cultural chameleon described the process of alternating cultures. Another use explained how some multicultural people might behave to solve cultural conflicts and stresses (Briley et al., 2005; Downie et al., 2006; Remenyi, Grant, & Pather, 2005). Vicent, Sanz, and Mocha (2009) used the chameleon metaphor to represent diversity

23

negotiations. Yilmaz (2001) explained chameleon behavior as adapting to changing surroundings, mainly to culture, religion, and ethnicity.

Through the intersectionality and interlocking frameworks, it was possible to see how the social identities of gender, ethnicity, and disability along with the social ideologies conflict, strengthen, and prolong one another. At the same time, there was a need to consider the background and situation because some social classifications are more evident in different situations (Browne & Misra, 2003; Hansen & Philo, 2007; Harrington, 2003; McDonald et al., 2007; Ransford & Miller, 1983; Rohmer & Louvet, 2009; Speicher, 2010).

According to Buchanan et al. (2009) and Shaw, Chan, and McMahon (2012), a person with membership in two or more protected classes might face multiplied acts of aggravation. The same aggravation might also take on a different aspect. The unique combination of social and cultural norms that go along with a dual or multiple group membership (e.g., disability, gender, and ethnicity) might take on dissimilar standpoint. For example, Shaw et al. (2012) discussed:

> Generally speaking, various combinations of specific characteristics, that is, being female, being older, having a behavioral disability, racial minority status, and working for either a small or very large company seem to place individuals at higher risk of experiencing disability harassment. (p. 88)

In public places, such as school or shopping mall, apparent physical features of race and gender are the central social identities conveyed. In private situations, such as with family, relatives, or friends, other social identities as sexuality or unseen disability might be more apparent based on the closeness (Pearson, 2012). With people with physical disabilities, as people who use a wheelchair, this assumption might be different. Rohmer and Louvet (2009) noted, "To describe persons in a wheelchair, disability is the most salient feature, more salient than gender" (p. 80).

McDonald et al. (2007) indicated that female and male characters change when considering the elements of race, disability, ethnicity, and gender. Stereotypes and cultural representations incline to place layers such as male and female. For example, McDonald et al. indicated that some people might perceive men with disabilities as inadequate men because they do not live up to the assumption of masculinity as adept and strong. Some people might perceive women with disabilities as weak, dependent, asexual, unemployed, and unable to marry and have children on her own. McDonald et al. also indicated that

24

people with unnoticed disabilities might not experience similar relationships between disability and gender because they do not encounter the same physical difficulties, and they could more readily perceived as average (e.g., able-body).

According to Hurd (2012) and Pearson (2012), several people recognize critical reflection on personal experiences as a necessary element to understand how people participate in society and how society defines them. Sharing personal experiences is the first step to understanding people's similarities and differences moving toward social justice. This understanding enabled me to sense how social classifications might influence the lives of people with multiple cultures. As Ryder, Alden, and Paulhus (2000) stated, "Demographics, although simple and concrete, do not tell the whole story" (p. 62).

Multiple cultural identities as a lens. Downie et al. (2006), Hong et al. (2000), and Vivero and Jenkins (1999) viewed the behavior of mixing identities concept as a response to social conflictive interactions and experiences constructed by the discourse of negative perceptions. Gavilán (2010) recognized the need to understand individual's identities in order to prevent cultural conflict. Briley et al. (2005) indicated that the contact with a particular cultural setting or cues, or reminders could influence people's behaviors. The influence could happen not only by adding accessibility of cultural rules but by also increasing the stimulus to behave in a way that is consistent with these rules. The switching behavior to fit the expectations of particular communities produces social approval and avoids embarrassment or humiliation (Briley et al., 2005).

Matsumoto (2007) proposed human nature, culture, and personality as three major sources of influence on behavior. Some scholars contended that mixed identities relates to a behavior demonstrated by a dishonest person, a person with low self-esteem, a person who has a mental health problem, or as a multiple-self problem (Hong et al., 2000; Ungvari et al., 2000). Numerous scholars also discussed the negative consequences of mixed identities as facing internalized struggles, tensions, problems with identities at work, and self-denials of personal desires (see Benet-Martínez & Haritatos, 2005; Hurd, 2012; Hong et al., 2000).

Other scholars argued that social influences, acculturation, cultural relations, and stresses from multicultural settings stem the risk of mixing identities. The social influences discussed included stereotyping, prejudice, refusing, or willingness to relate to social categorizations, internalization, and the treatment sensed. Some other scholars also indicated border identity, social classifications, roles, or dominance, in addition to emotional suffering,

25

diseases, stress, despair, cultural disturb, and burnout as problems associated with mixing identities (Barreto et al., 2003; Bazerman et al., 1998; Chiao et al., 2010; Hayes et al., 2011; Hurd, 2012; Kiely, 2004; Kreiner et al., 2006; Lau et al., 2005; Mezzich et al., 2009; Ngunjiri et al., 2010; Saayman & Crafford, 2011; Vivero & Jenkins, 1999).

Mixed behaviors. Multicultural people might mix behaviors from norm to norm, looking for safety and expressing flexibility (Barreto & Ellemers, 2000, 2003; Briley et al., 2005). Cultural setting provides a specific behavior or social norm. Mixing behaviors allows multicultural people to understand the culture's environment, permitting them to choose the appropriate behavior to adopt as they move from culture to culture (Barreto & Ellemers, 2000, 2003; Benet-Martínez & Haritatos, 2005; Briley et al., 2005; Hong et al., 2000; Matsumoto, 2007; see also Deaux & Martin, 2003). Matsumoto (2007) referred to these culture expectations as "general scripts of behavior" (p. 1300).

Briley et al. (2005) noted multicultural people might mix behaviors strategically, depending on social interactions, and might have different behavioral strategies to resolve concerns or to manage difficulties. Barreto et al. (2003) noted some of those strategies are not tactics to mislead or conceal behaviors, but to affirm rather than to hide their identities for evaluative reasons. Multicultural people might use their self-presentation to stress and sustain their identities (Barreto et al., 2003).

Researchers have focused on the ways multicultural people describe themselves from one social situation to another and how diverse behavioral tactics strongly associate with particular social situations (Robertson, 2006; Tanis & Postmes, 2005; see also Benet-Martínez & Haritatos, 2005; Hong et al., 2000). Different factors influence the extent to which multicultural people express some identification with a given social group (Robertson, 2006; Tanis & Postmes, 2005; Ward, Stuart, & Kus, 2011). According to Barreto et al. (2003), the way people see themselves is how they identify with a group and how they want other people to see them. Some multicultural people might feel motivated to influence how others view their social identities (Leary & Allen, 2011; Nezlek, Schütz, & Sellin, 2007).

Several debates on the effects of social situations on behavior usually involve the notion of oppression within society. Oppression happens in multiple forms. Forms of domination obstructing the opportunity to address power and privilege, and allowing the intersection of identities into multiple forms of oppression (Delgado, 2011; Hae Yeon & Ferree, 2010; McGibbon & McPherson, 2011). According to the literature reviewed,

26

oppressed people learn how to manage, negotiate, and mix identities to participate in social life, including cultural, public, and individual domains. Mixing identities could be a strategy used to manage the experiences of oppression (Campbell, 2011; Delgado, 2011; McGibbon & McPherson, 2011). Few researchers have examined the associations between social situations and mixing behaviors (Barreto et al., 2003; Barreto & Ellemers, 2000; Verkuyten & de Wolf, 2002; see also Benet-Martínez & Haritatos, 2005; Hong et al., 2000) of multicultural people.

Interpersonal networks and social categories as a lens. The literature showed that social identity is a system of cognitive and representation to share the characteristics of belonging, norms, and history of group membership in society. The social classification theory suggests that when demography is perceptible, some people might focus more on the differences than on the similarities (Chatman & Flynn, 2001; Crisp & Hewstone, 2001; Hogg, 2001a; Knapp & Dalziel, 2007). Scholars also indicated that people are rarely members of only one group and several social classifications could be noticeable simultaneously (Chatman & Flynn, 2001; Crisp & Hewstone, 2001; Gardner et al., 1999). A considerable categorical dimension forms the social identity theory including nationality, occupation, religion, race, gender, skills, and ethnicity (Deaux & Martin, 2003; Knapp & Dalziel, 2007).

Research showed that category membership creates a background for social identification with a category and membership to a group. The category has different meanings as from personal features to activities related to that particular category. The category could place a person in terms of other groups creating an evaluative and comparative structure based on the person's social position. Several people self-categorized themselves based on their immediate background and social experience (Chatman & Flynn, 2001; Crisp & Hewstone, 2001; Deaux & Martin, 2003; Flynn, Chatman, & Spataro, 2001; see C. Ho, 2007).

Deaux and Martin (2003) discussed that identity involves the elements of categorical membership and interpersonal context based on a mutual relationship to others. According to these scholars, people use many group identities to describe themselves (see Benet-Martínez & Haritatos, 2005; Hurd, 2012; Hong et al., 2000; see also Harrington, 2003). Some of the categories could be more important to the person and some might overlap (see Cramer & Plummer, 2009; Linder, 2011; Shen & Dumani, 2013; Trahan, 2011; Warner & Shields, 2013). Commonly, power and status define membership in a group, in which dominance or marginality set based on the social classifications of group members (Deaux & Martin, 2003; Meekosha, 2006; see Harrington, 2003).

A significant effect is that categories establish people's membership in everyday networks providing opportunities to relate with other similar people (Deaux & Martin, 2003; Flynn et al., 2001; Galupo & Gonzalez, 2013; Meekosha, 2006; see Knapp & Dalziel, 2007). Deaux and Martin (2003) indicated that interpersonal networks relate to people sharing a social category (e.g., education, occupation, or ethnicity). The network generates social support for specific identities and allows an interpretation of identities in a community.

Harrington (2003) indicated that some influencers on social interaction include social influence, social-political attitudes (e.g., authoritarianism, social dominance), styles of communication, stereotype information and insistence, and intergroup hostility. The influencers could involve on how people think and perceive their environment, attitude, and emotional determinants, and how some people understand others (see C. Ho, 2007; Knapp & Dalziel, 2007; Kramer, 1998; Melton & Cunningham, 2014).

Linking a category with network setting, as proposed by Deaux and Martin (2003), researchers could explore the background established by categorization, its connected cultural beliefs, and the relationship between interpersonal networks. The scholars indicated that using their proposed conceptual framework researchers could explore defining and negotiating identity intensely. Using the proposed framework scholars could investigate the reasons for lowered self-esteem, identification decreased, the reasons for choosing a category over another, unwillingness to identify with a specific categorization, and subjective identification. Including other elements resulting from the intersection of social categories and social networks.

Kramer (1998) discussed social situations as threatening people's fundamental sense of self, produce anxiety, and discomfort. Including being more vigilant about the credibility of others and are more cautious and perceptually prepared to encounter evidence of lack of trust. Kramer also noted that a large body of data suggested that one reaction people have to socially threatening information is to reflect about that information. The scholar also indicated that people involved in trust problems of this sort they not simply trust or distrust others, they rather measure how much trust and distrust are appropriate to a situation.

The decision to investigate cultural chameleon behavior supplementing intersectionality with interpersonal networks and social categories concept, and multiple cultural identities theories, took place after I learned that such behavior might develop to respond to social categorizations (Gavilán, 2010; Magnusson, 2011). My decision to use intersectionality was appropriate because it allowed me to look into race, class, gender, ethnicity, and disability as factors that could affect social, political, economic, and cultural ideas (Cramer & Plummer, 2009; McGibbon & McPherson, 2011). Other aspects to explore using intersectionality, interpersonal networks and social categories, and multiple cultural identities were poverty, immigration, and shared identities. In addition to providing ways to explore ideas that classify, categorize, and construct social values assigned to people (B. Cole, 2009; Cramer & Plummer, 2009; McGibbon & McPherson, 2011). The realization helped me to understand that using those theories as a framework, was appropriate to guide this exploration to understand cultural chameleon behavior.

Telling the Story. Writing autoethnography, telling the story, is the experience (Denzin, 2003). The analytic autoethnography used the concept of *Being There… Being Here* and narrative inquiry to explore my cultural experiences (Geertz, 1988; Fox, 2014; Spry, 2001; see also Coffey, 1999; Freeman, 2014). Geertz (1988) wrote, "Being There is a postcard experience ("I've been to Katmandu—have you?). It is Being Here, a scholar among scholars that gets your anthropology read… published, reviewed, cited, taught" (p. 130). Using photovoice method, the analytic autoethnography assisted in transforming the Geertz's concept of *I have been to Katmandu –have you?* to *I have been there living such a cultural experience –have you?*

The transformation aimed to connect the readers with myself as the subject. A moral connection in which I shared my cultural experiences to address, to inform, to implicate, and to solve cultural concerns that might be imperceptible for some (Barth, 2002; Butz, 2010; Chase, 2005; Geertz, 1988). Chang (2007) contended different styles of writing an autoethnography including analytical description, confessional self-exposure, and somewhere between "realist description and impressionist caricature" (2007, p. 10; see also Chase, 2005; Denzin, 2003). The narrative inquiry involving analytical and confessional self-exposure style seemed appropriate to use as the framework for this study. To transform a photograph into a postcard to share my cultural experiences related to gender, disability, and ethnicity. Transforming a photograph into a postcard, I aimed to gain a cultural understanding of others and myself during my social interactions (Chang, 2007; Denzin, 2003; Geertz, 1988).

Turning photographs into postcards also allowed me to separate myself from my past cultural experiences. The separation allowed me treating the data with a critically, analytically, and interpretatively perception. Allowing me to discover the cultural feelings emerging through photovoice of what I recalled, observed, and told others and myself (Chang, 2007; Geertz, 1973, 1988). Implementing the Being There Being Here concept as a framework helped me to confront the tensions between my internal self and the external perspectives of others through the academic literature, between social system and social control (Denzin, 2003; Geertz, 1973, 1988; Ngunjiri et al., 2010).

Definition of Terms

People from different disciplines that relate to the topic of multiple cultures might use common language to communicate, but they might have different conceptions about these terminologies. Some people unfamiliar with the terminology might find some words or terms used within the study difficult to follow. It is therefore necessary to define certain words and terms used within the autoethnography. The following are operational definitions of some of the words and terms used within the study.

Acculturation: Acculturation is the communication between individuals from different cultural backgrounds (J. Berry, 2001; Cox et al., 2010; Schwartz & Zamboanga, 2008). Acculturation, also known as the acculturation process, is the grade of participation with the original culture (Mezzich et al., 2009) that typically referred to the extent to which ethnic and racial minority groups attach to their original culture or to their new culture (Betancourt & López, 1993).

Acculturation strategies: The strategies involved within the concept of acculturation: integration, assimilation, separation, and marginalization (J. Berry, 2001; Cox et al., 2010; Schwartz & Zamboanga, 2008; see also Rudmin, 2003).

Acculturative stress: The tensions people might experience while adjusting to a different culture (Betancourt & López, 1993). Acculturative stress relates to physical, psychological, and social health decreasing in some people during the acculturation process (Mezzich et al., 2009). Another term for acculturative stress is marginality (Rudmin, 2003, p. 17).

Assimilation: Adjusting to a new culture but abandoning the traditional, meaning there is no desire to relate to the original tradition (Cox et al., 2010; Schwartz & Zamboanga, 2008). Assimilation is sometimes perceived as acculturated (Mezzich et al., 2009, p. 469).

30

Cultural interactions: The interactions and adaptations within cultural situations (Molinsky, 2007).

Cultural intersection: The intersection of two or more cultures (Cramer & Plummer, 2009).

Culture: The beliefs and values that influence traditions, norms, systems, and social situations (American Psychological Association, 2003).

Integration: Acquiring the new culture and retaining the original culture; relationships with others occur while maintaining the original culture (J. Berry, 2001; Cox et al., 2010; Schwartz & Zamboanga, 2008); some people refer to integration as bicultural (Mezzich et al., 2009).

Intersectional invisibility: People representing multiple suppressed cultures might become invisible because they do not fit within the models of their own groups (Purdie-Vaughns & Eibach, 2008).

Marginalization: Rejecting the new culture and discarding the traditional without a desire to identify with any culture (Cox et al., 2010; Schwartz & Zamboanga, 2008). Some people classify this strategy as "culturally marginalized" (Mezzich et al., 2009, p. 469).

Mixing identities: A strategy that some people with multiple cultures use for adjusting and fitting into different cultures (Chartrand & Bargh, 1999; Downie et al., 2006; Kiely, 2004).

Multicultural or multiple cultural identities: People representing more than two ethnic or racial minority groups (American Psychological Association, 2003).

Separation: Rejecting the new culture, but retaining the traditional culture, such that there is no communication with the larger culture but only with the original tradition (Cox et al., 2010; Schwartz & Zamboanga, 2008). Some people discuss separation as "culturally traditional" (Mezzich et al., 2009, p. 469).

Assumptions of the Study

The first assumption of the study was people with multiple cultures symbolizing many social classifications have similar cultural experiences during social interactions and experience conflict and stressors (Applegate, 1990; Viggiani, Charlesworth, Hutchison, & Faria, 2005). The second assumption was multicultural people turn into cultural chameleons to cope with stressors and conflict and to fit into a different culture (Briley et al., 2005; Downie et al., 2006; Stamm et al., 2004). The third assumption was multicultural people and cultural chameleons were stressed and had different needs specific to their cultural encounters (Chiao et al., 2010; Mezzich et al., 2009; Ungvari et al., 2000).

The fourth assumption was the analytic autoethnography could be pertinent to people with multiple cultures or cultural chameleons and the cultural chameleon is an adoptable behavior (Briley et al., 2005; Downie et al., 2006). The fifth assumption was the theory of intersectionality could be understood as a silent cycle spinning several social classifications as cultures forming one culture from its own (Allen-Collinson, 2013; Shaw et al., 2012). The sixth and final assumption was this study could be useful to professionals of different academic disciplines (Badley, 2014; Cramer & Plummer, 2009; Nelson et al., 2010; Schneider, 2011).

Limitations of the Study

Although this qualitative analytic autoethnography could have provided a foundation concerning cultural chameleon behavior related to people with multiple cultures, limitations existed. One limitation was that my story focused to explore the life of a person who represents multiple cultures by focusing on a woman who used a wheelchair and who emigrated from Mexico as a young adult. I am a person who represents different cultures and disadvantaged minority groups, but my experiences are different from those of other multicultural people. This difference indicates my cultural experiences might not pertain to people with physical disabilities, to people who use a wheelchair, to immigrants, or to women. My experiences might also not be associated to other people with multiple cultures or to other people from disadvantaged groups. This qualitative analytic autoethnography was my own story where I shared my cultural experiences focused on disability, gender, and ethnicity.

The explorative study included my narrative as a person with multiple cultural experiences. I narrated the introduction into a new culture, a new self, and the new journey of my life to achieve the American promise and the American dream to become a naturalized citizen of the United States. My experiences might not relate to individuals with backgrounds different from my own to disadvantaged groups, to social classification, or to social status. Such experiences are different for each person, differently internalized, and differently managed. My failures and successes during my multicultural interactions were different from the perceptions of other people with multicultural encounters.

A second limitation included the common idea related to the term culture or cultural identity. The term culture represented for many different people a set of two or more origins of birth only (e.g., Mexican-American, African-American, Asian-American, German-Russian, Mexican-African-American, or traditions from each country). Numerous people did not perceive social classifications or race and ethnic minority groups' categorizations as cultures; people perceived it as it sounds –a classification in society.

Delimitations of the Study

I had several topics in mind for my dissertation. Those topics included disability issues, educational concerns, cultural intersections, and identity perceptions among cultural group members. While searching for information and reviewing the literature, I discovered I did not want to study a topic that would not relate to my own experiences. Such resistance encouraged me to contemplate my own journey as an immigrant woman with disabilities. I carefully selected a qualitative analytic autoethnography to research cultural chameleon behavior using the intersectionality theory. I also selected and combined the theories of intersectionality, multiple cultural identities, and social categorizations to create a framework as a broaden lens to investigate the intersection of disability, ethnicity, and gender as coinciding factors.

The qualitative analytic autoethnography restricted my personal narrative to an examination of my life's events related to the research questions. My objective was to supplement existing knowledge concerning cultural chameleon behavior. The focus of the study was on people representing multiple cultures who might behave as cultural chameleons.

Although I represent more than three cultures, I focused on ethnicity, disability, and gender because these three cultures mostly influence my experiences during social interactions. Cramer and Plummer (2009) indicated the intersections of ethnicity, disability, and gender have different influences on how a person is perceived and how the person behaves. Harley et al. (2002) discussed race, class, and gender as a "constellation of positionalities" (p. 216) that confirm humiliations or privileges based on the person's place in society. The qualitative analytic autoethnography revealed insights that could contribute to the literature on why a multicultural person might turn into a cultural chameleon.

Summary

This qualitative analytic autoethnography provided a deeper understanding of the cultural experiences of a person with multiple cultures commonly defined as social classifications. The study involved exploring the reasons some multicultural people might turn into cultural chameleons during social interactions. Using the intersectionality, multiple cultural identities, and social classifications theories as a guide to help me answer the research questions enhanced the exploration. The analysis also provided some perspectives for future scholars who might explore this subject and its related topics. Chapter 2 contains a review of relevant research studies and the research method and design.

Chapter 2

Review of the Literature

The purpose of the study was to explore why some multicultural people might turn into cultural chameleons to fit in or to adjust to a different culture. The qualitative analytic autoethnography involved exploring the intersection of disability, ethnicity, and gender to understand cultural chameleon behavior that some multicultural people might adopt as a method to respond to conflict and stresses while adjusting to a different culture. This chapter contains a review of the relevant literature, provides information to understand cultural chameleon behavior in response to conflict and stresses while adjusting to a different culture by exploring the social classifications intersection of disability, ethnicity, and gender. The purpose of the literature review was to establish the need for the research study, to present a review of the literature related to the problem under study, and to determine the documentation of a clear and concise problem.

Documentation

Search engines and literature sources. The comprehensive literature review required the use of the Internet, online databases, articles, journals, and autoethnographies from ProQuest, EBSCOhost databases, and SAGE Research Methods Online, Dissertations and Thesis @ University of Phoenix, ProQuest Dissertations and Theses, SAGE Publications through the University of Phoenix electronic library, and QSR International's NVivo10 qualitative research software. The Internet searches primarily generated resource information from government agencies, multicultural studies, and professional organizations. The primary focus of the literature review was research articles and dissertations published between 2002 and 2014. Some historical literature before 2002 was necessary for the study.

Key terms to search relevant literature. Key terms used to search included *autoethnography, auto-ethnography, auto/ethnography, ethnography, ethnographic, narrative with qualitative method,* and *analytic and autoethnography*. The search also included *intersectionality, cultural intersection, intersection of cultures, interlocking, interlocking oppression and privileges, identity development, individual identity, collective identity, group identity, interlocking identities, gender, ethnicity, disability, identity, culture, multicultural, Latino/a identity, acculturation, cross-cultural, bicultural, multiple cultures, multiple identities, social situations, social classifications, social categorizations, cultural* *chameleon behavior, chameleonic-like behavior,* and *compound or mixed identity* to streamline the literature review and assemble pertinent data.

The literature review indicated the degree to which multicultural people shift their behavioral strategies during social situations to solve problems and to manage stress or conflict and the possible methods in which these behaviors occur. Reviewing relevant research studies revealed how scholars addressed the topics of social situations as influencing multicultural people to mix behaviors. The review involved looking at how scholars addressed those influences to mix behaviors as they relate to the factors of disability, gender, and ethnicity.

The focus of the literature review was the following research questions:

R1: What influences some people with multiple cultures to turn into cultural chameleons?

R2: How do I behave as a cultural chameleon when my physical disability or my ethnicity or my gender becomes my only attribute as a person?

R3: How and when do I perceive the need to behave as a cultural chameleon?

Historical Review

Mixing behaviors could occur when a cultural chameleon behavior is adopted to solve problems or concerns influenced by multiple identities, sense of belonging, or different life experiences (Briley et al., 2005; Downie et al., 2006). The cultural chameleon metaphor indicates that a multicultural person has compound identities intentionally or unintentionally developed (Downie et al., 2006; Hong et al., 2000). Some people with multiple cultural identities experiencing acculturation might switch cultural frames to manage the acculturation process depending on sociocultural cues (Hong et al., 2000; Luna, Ringberg, & Peracchio, 2008).

Briley et al. (2005) and Downie et al. (2006) indicated an adult with multiple cultures might not be concerned about playing the role of a cultural chameleon, but identifying the behavior might cause some distress. Some multicultural people might have different mental formations related to culture norms, including their own interpretations of the world and identities (Hammershøj, 2009; Hurd, 2012; Luna et al., 2008; see also Gardner et al., 1999). Some multicultural people might undergo uncertainty and struggles that might result from trying to meet cultural norms and expectations (Ekstedt & Fagerberg, 2005; Hurd, 2012; Kramer, 1998; Song, 2009; Thunman, 2012).

People with multiple cultural identities might encounter challenges with multiple cultures (Cramer & Plummer, 2009; Hurd, 2012; Ward et al., 2011). Those challenges might limit multicultural people's effective interactions and might lead to social conflicts and tension with oneself and others (Song, 2009; see also Ward et al., 2011; Verkuyten & deWolf, 2002). An individual's diversity expands beyond his or her own identities due to the interactions with each identity that could alter the attributes of each influencer (Bodenhausen, 2010; Deaux & Martin, 2003; Hong et al., 2000).

Intersectionality as a lens. The intersectionality concept originated in 1851 with Sojourner Truth's (Isabella Baumfree) speech *Ain't I a Woman?* in a Women's Rights Convention. The concept attempted to describe the exclusion of Black women from the White feminist dialogue, and antiracist discourse. In the 1990s, the concept reemerged in Black feminist scholarship when Kimberlé Crenshaw named the concept as intersectionality (Alexander, 2014; Bowleg, 2012). A theory associated with the intertwining system of domination permits others to understand how people struggle with multiple identities while trapped in the hegemonic systems of social classification (Rigoni, 2012; see also Hendrix et al., 2003).

Numerous scholars used an intersectionality approach to studying multicultural people (Alexander, 2014; Berg, 2010; Best et al., 2011; Elu & Loubert, 2013; Frost, 2011; see also LaPierre & Hill, 2013; Masselot & Bullock, 2013; Pérez Huber, 2010). Intersectionality helped some scholars to demonstrate how gender, ethnicity, and class are social categorizations fused forming. The theory of intersectionality could be a valuable tool for understanding the strategy of mixing behaviors. Primarily because the concept involves the experiences of people with multiple cultures, considers the implications and effects of social classifications, and studies power and privilege (Berg, 2010; Cramer & Plummer, 2009; E. Cole, 2009; Essed, 2010; Jones, Choe Kim, & Cilente Skendall, 2012; Lindstrom et al., 2012; Shaw et al., 2012; Staunces, 2003).

The theory of intersectionality, used as a lens to understand cultural chameleon behavior, provided an inclusive synopsis of the challenges associated with interconnecting identities. The synopsis allowed uncovering the dynamics of culture interactions on disability, gender, and ethnicity (Cantey, 2011; Frable, 1993; Lindstrom et al., 2012; Rigoni, 2012; Shaw et al., 2012). Intersectionality suggested the interactions between overlapping social classifications are significant systematic entities with important social consequences beyond basic demographic variables (Ojeda & Bergstresser, 2008).

Intersectionality originated to understand possible differences among people. Some differences might involve race, class, gender, ethnicity, and disability. In an autoethnography, Jones et al. (2012) provided some insights into intersectionality as the presumed reality of people with multiple identities. The central debate regarding intersectionality focused on whether people with multiple cultures encounter more discrimination than people with a single culture (Purdie-Vaughns & Eibach, 2008; Lindstrom et al., 2012; Shaw et al., 2012). The concepts of double and triple jeopardy also covered growing understanding of the effects of cultures intersection (Hayes et al., 2011; Lindstrom et al., 2012; Shaw et al., 2012).

Cramer and Plummer (2009) described the intersections of race, ethnicity, gender, and disability as strong influences on people's behaviors. Cramer and Plummer used intersectionality as the conceptual framework for their study to find why, how, and where a multicultural person decides to mix behaviors to make decisions. The results indicated having multiple suppressed identities influences multicultural people's judgments about which behavior to use.

People express different attitudes toward people with multiple social classifications. The intersection of cultures develops tensions, scissions, and counterexamples creating its richness comprising many cultures, and, at the same time, trapping those cultures making them as invisible and uncomprehensive single one. The theory of intersectionality aims to describe a way of hypothesizing the concerns of representing multiple cultures or memberships in many protected classes (E. Cole, 2009; Essed, 2010; Lindstrom, Harwick, Poppen, & Doren, 2012; Shaw et al., 2012).

Interlocking identities, privileges, and multiple levels of oppression. The concept of interlocking oppressions related to how different social classifications and oppressions developed through interacting with other people. Interlocking oppressions also related to the possible assumptions of the social classifications, and the interpretation of an individual's identity to other people (McKenzie, 2011; Pearson, 2012; Van Herk, Smith, & Andrew, 2011). Sarkisian, Gerena, and Gerstel (2007) indicated that feminist scholars who developed the interlocking concept were concern in bringing race, ethnicity, and class to gender studies.

Interlocking helps to explore and explain how the perception of race, gender, class, and other aspects establish one another in different conjoined ways as well (Barnett, 2007).

Interlocking stresses the need for people to understand and recognize their involvement oppressing one to another in order to reveal an association between the systems of oppression. Interlocking, in other words, suggests that people need to understand the ways they participate in oppressing others and accepting responsibility for how they use power and privilege (McKenzie, 2011; Pearson, 2012; Van Herk et al., 2011). Interlocking of race, gender, class, sexual identity, disability, and other aspects of oppression forces a re-examination of the meaning of social justice (McKenzie, 2011; Pearson, 2012; Van Herk et al., 2011).

Intersectionality and interlocking oppressions, although related, they are different. The literature review suggested intersectionality theories recognize multiple interlocking identities delineated by sociocultural power and privilege (Bowleg, 2008, 2012; Parent, DeBlaere, & Moradi, 2013). Intersectionality suggests that multiple social classifications intersect at subtle level to replicate multiple interlocking structures of privilege and oppression at a larger level socially structured. For example, on the micro level, a person might experience the intersection of gender, ethnicity, disability, race, sexual orientation, and class. On the macro level, the intersection could be racism, sexism, heterosexism, and ableism (Bowleg, 2008, 2012). Intersectionality also helps people to understand that the elements of identity work and connect as a socially constructed identity (McKenzie, 2011; Pearson, 2012; Van Herk et al., 2011; see also Foster et al., 2006). The oppressions of sexism, racism, heterosexism, ageism, ableism, to name a few, happen together to produce social disadvantage (Collins, 1990; McGibbon & McPherson, 2011).

Other scholars contended that using intersectionality, people focus on social classifications without taking into account how possible interactions with other people might affect an individual's subjectivity. Interlocking oppression goes further naming the systems of social classification taking into consideration how interactions with other people might affect a person's subjective. Specifically, interlocking oppressions helps people to understand how one person's characteristic of privilege could create another person marginalized identity (McKenzie, 2011; Pearson, 2012; Van Herk et al., 2011; see also Salazar & Abrams, 2005). In other words, understanding how people in terms of race, class, gender, disability, sexuality, ability, ethnicity, and other social classifications participate within society, and how society defines people, and how people identify themselves (McKenzie, 2011; Pearson, 2012). Pearson noted, "disability is a social identity, a social phenomenon, and part of the everyday process shaping race, class, gender, and sexuality" (2012, p. 104).

Interlocking also allows seeing social classifications overlapping, intersecting, and interlocking with one another. This observation also helps to identify the need to consider explorations based on the whole person rather than segmenting a person into distinct and separate social categories (Pearson, 2012; see also Bowleg, 2012). The literature review suggested that oppressions in society function jointly, intersecting in complex ways.

Some scholars also indicated that additive paradigms viewing each type of oppression as additive rather than interlocking, neglect to stress the control of power and privilege because identities intersect to manifold oppression (Collins, 1990; McGibbon & McPherson, 2011). Disability, ability, age, and many other traits of identity signify social classification, which is a strong determinant of a person's access to social and resources a person might need. Bowleg (2012) noted that although intersectionality emphasizes multiple social classifications as disadvantaged still the theory does not suggest that all interlocking identities experience equally disadvantages.

People who are not wealthy, heterosexual, white, male, Christian, young, and slim become the *Other*, the illegitimate, the abnormal, the inappropriate (Staunces, 2003). Based on the mainstream of Eurocentric, male patriarchy, and racialized domination, Collins (1990) developed a matrix to illustrate the deep-rooted additive models of oppression. The matrix of domination comprised few pure victims or oppressors. Collins recognized the need to explore how oppression functions on a lower level to understand oppression on an institutional and symbolic level. In such believed systems, a person must be Black or White.

Other persons of racial and ethnic minority groups' identity do not fit in this perspective and continually struggle with questions related to their identity. The emphasis on quantity and category happens along with the belief of ranking categories, requiring a privileged and a denigrated, where privilege is clear relative to the other. Staunces (2003) described the matrix of domination as an articulate system of different oppression structures, which oppresses the "non-wealthy, non-heterosexual, non-white, non-male, non-Christian and those who are not slim and not young" (p. 102).

Collins (1990) noted race, class, and gender as systems of oppression strongly affecting African-American women. The systems supported by economic, political, and ideological situations might not be the most central oppressions affecting many more people than Black women. For example, other people of color, poor White women, gays, and lesbians had similar sociopolitical reasons offered for their subordination. A more generalized matrix of domination constitutes race, class, and gender as axes of oppression categorizing Black women's experiences. Other groups might experience different magnitudes of the matrix (Collins, 1990).

Placing excluded groups in the center of analysis gives the opportunity to see the different amounts of disadvantage and privilege within the system. For example, penalized White women for their gender but privileged by their race. In other words, one social identity is more oppressive than the other is, such as being Black is more oppressive than being a woman (Collins, 1990; Pearson, 2012). Depending on the situation, a person might be the oppressor, the oppressor and oppressed, or member of an oppressed group. The issue is that adding an identity element indicates one social identity is more prevalent over the other separated by hierarchy (Collins, 1990; Pearson, 2012; see also Marshall & Read, 2003).

When multiple cultural identities compete, studies found that ethnicity outplays gender influenced by political attitudes. The phenomena not only occur among groups with cultural tradition of female subordination but also among groups where women experience greater autonomy from men (Marshall & Read, 2003). Pearson (2012) noted that with race, class, gender, disability, and sexuality there is a broad range of experiences not only one experience for a specific social classification. Pearson indicated that, although race, class, gender, disability, and sexuality might share some experiences, it is essential not to generalize one experience as a mutual experience. For example, would be inaccurate generalizing the experiences of White women within the middle-class status for those of all women in spite of social background.

Social classifications are complex issues related between people and different people with power. Social classifications do not consider only the powerless, the unprivileged as the *Others*, as Staunces (2003) noted, they also consider the circumstances for the people with more privileges and power. Staunces also indicated that the experiences of ethnicity and gender are not only types of minority encounters. The differences in power include being marked and unmarked, privileged and unprivileged, powerful and powerless. The majority also live in conditions framed by social classifications. Some feminist identity developed as a product of multiple oppressions. The multiple oppressions derived from minority group classification, from nontraditional socialization, and access to female role models within the family (Salazar & Abrams, 2005; Staunces, 2003).

Oppression referred to the massive and multi-layered injustices some groups of people experience (Young, 1990). The injustices are the result of insensible suppositions and the well-meaning response of people in normal everyday activities. According to Young (2000), oppressed people face a common condition. Although oppressed groups do not experience oppression in the same ways they undergo silence, challenges developing and implementing their abilities as well as to express their necessities, opinions, and emotions.

Collins (1990) argued that each person has a unique experiences, values, motivations, and emotions. Human ties could be freeing and empowering, but could be confining and oppressive. Cases of domestic violence, abuse, or any image illustrating women's internalized oppression represent domination on the personal level (Collins, 1990).

Young's (2000) noted the five faces of oppression criteria is not an oppression theory. The criterion is to determine if people or groups are oppressed. Including a way to challenge the certainty of some people's that they are members of an oppressed group when they are not, and as a way of tell others that they belong to an oppressed group when they disbelief.

Young's (2000) five faces of oppression involved the conditions of exploitation, marginalization, powerlessness, cultural imperialism, and violence indicating the way oppression works. In which exploitation referred to a controlled group, working or implementing their abilities and skills rendered to the type of work and for the benefit of other people (Dubrosky, 2013; Young, 1990). Marginalization referred to the deprivation of conditions for working or implementing abilities and skills in an environment of acknowledgment and collaborations. Marginalization also involved people who the system of labor cannot or might not use. People under the marginalization definition included elderly people, people who are in the first elder stages definition, and young people (e.g., Black or Latino who cannot find jobs). Several single mothers and their children, obligatorily jobless, numerous people with physical or mental disabilities, and American Indians mostly Native Americans on reservations as well (Young, 1990).

Marginalization, according to Young (1990), could be the most threatening systems of oppression because people experience exclusion from social life, possibly limited to what they need in their life, and exposed to extinction. People aging, people with mentally or physically disabilities, and people in poverty experience denigration, reprimands, demeans, and biased treatment by the policies and the people associated with welfare administration (Dubrosky, 2013; Young, 1990).

Powerlessness referred to the inability to develop abilities, cannot make decisions, or cannot have autonomy. Some people exercise little creativity or judgment in their work, they cannot have technical expertise or authority, and do not demand respect. Some people experiencing powerlessness might face unrespectable treatment based on the person's status and, particularly in public or administrative settings, express themselves uneasily (Dubrosky, 2013; Young, 1990). The powerful place the powerless into roles of subjection where they must take orders, avoid questioning or even asking. Young (1990) paraphrased Marx's idea structuring exploitation, which indicates that some people are powerful and wealthy because they profit from other people's work.

Exploitation, marginalization, and powerlessness referred to relations of power and oppression that happens within who works for whom, who does not work, and how the field of work outlines a position relative to others. These categories related to operational and institutional delimiting people's lives. The limitations could include the lack of needing material, accessibility of needed resources, and the opportunities to develop and exercise their abilities and skills (Young, 1990).

Cultural imperialism referred to the process of a dominant group's canon and beliefs establishing as the only norm and culture. The process could happen by stereotyping and marking a group out as the Other or the different. By controlling other groups, the dominant group reinforces its position (Dubrosky, 2013; Young, 1990). One injustice of cultural imperialism involved the puzzle of undergoing oneself as undetectable and being marked out as the Other. In other words, the experiences and perceptions of social life from oppressed groups is not evident enough to tap the dominant culture. The same dominant culture imposes its experiences and interpretations of social life on the oppressed group, who must belief such social life is the only existing social life (Dubrosky, 2013; Young, 1990).

The final element of the five faces of oppression is violence and referred to the systematic violence that some members of race and ethnic minority groups might experience. Many members of these groups might know they must fear of unintentional and unprovoked attacks on them or their property to damage, humiliate, or destroy the person. The attacks might also include harassment, bullying, ridicule solely to degrading, embarrassing, or slandering group members (Dubrosky, 2013; Young, 1990; see also Kaltman et al., 2011).

Interpersonal networks and social categories. The literature reviewed suggested that social classifications and networks are essential elements to achieve an inclusive social identity exploration. Numerous scholars indicated social categorizations as distinctions influencing drawing inferences that people use to understand and behave in the world they live (Hogg, 2001a; Knapp & Dalziel, 2007; Miller & Hoffmann, 1999). According to the reviewed literature, categorization is the most basic and necessary cognitive method. The method helps to streamline the environment and accelerate the process of information (Hogg, 2001a; Knapp & Dalziel, 2007).

Social categorization referred where people place themselves and others to distinguish among categories, involves comparisons among people, including the self (Hogg, 2001a; Knapp & Dalziel, 2007; Miller & Hoffmann, 1999). The literature showed that people tend to think of themselves and others as being part of different social categories. In other words, as Knapp and Dalziel (2007) explained, people use accessible and suitable categories based on their goals, situation, and current setting (see Hogg & Terry, 2000; Melton & Cunningham, 2014; see also Miller & Hoffmann, 1999).

According to Knapp & Dalziel (2007), categorization biases and the resulting behaviors, social identification and the resulting behaviors, self-reinforcement of categorization bias and social identifications influence people's responses. The forces of cognitive consistency, social scripts, and behavioral norms to represent a group might influence people. The influence might develop when people become aware of noticeable social categories and place themselves in those categories (Knapp & Dalziel, 2007). The categorization biases might develop based on the noticeable social categories. The perceptible classification might produce an overemphasis of group's similarities, differences compared to other social groups, and more positive evaluation of the groups people belong (Knapp & Dalziel, 2007). The resulting behaviors based on the category biases could alter the person's interests from self and the group (Knapp & Dalziel, 2007).

When people identify with social categories and place themselves within those categories, one or more, they might attribute worth to such category. People might also assume the category as self-concept, and might identify with such category when the differences with other categories are important and self-relevant (Hogg, 2001a; Knapp &

Dalziel, 2007). The behaviors resulting from the social identification base on a positive sense of self, people tend to act in different ways creating favorable differences between their identifiable group and other groups (Knapp & Dalziel, 2007).

Numerous scholars discussed that people not only process information as passive perceiver but also process information actively. In other words, based on the self-reinforcement of categorization bias and social identification, people could depersonalize themselves and one another. People might also search for information validating their negative perceptions of each other and their positive views of self (Knapp & Dalziel, 2007; Salazar & Abrams, 2005).

Several scholars discussed that people not only make sense of the world and the environment as motives for social categorization but also for self-enhancement or self-esteem, and lessening uncertainty (Hogg, 2001a; Hogg & Terry, 2000; Kramer, 1998). The motivations might be the influence from the effects of social categorization, which encloses in-group identification, sense of belonging, and self-definition in-group membership. Including in-group loyalty, preference, conformity, normative behaviors, affection, and solidity (Hogg, 2001a; Hogg & Terry, 2000; see also Mannarini, Rochira, & Talò, 2012; Miller & Hoffmann, 1999; Salazar & Abrams, 2005).

Social categorizations not only provide a mechanism for explaining and predicting people's behavior, but also might contribute to social stereotyping and prejudice. Social categories might help to define between friends or enemies, cooperate or compete, help or harm, and so on. Social classifications might also serve to support interpretations on how people relate to one another (see Rhodes, 2013). Salazar and Abrams (2005) discussed different models to explore identity development within race and ethnic minority groups as racial identity, feminist identity, gay and lesbian identity, racial/cultural, and social class (e.g., Corrigan & Matthews, 2003; Flynn, 2012; Pope et al., 2004; Sarkisian & Gerena, 2005; see also Coffey, 1999).

Salazar and Abrams (2005) indicated a person could be a member of a majority group with respect to several identities (e.g., White, middle class, female). A person could also be a member of a marginalized group with respect to one or more identities (e.g., lesbian, with a disability; see Berg, 2010; Rohmer & Louvet, 2009; Shen & Dumani, 2013; see also Browne & Misra, 2003; Pope et al., 2004; Ransford & Miller, 1983). Salazar and Abrams also noted that each of the racial or ethnic group experience identity development in different ways,

45

although might be several similarities as how marginalized groups move through the identity development process. The authors also considered that people with disabilities, women, sexual minorities, and so forth might not experience the same identity development as ethnic or racial identity (Berg, 2010; Rohmer & Louvet, 2009; Pope et al., 2004; Shen & Dumani, 2013). For instance, racial and ethnic minority groups might not experience the same identity development process, the ethnic or racial identity, or another cultural identity. Sexism or homophobia is not the same experience of racism (Salazar & Abrams, 2005; see also Barnett, 2007; Browne & Misra, 2003; Demos & Lemelle, 2006; Ovadia, 2001; Pope et al., 2004).

The groups experiencing marginalization, the attitudes, and beliefs might affect the identity development of racial and ethnic minority groups. Healthy identity "in members of these groups is contingent upon the individual's ability to develop an accurate self-identity in spite of the oppressive milieu in which the individual's exists" (Salazar & Abrams, 2005, p. 49; see Galupo & Gonzalez, 2013). People who represent marginalized groups might experience racism, sexism, ableism, heterosexism, and privilege over them. Some members of marginalized groups might also experience some people speaking negatively about them, avoiding them, discriminating them, attacking them verbally and physically, and trying to eradicate them (see Brown, 2012; Collins, 1990; Dubrosky, 2013; Galupo & Gonzalez, 2013; Hae Yeon & Ferree, 2010; McGibbon & McPherson, 2011; Moriizumi, 2011; Shen & Dumani, 2013; Söder, 2009; Strolovitch, 2006; Young, 1990).

The literature showed identity as a possible cyclical for some people identified with marginalized or social categorized groups. Some people might go thought the identity stages of conformity, dissonance, resistance and immersion, introspection, and integrative awareness as cycle (Case & Hunter, 2012; Salazar & Abrams, 2005; see also Corrigan & Matthews, 2003; Elsbach & Kramer, 1996; Garcia, 1981; Holcomb, 1997; Hogg, 2001a). Conformity related to the individual who respects the majority culture as superior. Internalizes the values and negative messages about self and the members of his or her group. According to Salazar and Abrams (2005), the person might distance from other members in the same group, motivated to be an exemption, "See how different I am from the rest of them?" (Salazar & Abrams, 2005, p. 52). Salazar and Abrams explained that denial might be necessary for some people's survival and sanity because of the constant oppression.

The dissonance stage might be rapid or gradual. This phase could be the result of a national event. The person experienced discrimination directed toward self or significant others. The person met someone who challenges negative stereotypes. Salazar & Abrams (2005) explained that moving away from the community that isolated or sheltered them expands their perception. What the person might deny or ignore moves in front, his or her former reality becomes conflicting. The person might begin questioning stereotypes and become suspicious of majority culture members. For example, the person might state, "This is racism, this is sexism, this is homophobia. Why should I feel ashamed of who I am?" (Salazar & Abrams, 2005, p. 52).

Resistance and immersion referred to high emotion such anger and shame, which in many instances people expresses it superficially as injustice against self and against members of the same group. Salazar and Abrams (2005) noted the shame is not about internalized stereotypes but about believing those stereotypes, and after reexamination the person might become proud. For example, an inner change might include an "ethnic minority individual who rejects majority attire in favor of dressing in clothing that reflects the individual's ethnic status (Salazar & Abrams, 2005, p. 52; see also Case & Hunter, 2012). The person might want to discover his or her by immersing into it. In this situation, as Salazar & Abrams (2005) explained, when a person is experiencing resistance and immerses might cause a problem. Knowing that oppressive systems inform his or her identity and history, the same mechanisms the person wants to scape. According to some scholars, "Some measure of separatism may be necessary for healing. The strong emotion of this stage is an important part of growth, but requires a lot of energy to sustain" (Salazar & Abrams, 2005, p. 52).

Introspection referred to the energy and attention directed externally becomes internally. During the introspection stage, the focus is on the "selfhood" (Salazar & Abrams, 2005, p. 53). For example, as a person of color, sex preferences, a person with disabilities, and so forth. In this stage, a person might seek to detect balance becoming more analytical of the group and reluctant to continue giving something up for acceptance.

The integrative awareness related to when the person experiences inner security, autonomy, peace, and balance. The person could embrace the aspects of his or her own culture and of the majority culture, and not accepting others. The person might understand that oppression diminishes not only the oppressor but also the oppressed (see Flynn, 2012). The person might develop tolerance for uncertainty and might be able to navigate among cultures without losing the selfhood. According to Salazar and Abrams (2005), social action might become part of the person, but the multiple perspectives could be complicated because sustaining awareness is challenging mentally and emotionally.

Multiple and intersecting identities might interlock and, sometimes, become inseparable. The identity development might be different for each person. A person with multiple cultures identities might experience identity development of one identity difficult, and even more complexity when such identity relates to another and another identity (Salazar & Abrams, 2005; Shen & Dumani, 2013; Warner & Shields, 2013).

Multiple cultural identities. Multiple cultural identities also known as multicultural identities is a term mainly used to describe people with multiple origins or traditions. According to Verkuyten and deWolf (2002a), people with multiple cultural identities cannot control the way some people are marked, described, and constructed. Cultural identities might be distinctively represented within each multicultural person, yet, most scholars exploring cultures, do not incorporate self-representations or social classifications within the connotation of cultures. Scholars of cultural research suggested the need to understand how multiple cultural identities interact and influence a multicultural person (Chao & Moon, 2005; Chao, Chen, Roisman, & Hong, 2007; Chiu, Gelfand, Yamagishi, Shteynberg, & Wan, 2010; Downie et al., 2006; Hong et al., 2000; Hurd, 2012; see also Flores & Huo, 2013; Salazar & Abrams, 2005; Shen & Dumani, 2013).

Several people with multiple cultures might not have internal conflicts representing more than a few cultures. The conflict might develop based on society's demands and expectations from them and from each cultural identity group they represent (Benet-Martínez & Haritatos, 2005; Hong et al., 2000; Ward, Bochner, & Furnham, 2001; see also Levy & Plucker, 2003; Verkuyten & deWolf, 2002). Certain demands or expectations might include being culturally authentic, being faithful to the group, speak the language, and follow the norms, in addition to others. The demands and expectations might develop cultural conflict and cultural distance as two separate aspects of the dynamic intersection of cultural identities (Benet-Martínez & Haritatos, 2005; Deaux & Martin, 2003; Leung & Chiu, 2010). Knell (2006) quoted an anonymous third culture individual (TCI) stating, "I am the one who wears a thousand masks, one for each day and time. I am the one who learned to be all I'm expected to be, but is still not sure of who I really am" (p. 82; see also Lyttle, Barker, & Cornwell, 2011). People with multiple cultures might see as necessary to manage their responses to

48

each situation to reflect an appropriate reaction (Downie et al., 2006; Hong et al., 2000; see also Hurd, 2012).

Various scholars discussed that managing multiple cultural identities might include conflict resolution built from diverse demands –internal and external. Managing multiple identities requires evident, mindful flexibility, and delicate compliance to what the culture needs based on the situation (e.g., self-esteem intensities or moderations, adaptations in discipline, identity neglect; see Ellison, Finch, Ryan, & Salinas, 2009; Flores & Huo, 2013; Hendrix et al., 2003; Sacharin, Lee, & Gonzalez, 2009). Managing multicultural identities might also require the skill to choose among identities to stress what the person desires based on the self (Benet-Martínez & Haritatos, 2005; Levy & Plucker, 2003; Sacharin et al., 2009). The lack of knowledge or the resistance to manage multiple cultural identities might turn into "cultural denial" (Cheryan & Monin, 2005, p. 718).

According to different scholars, there are numerous strategies offered to deal multiple cultural identities. According to Hong et al. (2000), there is not enough information available as to how people chose managing those strategies. People with multiple cultural identities might negotiate their multiple cultures through integration, interchange, or interactions based on the society's norms (Shen & Dumani, 2013; Verkuyten & de Wolf, 2002a). The negotiation might also include managing the attitudes toward multiple cultures believed by the majority or dominant group (Deaux & Martin, 2003; Downie et al., 2006; Hong et al., 2000; see Shankar, Elliott, & Fitchett, 2009; Ward et al., 2001). The literature review on multiple cultural identities revealed that negotiating multiple cultural identities might bring noticeable behaviors when adjusting to cultural settings. Negotiating identities might develop internal uncertainties related to identity commitments and cultural associations as well (Adam et al., 2010; Benet-Martínez & Haritatos, 2005; Chiu et al., 2010; Downie et al., 2006; Flores & Huo, 2013; Hong et al., 2000; Ward et al., 2001; see also Ellison et al., 2009; Verkuyten & deWolf, 2002a).

To date, many acculturation models, previously defined as cultural shock (Ward et al., 2001), stress that people learn and practice a new culture. People retain the information and practices of their traditional cultures. Cultural identities could exist together within a person without unfavorable psychological concerns (e.g., Ryder et al., 2000; Verkuyten & deWolf, 2002; see also Ozyurt, 2013; Ward & Rana-Deuba, 1999). Certain scholars noted that new cultural members might use different identity strategies depending on the setting, the place's diversity, and the dominant group's perception and value to the new member's identities (Deaux & Martin, 2003; Kim & Hubbard, 2007; Lee, 2008; Shen & Dumani, 2013).

Current acculturation models also imply that people with multiple cultures might develop and alter their multiple cultural identities. This could happen when responding to changing situations to sense association with the person's previous experiences, based on current goals, and his or her potentials (e.g., Lee, 2008; Maddux, Adam, & Galinsky, 2010). Hong et al. (2000) noted that several authors focused on the negative consequences of identity alterations. Used descriptive terms such as culture shock, acculturative stress, identity confusion, cultural denial, chameleonic-line behavior, among others (Cheryan & Monin, 2005; Downie et al., 2006; see also Furham, 2012; Ward et al., 2001). The descriptive negative viewpoint illustrated managing of multiple cultural identities as negative experiences resulting from the cultural differences awareness. Including the intention to retain or to reform the current identity based on the new cultural experiences (Downie et al., 2006; M. Ho & Bauderb, 2011). The negative experiences might occur only at particular transitional phases of multicultural development (Hong et al., 2000).

The actual perspective stresses to consider recognizing and investigating the processes involved in multiple cultural identities' development and management. Recent studies indicated that knowing different cultural traditions helps the person to develop self-awareness of his or her own cultural attraction (Ozyurt, 2013; Song, 2009; Zaharna, 1989). The awareness might also allow people to compare, to distance themselves, or to choose from the available cultural identity options (Dickerson, 2000; Mossman, 2012; Verkuyten & deWolf, 2002a). Overtime, people might create a set of adjustment, leading to constant identity shifts or the internalization of new cultural identities (Hong et al., 2000).

Existing research on cultural identity negotiation indicated specific strategies for identity negotiation as acculturation, integration, assimilation, and marginalization (J. Berry, 2001; Cox et al., 2010; Schwartz & Zamboanga, 2008). Various scholars suggested the identity negotiation as similar for multiple identities negotiation but at the same time as different. Hong et al. (2000) organized existing research and theory on multiple cultural identity negotiation models as integration, alternation, or synergy.

In the integration model, Hong et al. (2000) noted the identity elements from multiple cultures merge into the other cultures making a unitary multiple cultural identity (Benet-Martínez & Haritatos, 2005; Tadmor, Galinsky, & Maddux, 2012; Verkuyten & deWolf,

2002a; Ward et al., 2011). The integration model described people with multiple cultures as having highly developed identities in each one of their cultures, and they use them in suitable ways in different settings (Hong et al., 2000, 2003). The alternation model, Hong et al. (2000) indicated that people with multiple cultures switch identities continuously depending on the appropriateness of the identity with the immediate setting. The model of synergy relates to the new identities formed because of contact and recombination with different cultural models creating a new identity (e.g., cultural hybridization; Bhabha, 1994; Clandinin, 2007; Kim & Hubbard, 2007; Sussman, 2000).

Hong et al. (2000) specified that when people with multiple cultural identities negotiate their identity they do it more than to gain knowledge of the culture. They reflect on cultures, and evaluate the significance based on previous cultural experiences. According to these scholars, multiple cultural identity is a product of consideration and constant personal development.

The reviewed literature suggested that an assimilation effect is created when people with multiple cultural identities do not encounter identity challenges. If they sense problems, they might increase awareness of the interaction. They trigger a compatible and flexible identity, and retell themselves of the feelings and values attached to their cultural identities (Hong et al., 2000). Being aware of the differences and disadvantages, some people members of the racial and ethnic minority groups might develop a separate cultural identity to fit in the majority group or dominant culture.

For example, a participant of an ethnographic study stated:

As a result of all these differences and having been forced to adapt to this new culture, I have developed another cultural identity which is capable of surviving in this new environment … This identity functions like a second personality that appears when it is necessary to adopt a culturally appropriate behavior in the new culture. (Sparrow, 2000, p. 192, as cited in Hong et al., 2000, p. 339).

In sum, as multiple cultural identities, Hong et al. (2000) suggested that people might be adept of having mentally representation of multiple cultures and might be able to adjust to those cultures. Hong et al. also proposed that culture is different within individuals forming a population described by demographics, national, or ethnic individualities. The scholars also noted that understanding multiple cultures is valuable because the knowledge people with multiple cultural identities possess equips them with revealing tools of empathetic experiences.

Hong et al. (2000) also noted the encounters with multiple cultures could also raise identity distresses. The distresses raised primarily in conditions where people with multiple cultural identities need to show loyalty to the culture or the others. This includes when people with multiple cultural identities face domination, ambiguity, rejection, and so forth. In this case, the identity negotiation is encouraged by power within relations in society.

Mixing behaviors. Although theories of the social identity model provided possible reasons for mixing behaviors, a different perception also showed promise. According to Briley et al. (2005), a cultural setting could influence behaviors by increasing openness to those culture norms, in addition to the level of the person's motivation to behave in a certain way, harmonizing with those norms. The effects of mixing behaviors might reflect motivations, primarily when the behavior is socially noticeable (Molinsky, 2007).

Barreto et al. (2003) provided a different point of view by noting multicultural people might shift behaviors strategically to emphasize and to confirm their identities perceived as concealed or pretentious by some people. Ghavami, Fingerhut, Peplau, Grant, and Wittig (2011) indicated affirmation brings a greater sense of identity. Cook, Purdie-Vaughns, Garcia, and Cohen (2012) advanced the notion that social environments often expose multicultural people to social threats such as negative evaluation and rejection.

Barreto et al. (2003) noted one problem a person with multiple cultures might encounter is managing "gatekeepers" (p. 301) of either a native or a dominant culture who decide the norms for identity or membership to a culture. Self-identity and external categorization develop an identity threat based on differences between people (Badea, Jetten, Czukor, & Askevis-Leherpeux, 2010; Barreto & Ellemers, 2003). Immigrant group members often encountered differences between their self-perception and acknowledgment by the hosting culture, principally because the focal concept was that people have only one culture or identity (Barreto et al., 2003; Hernandez, 2009; Pohlert, 2008). Immigrants might have multiple identities, but others might perceive them only by their origin or native identity (Barreto et al., 2003; Yoon, 2011). People with disabilities using a wheelchair are instantly labeled by the disability (e.g., wheelchair) and not by any other possible membership group (e.g., origin, ethnicity, race, or gender; Rohmer & Louvet, 2009).

The differences in how people with multiple cultures perceive themselves and how others perceive them, including the hosting culture, often include discrimination, stereotypes, and stigma (Barreto & Ellemers, 2003; Sinclair, Hardin, & Lowery, 2006). For multicultural people, compound identification often happens simultaneously, such that disclosing identities might create uncertainties based on discrimination, stereotypes, and stigma, which might develop into significant identity intimidation (Barreto et al., 2003). Lam, Hector, Fong, and Corrigan (2006) advanced the notion that stereotypes occur throughout ethnic, religious, social class, gender, or disability groups. J. Berry (2001) also noted marginalization could result based on experiencing cultural loss, exclusion, or discrimination.

Some people with unnoticeable (hidden) disabilities might choose not to disclose their disability to avoid distress caused by discrimination, rejection, or stigmatization. In an autoethnography, Goldin (2012) recalled the following comment by a doctor: "If you choose to disclose the nature of your body, you must be ready for a fight" (p. xii). Disclosing could involve awareness of being in such situation. Disclosing could also entail evaluating the sensitivity of the culture norm behavior, knowing that disclosing could develop a threat against the person or could affect the person's self-esteem (Barreto et al., 2003; Tajfel, 1982; see also Ellemers, Spears, & Doosje, 2002; Tajfel, Richardson, & Everstine, 1964).

The desire and motivation to fit into a culture might encourage a person to know more about a culturally scripted behavior (Briley et al., 2005). The culturally scripted behavior implicating stereotypes might influence a multicultural person to mix behaviors to fit in or to adjust to a culture (Alves et al., 2006; Molinsky, 2007). The decision to accept or reject the stereotype could bring negative consequences to an individual's life (Briley et al., 2005; Ellemers et al., 2002; Tajfel, 1982; Tajfel et al., 1964).

Tensions and conflicts could also develop during mixing behaviors as a disruption that forms during the intersection of cultures, which opinions of social identities, perceptions of social categorizations, and the dynamics related to diversity could influence (Bodenhausen, 2010; Padilla, 2001; Torres & Rollock, 2009). Falk, Dunn, and Norenzayan (2010) inquired into personal emotional assumptions, indicating that people make choices based on what makes them more comfortable based on the culture norm. Briley et al. (2005) noted after multicultural people identify a culture, they might have to adjust to acceptable behavior and might need to change behaviors based on the use of language, beliefs, morals, desires, perceptions, resources, abilities, disabilities, stereotypes, or social threats (Badea et al., 2010; Luna et al., 2008; Sinclair et al., 2006).

Disability. Study findings historically showed that people with disabilities have experienced biased assumptions, detrimental stereotypes, unfounded fears, discrimination, and misconceptions (Esmail, Darry, Walter, & Knupp, 2009). People with disabilities have motives to interact socially and must resolve complex social problems to survive, as every human does (Matsumoto, 2007). Despite such experiences, people with disabilities continue their daily living activities and secure healthy styles.

The focus of research on disability has been how history and social perceptions affect not only the identity of a person with disabilities and how that person makes meaning of self. In an autoethnography, Schneider (2011) described developing resentment and annoyance toward his disability, meaning toward himself, because the disability is part of his identity. Bahm and Forchuk (2009) indicated the perceptions of stigma and discrimination have harmful effects to people who experience them.

Rohmer and Louvet (2009) indicated that in society, a physical disability defines a person as an identity symbol. Rohmer and Louvet also showed that people from racial minority, ethnic minority, and suppressed groups with disabilities who use a wheelchair are reduced to their classification group. Women and men using a wheelchair suffer the loss of gender and ethnicity because people describe them by their disability, not by their respective gender or ethnicity (Rohmer & Louvet, 2009). These issues further compound the notion of identifying as a person with disabilities, forcing the person to behave as the culture expects. People with disabilities could face rejection or discrimination if they do not behave as scripted (Ramey, 2007; Rembis, 2010; Smart, 2009; Voigts, 2009).

Multicultural people with disabilities could encounter additional difficulties based on the disability and their ethnic minority groups' identities (Molina, 2006; Schneider, 2011; Voigts, 2009). Molina (2006) considered the intersection of race, immigration, and disability as a cycle that never ends and indicated race and disability support one another. Dietz-Uhler and Murrell (1998) noted when something threatens a person's positive identification, self-esteem is at risk, which obligates the person to manage the threat to rebuild or to maintain self-esteem.

There was evidence that stigma, discrimination, rejection, and labeling represent a social threat for multicultural people with disabilities (Bahm & Forchuk; 2009; Nario-

Redmond, 2010; Rohmer & Louvet, 2009). Other scholars noted that people with disabilities are isolated not only within society but also from family and friends (Brewer & Kramer, 1985; Frable, 1993; Simpson, 2010; P. Smith & Routel, 2010). The isolation from family and friends might develop based on tensions between their own identity and those of a dominant culture, which influences them to shift identities to accomplish what they might want for their lives or for social interactions (Brewer & Kramer, 1985; Frable, 1993; Simpson, 2010; P. Smith & Routel, 2010).

Smith-Sullivan (2008) discussed tensions between identity and family and friends could include uncomfortable feelings such as being judged, patronized, shamed, unheard, misunderstood, or dismissed. Many people with disabilities are not legally capable of representing themselves, regardless of their race, based on the definition of independent and able-bodied (Molina, 2006). Ciol et al. (2008) explained that race and ethnicity influence the way people report a disability, indicating that social environments such as social support might influence the perception of a physical disability. The factors that connect and interconnect difficulties for people with disabilities might cause them to conceptualize, accept, conform to, or reject social roles scripted for them (Claidière, Bowler, & Whiten, 2012).

Scholars investigating disability made a notable agreement and developed a disability culture, educating not only professionals within the disability discipline, but also other scholars and communities on the issues people with disabilities encounter. The literature review on disability provided an endless list of themes:

- People with disabilities encounter difficulties worldwide (Coleman & Croake, 1987).
- The disability concept carries history (Esmail et al., 2009; Loewen & Pollard, 2010).
- People with disabilities experience stigma from other ethnic minority groups and others with disabilities (Bahm & Forchuk; 2009; Nario-Redmond, 2010; Ramey, 2007; Rembis, 2010; Rohmer & Louvet, 2009).
- People with disabilities lose gender because people label them by the disability or they are unnoticed (Esmail et al., 2009; Rohmer & Louvet, 2009; Stone, 2005).

55

- People with disabilities encounter visible and hidden social stigmas (Campbell, 2011).

- People with disabilities encounter more discrimination if they are members of other racial or ethnic minority groups (Taub, McLorg, & Fanflik, 2004).

People with disabilities might encounter challenges when something threatens their positive identification and self-esteem. Nario-Redmond (2010) explained people with disabilities face stereotypes such as unappealing, inspiring, or heroic. Much research also indicated that people with disabilities, as does every person encountering social identity threats, must manage the threat to rebuild or maintain self-esteem against stigmatization, rejection, and discrimination (Cook et al., 2012; Dietz-Uhler & Murrell, 1998).

Some scholars offered a different definition of disability focusing on the restricting nature of culture and setting other than the limitations of the person with a disability. The proposed definition is the *explanatory legitimacy theory* (ELT). The ELT theory roots on past and present diversity studies and debates. Within the ELT, scholars define disability as a contextually embedded, active substantial category of human diversity introducing description, explanation, and legitimacy as interactive elements. The ELT interactive element of description involves the complete scope of human activity, appearance, and experience, explanation is the set of explanations for different doings, appearance, and experience, and legitimacy suggests judgment about acceptability and worth (Gilson & DePoy, 2006; see also Cramer, Gilson, & DePoy, 2003).

According to Gilson and DePoy (2000), defining disability as culture surpasses inner factors of disability, incorporates social and political definitions, and generates a cultural discourse that symbolizes the group of people with disabilities. Cultural views of disability suggest that people who define themselves as having a disability belong to a unique group sharing experiences, values, understood rules, language, and dialogue (Devlieger & Albrecht, 2000; Gilson & DePoy, 2000). Yet, "Our findings and these hypotheses suggest that (a) disability may have different salience and meaning across minority groups and (b) social support and coping strategies may also differ markedly" (Devlieger & Albrecht, 2000, p. 59). Devlieger and Albrecht also suggested disentangling the effects of poverty and social class from those of race and ethnicity to understand the dynamics of defining and dealing with disability.

Some people could implicitly assume that disability culture is common to all people with disabilities and that people experience the disability in a similar way. For some people with disabilities, the concept of disability might be similar to other groups with disabilities, but in some cases is different in the importance, concerns, and life expression, such as for some people with disabilities from different race/ethnic minority groups or social status (Devlieger & Albrecht, 2000). Viewing disability as culture has some advantages, but the drawbacks and limitations are significant.

Several people understand the phenomenon of disability in different ways. Many disability models exist including the social, medical, principle of normalization, social role valorization, limits, expert or professional, rights-based, tragedy or charity, religious or moral, economic, customer or empowering, rehabilitation, disablement, political, cultural, consciousness, and integrated models (Bampi, Guilhem, & Alves, 2010; Barnartt, 1996; Gilson & DePoy, 2000; LoBianco & Sheppard-Jones, 2007; Nevin, Smith, & McNeil, 2008; Oliver, 1986; Roush & Sharby, 2011; Scullion, 2010). The two predominant disability theory models, which emerged over the last 50 plus years, are the medical and social models (Gilson & DePoy, 2000; LoBianco & Sheppard-Jones, 2007).

The medical model emphasizes the manifestation of the physical or mental limitations. The model defines a person as having a disability if she or he has a physical or mental limitation affecting one or more major life activities, has a record of such impairment, or medical professionals consider the person as having such impairment (Cramer & Plummer, 2009; LoBianco & Sheppard-Jones, 2007; Scullion, 2010).

The medical model might include the need of using a mobility aid (e.g., a wheelchair, cane, braces), not able to communicate because of the disability, learning disability, visual or hearing impairment, or the person is not able to do daily living activities (Oliver, 1986, 1996; LoBianco & Sheppard-Jones, 2007). In essence, in the medical model professionals consider a person with a disability as ill or unhealthy someone who needs fixing with therapy, medicine, surgery, or special treatment to adapt to the environment (LoBianco & Sheppard-Jones, 2007; Peters, 2006; Turnbull & Stowe, 2001).

The social model of disability looks at how society responds to a person with a disability. The model indicates that an ample response from society could eradicate disability. Supporters of the social model suggest that society's inability to remove the environmental barriers encountered by a persona with a disability obstructs people with disabilities. In sum, the social model focuses on social attitudes and opportunities rather than impairment (Anastasiou & Kauffman, 2013; Bampi et al., 2010; LoBianco & Sheppard-Jones, 2007; Peters, 2006; Turnbull & Stowe, 2001).

The medical and social model contrast in terms viewing the needs of people with disabilities. The medical model focuses on finding a cure and the social model focuses on finding inclusion, but these models also provide different definition of the disability concept. Either including that, the social factors as working, married, or active member in the community might make a person with a disability seem to self or to others as being less disabled (LoBianco & Sheppard-Jones, 2007).

Ethnicity. The literature on ethnicity was extensive, but did not investigate inner dynamics influencing mixing behaviors. According to Peipina (2009), ethnic identity is a critical component in the organization of groups of ethnic identities and is a national self-identification. Several scholars discussed ethnicity as not only to one of the most important identities within a group's identity, but also as dynamic changing upon time and context. According to some researchers, the core of ethnic identity involves the sense of belonging to a group, as group member, in which the sense of fitting in develops over time through exploration, learning, and loyalty (Peipina, 2009; Phinney & Ong, 2007). Some scholars explained ethnicity of a group as the result of religious belief and practices (Willem, 2009).

Numerous scholars agreed to three main views on ethnicity as elemental, circumstantial, and constructivist discourses. In the elemental discourse, ethnicity involves language, kinship, region, custom, and religion, described as a persistent and immutable element of social identity, and the one that determines the people's behavior. In the circumstantial view ethnicity is the result of specific interests, goals, agendas, specific circumstances, and focus on the limits that delineate and define the group, and not so much on the culture, which could be found within it (Phinney & Ong, 2007; see also Merritt & Harrison, 2006).

In the constructivist view, ethnicity is an identity formed through interaction and in dialogue with members of a group and with other people outside the group. They all work to achieve goals and to realize interests including economic ones (Cramer & Plummer, 2009; Cohen, 2009; Peipina, 2009; Phinney & Ong, 2007). For example, the U.S. Census Bureau defined ethnicity as relating only to Hispanic or non-Hispanic origin, which some scholars disagree because they would favor a broader definition to include language, heritage, transmitted norms, values, beliefs, behavior, and the like (Cohen, 2009; Peipina, 2009).

Applegate (1990) noted ethnicity is an inner process and representation that shapes people's sense of self and others as an internalized and transmitted representation that is unique and individual. Phinney and Ong (2007) noted ethnic identity changes with time, based on situations, and involves values, behaviors, and attitudes. Some scholars exploring ethnicity contended ethnicity serves to set social boundaries based on certain groups' behaviors (Acharya, 2010; Friedkin, 2010; Orbe & Drummond, 2009; Soto et al., 2012).

The labels constructed in the Unites States for social and political matters describing race are "African Americans, Asian Americans, European Americans, Hispanic or Latino Americans, Native Americans, and Multiracial Americans" (Orbe & Drummond, 2009, p. 439). Purdie-Vaughns and Eibach (2008) noted these definitions might discourage people with intersecting cultures from belonging to their culture groups because such definitions are androcentric, ethnocentric, and heterocentric. These definitions illustrate the person as male, as a member of the dominant ethnic group, and as heterosexual (Purdie-Vaughns & Eibach, 2008). Ethnicity for multicultural people overlooks the intersectionality of cultures because the person might not be multiracial or multiracial American. Multicultural people might belong to more than one race group or might not fit within the Americans descriptor.

Ethnicity has been used in different forms related to race. Some scholars defined ethnicity based on cultural characteristics (Orbe & Drummond, 2009; Soto et al., 2012). According to Yoon (2011), ethnicity seems to have more than one meaning because it highlights people's differences. Chao (2012) explained ethnic identity as "an individual's sense of being a person definable in part by membership in an ethnic group" (p. 51).

Rohmer and Louvet (2009) discussed the problem of defining ethnicity as a superordinate category involving different degrees of salience depending on the person's social categorization. The omission of racial or ethnicity experiences is an example of oppression and silencing the person (Cantey, 2011; Soto et al., 2012). Aldarondo (2001) described the struggles multicultural people encounter and explained those challenges come from society's pressure to have one identity instead of multiple. Aldarondo also noted race and ethnicity are two terms under transformation, in which many instances do not apply because many individuals have multiple heritages, have multiple ethnic and racial backgrounds, and have multiple religious beliefs.

Although Torres et al. (2012) focused on Latino participants, the study showed that people with multiple cultures reevaluate their ethnic identity based on life events or different environments. Torres et al. indicated managing modifications within the culture setting and the identity's context of diverse situations influenced those changes. Some changes and diverse situations include employment relocation, marriage, or major life events (Torres et al., 2012).

Ethnic identity is multidimensional and emerges from a sense of belonging to a group, a culture, and a culture's settings, and it develops over time (Phinney & Ong, 2007). Immigrants face challenges negotiating racial and ethnic identity as American Latinos because they have multiple identities (Collins, 2001). Race and ethnicity play an important role in the life of multicultural people (B. Cole, 2009; Collins, 2001; Phinney & Ong, 2007). Some researchers also discussed Latinos or Latinas and Hispanics as encountering more challenges than other ethnic groups in the United States (Sarkisian & Gerena, 2005).

Gender. Gender identity is how a person identifies socially and involves attitudes, rights, responsibilities, and behaviors that society links or expects from men or women (Moin, Duvdevany, & Mazor, 2009; Nario-Redmond, 2010; Sultana, 2011). Parent et al. (2013) discussed gender as a set of socially formed standards of community, identity, and implicit and explicit behaviors assigned to people base on their noticeable biological sex. According to Cantey (2011), an interconnection exists between sexuality and gender. Muehlenhard and Peterson (2011) noted that gender is a more flexible concept because it identifies women and men based on psychological, social, and cultural differences.

Gender encounters disproportionate stereotypes developed for groups with certain societal roles (Marshall & Read, 2003; Nario-Redmond, 2010; Parent et al., 2013). Purdie-Vaughns and Eibach (2008) discussed the association between gender roles and ethnicity to low-income immigrant ethnic minority women encountering more disadvantages due to their ethnicity, gender, class, and citizenship. According to the literature, gender is a key factor that society uses to identify groups for self-identification and communication (Bodenhausen, 2010; Hughey & Vidich, 1992; Parent et al., 2013; Yoon, 2011; see also Merritt & Harrison, 2006).

In some cultures, traditional beliefs about gender roles place women under men's influence (Marshall & Read, 2003; Sultana, 2011). In such cases, women's role includes being passive, refined, delicate, dependent, and pure while men's role includes being active, independent, and strong (Sultana, 2011). According to these traditions, women are homemakers and wives, have children, and their place is as a daughter or sister (Sarkisian & Gerena, 2005; Sultana, 2011). These women follow traditional cultures influenced by traditional thinking or power where the cognitive, strategic, and emotional components of social situations still prevail (Marshall & Read, 2003; Sarkisian & Gerena, 2005; Sultana, 2011).

Classifying a person based on gender and ethnicity is a silent type of social classification (Bodenhausen, 2010; B. Cole, 2009; Rohmer & Louvet, 2009). Women who encounter categorization within their job might have to silence their gender identity and express no involvement with women's social position because showing support would weaken the way their coworkers treat them (Barreto & Ellemers, 2002). Such women resist associating with external classifications and self-identity to avoid further or future categorizations (Barreto & Ellemers, 2002).

For women with disabilities, gender could be a factor worsening the discrimination against them and could lead to marginalization (Nosek & Hughes, 2003). Some women using a wheelchair lose their gender, and people describe them by the wheelchair and not by their gender or ethnicity (Ortoleva & Knight, 2012; Rohmer & Louvet, 2009). Women and men with disabilities might lose their gender due to their use of a wheelchair and their experiences could worsen as a multiethnic person (Esmail et al., 2009; Rohmer & Louvet, 2009; Stone, 2005).

Cheng (2009) noted people with disabilities encounter major and stereotypical ideas of gender functioning. Cheng indicated disability, feminist, and gender theories discussed the intersections of gender, race, ethnicity, sexuality, able-ism, and males' power over females as intersectional. Women with disabilities who are cross-cultural might be unrecognized in different sectors in society (Cheng, 2009). Chao (2012) also discussed gender roles as social constructions of multiple complex attitudes, expectations, and beliefs.

The intersectionality of disability, gender, and ethnicity creates higher sums of conflict and stress for multicultural people (Cramer & Plummer, 2009; Ortoleva & Knight, 2012). Intersectionality not only limits multicultural people's daily activities but also interferes with their self, social interactions, and communication (Cantey, 2011; Nario-Redmond, 2010). The next section contains discussions of self-leadership as it relates to intersectionality and mixing behaviors.

Self-leadership strategy. Self-leadership could be an important strategy for multicultural people to possess (Neck & Manz, 1992; Unsworth & Mason, 2012). Self-leadership is a strategy that helps people navigate difficult situations and walk through stressed environments (Boss & Sims, 2008; Neck & Manz, 1992; Unsworth & Mason, 2012). Self-leadership confirmed the strategy of mixing identities as internal dialogue needed to understand a behavior during social interactions (Alves et al., 2006; Manz, 1986; see also Chao et al., 1994). Alves et al. (2006) explained self-leadership as having different connotations depending on cultural settings and norm behavior, and its implementation might include a wide variety of uses.

Lash and Hodgetts (1992) reviewed the book *Mastering Self-Leadership: Empowering Yourself for Personal Excellence* written by Charles C. Manz, who indicated people could control their own destiny with self-leadership. Self-leadership is a talent not only for leaders, employers, or employees but also as a personal skill (Lash & Hodgetts, 1992). Research also revealed self-leadership allows a person to avoid possible stressors and conflicts resembling pressure (Boss & Sims, 2008; Friedkin, 2010; Neck & Manz, 1992; Unsworth & Mason, 2012). Some stressors include anxiety and uncertainty, and highly affecting behaviors and self-leadership might produce a guiding effect on those behaviors (Gudykunst, 1983; Matsumoto, 2007).

Emotion control regulation appears to be similar to self-leadership, and both involve self-regulation, but these strategies' concepts are different (Boss & Sims, 2008; Friedkin, 2010; Unsworth & Mason, 2012). Emotional control regulation allows self-control, aiming for positive responses and feelings (Nelson et al., 2010). Self-leadership involves self-thinking, self-talking, self-mental imagery strategies, and self-influencing (Curral & Marques-Quinteiro, 2009; Unsworth & Mason, 2012). Self-regulation explains how people behave (Alves et al., 2006).

The main concept of self-leadership is that people could control self-thinking because they have the power to do it (Haseli, Vaezmousavi, & Seddighi, 2012; Theodorakis, Hatzigeorgiadis, & Chroni, 2008). Self-leadership originates from self-talking, self-verbalization, and self-imagery influencing personal effective performance in different activities and tasks (Curral & Marques-Quinteiro, 2009; Neck & Manz, 1992; Theodorakis et al., 2008). Self-talk is an approach used to speak mentally to oneself to compare and understand the relationship between ideals, principles, goals, and objectives; self-leadership is an internal voice guiding and speaking to the self (Chohan, 2010; Curral & Marques-Quinteiro, 2009). Chohan (2010) described the strategy of self-talk as "the inner voice" (p. 10).

Haseli et al. (2012) studied athletes' performance and described self-leadership as an intrinsic personal dialogue. The internal conversation helps the person to explain, determine, modify, and evaluate inner feelings and provides guidance on what to do (Cojocaru, 2013; Haseli et al., 2012). Theodorakis et al. (2008) also performed studies on self-talk within athletes and confirmed the strategy as a tool to improve interest and self-assurance, to control mental and emotional responses, to control determination, and to generate responses.

Numerous scholars have described self-leadership as a mechanism leading through constant self-influence (Boss & Sims, 2008; Neck & Manz, 1992). The concepts of constant influencing the self or self-management might appear similar to self-leadership (Boss & Sims, 2008; Manz, 1986; Neck & Manz, 1992). Manz (1986) noted self-leadership recognizes the difference between what people want to do and what they should do and the reasons influencing them to choose certain behavior.

The literature also indicated self-leadership is a tool to regulate emotions, to lessen the effects of failure, and to help move into recovery. Failure is part of a person's life and people respond to failure in different ways (Boss & Sims, 2008). Boss and Sims (2008) noted failure could control some people's actions; some people might recover quickly whereas others' self-esteem and self-assurance are affected. Emotional intelligence and emotion regulation relate to emotions and feelings, whereas the focus of self-leadership is on behavior and reasoning; it also slightly touches emotions (Boss & Sims, 2008). The essential notion of self-leadership is that people go to the inner self to find what they think is necessary to control and to encourage their conduct and thought (Manz, 1986; Neck & Manz, 1992).

The inner voice is a powerful personal process, as thoughts are unique and internal (Chohan, 2010; Jemmer, 2011). Thinking and communicating with the inner voice could affect and influence feelings, behaviors, and attitudes because the inner voice could convey positive or negative messages (Chohan, 2010). Houghton and Yoho (2005) noted self-leadership involves enjoyment when doing something, whereas positive thinking refers to recognizing, handling, and changing irregular beliefs and expectations to facilitate the thinking process.

Jemmer (2011) indicated self-talk is intrapersonal communication to coordinate body with brain to regulate behavior and could have psychophysiological structures interfering with how people see themselves compared to the way they interact with other people. People could feel acute feelings when self-talk is about such feelings (Jemmer, 2011). A cross-cultural comparative study also showed the influence of people's patterns and personalities as playing a strong role on cultural adaptation (Genkova, 2012).

Self-talk as a strategy for self-leadership involves allowing a person to evade pressures and problems (Boss & Sims, 2008; Unsworth & Mason, 2012). According to Genkova (2012), the strategy helps people balance their environment and make it comfortable to meet their personal needs. Although Jemmer (2011) described self-talk as having two ends, numerous scholars have specified self-leadership is a good strategy to implement an inner voice for personal improvement and guidance and as a tool to reflect about possible outcomes and evading conflict (Boss & Sims, 2008; Cojocaru, 2013; Neck & Manz, 1992; Unsworth & Mason, 2012).

When people want others to accept them, they feel motivated to present themselves by using self-presentation objectives (Nezlek et al., 2007). The objectives might involve positive relations and a good reputation related to social interactions and tasks, which are factors that relate to the self-leadership concept (Nezlek et al., 2007). Hogg (2001) discussed social identity and viewed leadership as processed by social categorization and the processes associated with social identity and self-definition.

The literature review showed that the focus of studies on self-leadership was on business management involving employers, employees, organizations, and entrepreneurs (Neck, Ashcraft, & VanSandt, 1998; Neck & Manz, 1992). Curral and Marques-Quinteiro (2009) explored self-leadership within innovation. Tabak, Çelik, and Türköz (2011) also indicated managers and employees in the public sector had high self-leadership perceptions. The focus of self-leadership is on performance improvement rather than social and cultural expectations (Alves et al., 2006).

Self-leadership provides multicultural people with autonomy and decision-making ability to achieve their goals. Researchers have indicated different concepts related to self-leadership in which some ideas related to how people behave or should behave and also revealed self-leadership theory includes enhancing strategies to focus a behavior (Alves et al., 2006; Neck & Houghton, 2006). The enhancing strategies involved self-observation, self-goal setting, self-rewards, self-punishment, and self-cuing (Alves et al., 2006; Neck & Houghton, 2006).

As related to multicultural people, self-observation could help to develop awareness regarding when and why to behave. Self-goal setting could help to decide which objectives to reach and how; self-rewards could help to compensate for motivation; self-punishment could help to provide constructive feedback to self; and self-cueing could help to monitor the self's external environment (Alves et al., 2006; Neck & Houghton, 2006). Multicultural people might use some or all of these self-leadership-enhancing strategies when mixing behavior during social interactions.

Qualitative Analytic Autoethnography

Numerous concepts are attainable from existing research in autoethnography. *"The autoethnographic* means telling a story about how much we –children and parents researchers and subjects, authors and readers— worry about fitting in, about normal, about being accepted, loved, and valued" (Adams & Jones, 2011, p. 114; see also Bochner, 2010; Butz, 2010; Denshire, 2014; Denzin, 2003; Garratt, 2014; Ngunjiri et al., 2010). An autoethnography is the study of self, consisting of profound ethical questions and self-relation to others (Atkinson, 2006; Adams & Jones, 2011; Chang, 2007, 2008; Crawford, 1996; Denshire, 2014; Doloriert & Sambrook, 2012; Ellis, 2007; Hughes et al., 2012; Jefferies, 2012; Holman Jones, Adams, & Ellis, 2013; Maydell, 2010; Schneider, 2011; Tolich, 2010; Warren, 2009).

According to Doloriert and Sambrook (2012), in etymological terms, autoethnography derived from Greek words *auto* meaning the self, *ethos* meaning nation, and *grapho* meaning to write. Autoethnography means "to write (research) about a nation (group of people) and the self (the researcher)" (p. 83). As a genre of writing and research, autoethnography is a form of qualitative research combining autobiographic and ethnographic methods (Anderson, 2006; Berger, 2001; Butz, 2010; Chang, 2007, 2008; Jupp, 2006). According to Jupp (2006), autoethnography includes researching, writing to self-reference, starts with personal experiences and studies "'us' in relationship and situations" (Ellis, 2007, p. 13; see also Berger, 2001; Crawford, 1996; Denshire, 2014; Ellis, 2004, 2008; Ellis & Bochner, 2006).

Autoethnographers narrate personal experiences associated with a broader situation based on cultural concerns sustained by academic research. Martinez and Merlino (2014) expressed:

We believe that the beauty of autoethnography is that it "creates a space for a

turn, a change, a reconsideration of how we think" (Holman Jones et al., 2013,

p. 21). It has the potential to question al representations that are stuck to our

brains with the think glue of culture. It allows us to reflect to on our own

points of view as people as well as social researchers. (p. 996)

As noted by Hamilton et al. (2008), the writer's position of self is a critical component of an

autoethnography because the writer's situatedeness illustrates, connects, and reflects on

actual life events. The possibility exists that the self-truth could emerge from understanding

the culture's situation and the autoethnographer's reality (Adams & Jones, 2011; Crawford,

1996; Doloriert & Sambrook, 2012; Ellis, 2000; Bochner, 2012; Jefferies, 2012; see also

Bochner, 2010; Hughes et al., 2012). Murphy-Keith (2013) shared:

Through critical autoethnography I am able to connect the micro (personal

experience) with the macro (cultural messages/expectations) with the ultimate

aim of changing both my life and my broader social environment for the

better. In critiquing the discourses around Lolita specifically, I make it clear

that my experiences are not rare or on the periphery of society but are central

and damaging. (p. 103)

The importance of the writer's position as the autoethnographer is being part of the

narration by making the writer noticeable and enthusiastic within the context (Adams &

Jones, 2011; Anderson, 2006; Chang, 2007, 2008; Ellis, 2000; Ellis & Bochner, 2006; see

also Atkinson, 2006; Butz, 2010; Crawford, 1996; Warren, 2009). According to

Asdornnithee (2010):

Autoethnography is a research method which makes the author's inner

experience explicit, based on the belief that one's own inner experience has a

part in determining the outer reality and in influencing another if appropriately

conveyed. (p. 89)

Schneider (2011) put forward the notion that an autoethnographer must establish a

connection between the personal cultural experiences shared and the related cultural

influences within societies. This notion provides the opportunity to share personal cultural

experiences while learning a particular cultural experience (Adams & Jones, 2011; Ellis &

Bochner, 2006; Moisander & Valtonen, 2006). Lewis-Beck et al. (2004) discussed writers

taking their insights into a larger culture by integrating creative writing to narrate personal cultural experiences. Bochner (2012) argued, "Autoethnographies attempt to make social science something more than an end in itself" (p. 155; see also Crawford, 1996).

Researchers have also indicated the limitations of an autoethnographic approach for the writer. The studies cited in Maydell (2010), Tolich (2010), and Lewis-Beck et al. (2004) showed some potential problems for a study, including the writer's dual membership (insider and outsider), the interpretation of the dilemma's intensity, the claim of objectivity, and personal affliction. Ngunjiri et al. (2010) advanced the notion of these dilemmas and related ethics, accountability, exposure, self-disclosure, and vulnerability to those problems. Allen-Collinson (2013), Ellis (2007), Ellis et al. (2011), and Hughes et al. (2012) also noted that a critical factor that an autoethnographer needs to recognize is the requirement to protect others by altering identifiable information.

Some researchers indicated the political concerns of an autoethnography. Including that, an autoethnography is not a traditional research method, is an evocative or analytical method, and uses first person when writing narratives involving the researcher and the topic (Anderson, 2006; Atkinson, 2006; Boyle & Parry, 2007; Doloriert & Sambrook, 2009; Prince, 2006). Scholars also discussed autoethnography as representing not only a political or personal risk but also professional by exposing the self through the process; making the narrator vulnerable (Boyle & Parry, 2007; Ellis et al., 2011). Some scholars indicated that writing an autoethnography, in some cases, "can be considered the most dangerous fieldwork of all" (Boyle & Parry, 2007, p. 186).

The concept derived from the idea that autoethnography moves to the writer, back and forth, from individual situatedness within the out-world to the inner self (Boyle & Parry, 2007; Ellis, 2008). In addition to the risks and challenges involved with conducting such a study, an autoethnography provides the opportunity to explore topics that need profound expression with emotions that sometimes only the inner self can touch, such as spirituality, pain, social identity, gender, grief, or health (e.g., Poulos, 2014; see also Bochner, 2010; Ngunjiri et al., 2010; Warren, 2009). Duarte (2007) and Klinker and Todd (2007) noted an autoethnography study is an opportunity to explore oneself in a culture where the self is struggling to flee.

The assumption of using an autoethnography is that the autoethnographer is willing to tell his or her life's personal truths (Adams & Jones, 2011; Badley, 2014; Chang, 2007, 2008; Denshire, 2014; Denzin, 2014; Ellis et al., 2011; see also Atkinson, 2006; Crawford, 1996).

67

According to Murphy (2008), "Some have referred to autoethnography as the process of admitting one's own fears while using the daily drama of people's lives as a powerful way both to shape and show cultural construction in action" (p. 166; see also Crawford, 1996; Tedlock, 2005; Warren, 2009). Denzin (2014) paraphrased Stacy Holman Jones, Tony Adams, and Carolyn Ellis' concept of autoethnography:

> Autoethnography is the use of personal experience and personal writing to (1) purposefully comment on/critique cultural practices; (2) make contributions to existing research; (3) embrace vulnerability with purpose; and (4) created a reciprocal relationship with audiences in order to compel a response. (p. 19)

According to Ellis and Bochner (2000), autoethnography is difficult to define and apply based on its meaning and application. For decades, numerous scholars use different terms to describe concepts and definitions similar to autoethnography. For example, in 1982, Zola used the term socioautobiography, and Brandes used ethnographic autobiography to describe autoethnography (Ellis & Bochner, 2000; see also Badley, 2014; Chang, 2007; Crawford, 1996; Denshire, 2014; Doloriert & Sambrook, 2012; Ellis, 2008; Hughes et al., 2012; Moisander & Valtonen, 2006; Ngunjiri et al., 2010). In 1984, Ohnuki-Tierney used the term native ethnography.

In 1985, Conquergood used the term performance, and McCall used group storytelling. In 1986, Marcus and Fishcer used ethnographic poetics, Tyler used postmodern ethnography, Clifford and Marcus used writing culture, and Clifford and Marcus used ethnography. In 1988, Van Maanen used confessional tales, literary tales, and impressionistic accounts, and Pollock used performativity and performative. In 1989, the Personal Narratives Group used the term personal narratives, Lejeune used ethnobiography, Jackson used radical empiricism, Denzin used interpretative biography, and group storytelling by McCall (Denzin, 2014; Ellis & Bochner, 2000; see also Butz, 2010; Denzin & Lincoln, 2002; Doloriert & Sambrook, 2012; Riordan, 2014).

In 1990, Van Maanen used lived experience. In 1991, Krieger used personal essays, ethnographic memoir, and Tedlock used narrative ethnography. In 1993, Hawkins used the term auto-pathography, Goldman used collaborative autobiography, and AbuLughod used narrative ethnography (Ellis & Bochner, 2000). In 1994, Denzin used the terms personal experience narratives, self-stories, and interpretative biography, Richardson used narratives of the self, and Adler and Adler used complete-member research and auto-observation. In

1995, Ellis used the term ethnographic short stories and self-ethnography, and Church used critical autobiography.

In 1996, Crawford used the term personal ethnography, Payne used autobiology, new or experimental ethnography, and Ellis and Bochner used sociopoetics (Ellis & Bochner, 2000). In 1997, Denzin used experimental texts, Richardson used writing-stories, Riemer used opportunistic research, Bochner, Ellis, and Tillmann-Healy used evocative narratives, DeVault used reflexive ethnography, Gubrium and Holstein used emotionalism, Reed-Danahay used autobiographical ethnography, self-narrative, and ethnic autobiology, and indigenous ethnography by Gonzalez and Krizek. In 1998, Ellis used the term first-person accounts (Denzin, 2014; Ellis & Bochner, 2000).

In 2003, Denzin and Pelias used the concept performance (auto)ethnography. In 2005, Saldaña used the concept of ethnodrama, Madison used critical performance (auto)ethnography, and in 2006, Davies and Gannon used collective biography. In 2009, Jackson and Mazzei used the concept of deconstructive (auto)ethnography. In 2011, Spry used the concept of reflexive self performing itself, Wyatt used the concept collective biography, and Saldaña used the concept of ethnodrama, and in 2012, Norris and Sawyer used duoethnography.

Denzin (2014) discussed new forms of (auto)biographical methods presented by different scholars. The methods included narrative ethnography, meta-autoethnography, and collaborative autoethnography. Some scholars offered the form of co-constructed decolonizing autoethnography, duoethnography, collaborative writing, ethnodrama, and performance ethnography. Other new forms offered included sociopoetics, performance writing, writing stories, ethnographic fiction, polyvocal texts, and mystories. Recently, scholars chose the term autoethnography to describe studies and procedures connecting the personal to the cultural (Ellis & Bochner, 2000; see also Doloriert & Sambrook, 2012). Denzin discussed a new interest in interpretive method to the study of culture, biography, and groups.

Chang (2007) suggested putting attention for five drawbacks when doing autoethnography:

> (1) excessive focus on self in isolation of others; (2) overemphasis on
> narration rather than analysis and cultural interpretation; (3) exclusive reliance
> on personal memory and recalling as a data source; (4) negligence of ethical

standards regarding others in self narratives; and (5) inappropriate application

of the label 'autoethnography.' (p. 216)

The first drawback relates to culture and autoethnographers need to understand that an autoethnography is not a self-revealing story based on self-centered reflection. The second downside relates to the researcher needing to focus on the research purpose to avoid settling for large narratives without cultural exploration and clarification (Chang, 2007).

Third concern, Chang (2007) advised not to depend on personal memory as the only data source because, although memory is a unique source of information, autoethnographers need to support their reasons with broad-based data. According to Chang, multiple foundations of data can offer sources for triangulation that could help enhancing the accuracy and validity of the autoethnography context. The forth concern, links to confidentiality indicating that not because researchers use autobiographical stories means they do not need to follow confidentiality rules. Chang also highlighted that autoethnographers need to be aware that they have a responsibility to adhere to confidentiality as an ethical principle, like any other researcher of human subjects do.

The fifth and final drawback refers to the confusion of using the term autoethnography when is not. Chang (2007) indicated that it is the researcher's task to learn more about the multiple practices of autoethnography and to outline its use clearly enough to avoid confusion. Chang indicated that an autoethnography helps to unite, to comprehend, and to growth.

Telling of the story performing autoethnography. Writing autoethnography, also referred as performing autoethnography, could vary in writing styles depending on the autoethnographer's purposes and audience (Chang, 2007; Crawford, 1996; Denshire, 2014; Ellis, 2008; Riordan, 2014). The acknowledged tales originating from ethnographic writing involves styles as realistic, confessional, and impressionist accounts providing alternatives in autoethnography writing (Chang, 2007; Coffey, 1999; Denshire, 2014; see also Moisander & Valtonen, 2006). Ellis et al. (2011) indicated the autoethnography writing style depends on the study's emphasis to others, the autoethnographer's self, the interaction, the analysis, the interview, and the power of interactions.

Numerous scholars indicated autoethnography involves analytical description, realistic description, impressionist caricature, and confessional self-exposure (Chang, 2007; Moisander & Valtonen, 2006; Riordan, 2014). An autoethnographic writing style, which according to Riordan (2014) is performative by its type, could help people who might experience struggles describing the experiences (see Butz, 2010; Moisander & Valtonen, 2006; see also Denshire, 2014; Fox, 2014; Murphy-Keith, 2013). Chang (2007) suggested an autoethnographer planning to use ethnographic tales might need to modify the selected tale based on the concept that autoethnography is a cultural study of self and others.

Some autoethnographic types are layered account, co-constructed narratives, personal narratives, narrative inquiry, indigenous/native ethnographies, complete member texts, and narrative ethnographies. Including reflexive interviews, dyadic interviews, reflexive ethnographies, and interactive interviews (Ellis, 2008; Ellis et al., 2011; see also Coffey, 1999; Denzin, 2003; Denzin & Lincoln, 2002; Riordan, 2014). The following paragraphs provide brief details of some of the autoethnographic accounts discussed by different scholars.

Ellis et al. (2011) indicated that when using a layered account the narrator focuses on his or her experience along with data, abstract analysis, and related literature. The account stresses the research process and uses vignettes, reflexivity, polyvocal, and self-examination (e.g., Mizzi, 2010; Haynes, 2011; see Ellis et al., 2011; Ellis, 1991, 2008; see also Coffey, 1999; Dutta, 2014; Gale, 2014; Riordan, 2014). The layered account involves altering the narrator's voice splicing the formal writing with ethnographic and autobiographical materials, self-reflexive texts, and other narrator's claims (Riordan, 2014; see also Denshire, 2014; Ellis, 2008; Ellis et al., 2011).

The co-constructed narratives relates to the meaning of interpersonal experiences involving each narrator writing the personal experience around an epiphany, sharing, and responding to the shared story by the other narrator (Riordan, 2014; see also Denshire, 2014; Ellis, 2008; Ellis et al., 2008; Ellis et al., 2011). Ellis et al. (2011) indicated co-constructed narratives perceive friends, family, and or intimate partners, including how they collaboratively cope with uncertainties, hesitations, and conflicts (e.g., Cann & DeMeulenaere, 2012; Ellis et al., 2008; Ellis & Rawicki, 2013; Gearity & Mertz, 2012; see Clandinin, 2007; Pensoneau-Conway & Toyosaki, 2011).

Personal narratives are stories narrated by the narrators who view themselves as the phenomenon and write evocatively focusing on their educational arena, exploration and personal lives (Ellis et al., 2011). Personal narratives offer understanding of the self or some intersections in life with cultural context, link participants as co-researchers, and invite readers into the narrator's experiences to reflect, to understand, to learn, and to cope (Ellis, 2004, 2008; Ellis et al., 2011; see also Ellis & Bochner, 2000; Fox, 2014; Garratt, 2014; Pensoneau-Conway & Toyosaki, 2011; Trahar, 2009). According to Ellis et al., the personal narratives are debatable for traditional science research mainly if the narrative does not have traditional analysis and connection with the academic literature.

Indigenous/Native ethnographies are autoethnographic forms to speak and eradicate power in research. In the colonial background, ethnographers had the power, the right and the authority to study, claim, and publicize knowledge gained from other cultures. The ethnographers were mainly members of dominant cultures and were perceived as outsiders coming inside to help native people (Ellis, 2008; Ellis et al., 2011; Pensoneau-Conway & Toyosaki, 2011; see also Chang, 2007; Denshire, 2014; Denzin, 2003). Ellis et al. discussed that indigenous/native ethnographers work today to create their own personal and cultural stories because they are no longer at the service of dominant cultures of ethnographers.

Narrative or reflexive ethnographies focus on different culture or subculture. The author's personal experiences are essential to illuminate the studied culture while reflecting and looking deeper at the self in social interactions (Ellis, 2008; Ellis et al., 2011). The reflexive ethnographies vary from studying researchers' own experiences to studying the researchers' experiences with other participants. Personal stories refer the stories focusing on the researchers' off-stage experiences as to study others (e.g., ethnographic memoirs or confessional tales). Ethnographers use the self to study the other and reflexive ethnographers use their whole being including bodies, senses, feelings, and moments to learn about the other (Ellis, 2008; Ellis et al., 2011).

Complete member account includes detailed exploration of groups where the authors are full members or became identified and accepted members during the study, and the authors became part of the studied phenomena (e.g., Garratt, 2014; Griffin, 2009; Struthers, 2012; see Anderson, 2006; Butz, 2010; Chang, 2007, 2008; Doloriert & Sambrook, 2012; Ellis, 2008; Ellis et al., 2011; see also Denshire, 2014).

Modern narrative inquiry, according to Chase (2005), can be a mixture of interdisciplinary analytic lenses, different disciplinary methods, and can be a traditional and modernize method. The mixture orbits around the personal experiences as the authors' narrate their stories (Chase, 2005). Chase indicated that a narrative could be verbal or written and might elicit or hear information during fieldwork, interviews, or a natural conversation. In any of those situations, Chase discussed that a narrative might be:

> (a) a short topical story about a particular event and specific characters such as an encounter with a friend, boss, or doctor; (b) an extended story about a significant aspect of one's life such as schooling, work, marriage, divorce, childbirth, an illness, a trauma, or participation in a war or social movement; or (c) a narrative of one's entire life, from birth to the present. (p. 652)

The literature review suggested autoethnographers developed, and continue developing, a range of different methods helping them to bring the context to life. Some of the methods identified during the literature review included idiomatic expressions or metaphor (i.e., figurative language) to describe unfamiliar ideas, using graphics or images to create interest, and using different fonts and size fonts to distinguish different voices. Using different components, mixed tenses to develop drama or suspense, and using icons or symbols to clarify information as well (Riordan, 2014; see also Denzin & Lincoln, 2002).

Ethnography is about experiencing and remembering, as autobiographical practice does. According to Coffey (1999), ethnographic research is an experienced reality depending on the experiences of being there (see also Fox, 2014; Geertz, 1988; Spry, 2001; see also Chase, 2005). Coffey indicated that memory goes beyond any collected text or artifacts, and some times souvenirs or items help people to remember and recreate more than the collected items. Socially shared resources organize the personal experience of autobiographical memory and people draw on cultural significance and language to form memories. The cultural significance and the language become a framework for remembering (Coffey, 1999).

Current Findings

The literature review revealed that cultural intersection could include experiences relating to race, ethnicity, social class, and disabilities and could generate conflicts and stresses within multicultural adults (Constantine, 2002; Song, 2009). Intersectionality for women using a wheelchair escalates when race or ethnicity, disability, immigration, and gender are involved, and other dynamics such as social class, education, or basic daily activities interrelate (Taub et al., 2004). Several studies on the possible conflicts of cultural intersection also elaborated on the association of social class, classism, privilege, race, and racism involving other people or oneself (Constantine, 2002; W. Liu, Pickett, & Ivey, 2007). The studies also indicated adults implementing cultural chameleon behavior might need to

73

adapt to different cultures at one time or to switch behaviors quickly based on different situations (Bodenhausen, 2010; Deaux & Martin, 2003).

Different findings also noted the importance of understanding the multifaceted ways that identity develops, as discourses of social dissimilarity and imbalance strongly affect identity. Existing research demonstrated that social perception often differs based on the intersection of diverse social identities affecting members of multiple marginalized groups in complex ways. The concepts of self and identity are never neutral; take multiple forms, and sometimes take opposing forms. An individual identity varies and shifts throughout a lifetime (Deaux & Martin, 2003; McKenzie, 2011; Shen & Dumani, 2013).

The literature review revealed some scholars creating three ways to represent the self as the individual self, relational self, and collective self. The personal traits describe the individual self; the personal relationships with others exemplify the relational self, and the memberships in social groups or classifications portrays the collective self (Brewer & Gardner, 1996; Sedikides & Brewer, 2001; Hong, Wan, No, & Chiu, 2010). Hong et al. (2010) added cultural identity outlined by self-definition referring to a group of ideas and traditions shared or commonly spread in certain population or as a "tradition of knowledge" as Barth (2002, p. 2) indicated.

Hong et al. (2010) contended cultural identity and collective identity as two different concepts. Collective identity is when a group shares, voluntary or by involuntary, a particular tradition of knowledge. For example, voluntary sharing identity could involve religion as distributed within its members around the world, and involuntary when the person did not have the option to decide, for example, gender, race, or baptized at birth.

The literature review also revealed that, although cultural and collective identities are different, cultural identification and collective identification relate. Hong et al. (2010) argued identification as the degree to which an individual establishes a unit relation between the self and the relevant identity. People who identify with a tradition of knowledge and with a group membership believe that an essential part of their self-definition. When people identify with the tradition of knowledge they believe to define a collective identity. For instance, people from Mexico who are Catholics define the ethnic Mexican collective group, and with the group of catholic Mexicans.

Hong et al. (2010) also claimed that people acquire tradition of knowledge through cultural learning, personal experiences, or by observing. Acquiring knowledge increases in perceptive accessibility because of its repetition and application to understand the personal experiences and to organize social actions. Some people might identify with such tradition of knowledge, some might not, in other words, learning, and acquiring certain knowledge tradition does not mean the person identifies with such knowledge.

Some findings also indicated that culture is a cognitive place for understanding different experiences and reaching personal goals, but does not strictly regulate a person's behavior. When people with multiple cultural identities alternate their cultural identity, they might not just bring back their knowledge about the appropriate culture, they might reflect on their cultural traditions, compare the traditions, and evaluate their importance related to cultural experiences, past and current (Cohen & Gunz, 2002; Geertz, 1973; Hong et al., 2010). A multiple cultural identity might be a product of reflecting and a constant personal plan. If there is a conflict of identities, where the person's identity is in question, she or he might increase awareness of intercultural experiences in society, activate perceptions related to the compatible identity, and remember any feelings and values attached. In sum, negotiating identities is a process; it might not be a reaction to a situation or setting (Hong et al., 2010).

Bodenhausen (2010) noted the need for research on the role-play of social identity innately involved in the cultural connection process. According to Bodenhausen, focusing only on factors such as racism, sexism, ageism, and other forms of prejudice might lead to missing the focus and the function of identity during the assimilation process. Constantine (2002) also indicated perceiving a group as a whole could lead to missing the intersection of group members' identities, which might shape members' experiences and realities. Matsumoto (2007) explained different social situations might provoke different behaviors, and those behaviors might create sub behaviors related to the same social situation.

The current findings also included a discussion on tensions and conflicts defined as the disruption that occurs when two or more cultures cross each other (Padilla, 2001; Torres & Rollock, 2009). Social identities could influence the disruption regarding how people perceive the multicultural person, social categorization, and dynamics related to group diversity (Barreto et al., 2003; Bodenhausen, 2010). Multicultural people might feel the need to switch between individualist and collectivist cultures or their own beliefs to fit in certain cultures (Barreto et al., 2003; Campbell, 2011; Falk et al., 2010).

Matsumoto (2007) noted when people encounter several situations with different scripted social roles, they adapt through altering their cultures. This intersection might cause stresses and conflicts if the person feels obligated to respond or to meet society's expectations (Falk et al., 2010; L. Liu et al., 2012). People might have to confront different challenges involving immigration status, race, national and ethnic origin, religion or no religion, socioeconomic levels, and social class, among other names used to identify a culture (Cohen, 2009).

People with multiple cultures might encounter conflict and stress with collectivistic or individualistic beliefs and with other cultures because the effects of culture are recurrent and continuous and produce uncertainty and anxiety when judging oneself or others (Alves et al., 2006; Hong et al., 2000; Matsumoto, 2007). Purdie-Vaughns and Eibach (2008) introduced the idea of "intersectional invisibility" (p. 378), noting that people with multiple suppressed cultures become invisible when clashing with the models of their minor groups. In sum, people might have different beliefs about a group's scripted behavior, and accepting or rejecting the behavior might affect them (Frable, 1993; Gudykunst, 1983; Matsumoto, 2007).

The intersection of multiple cultures revealed that multicultural people might encounter an intersection of more than two cultures (Constantine, 2002; Song, 2009). The uniqueness of the multicultural population forces them to select a strategy for acculturation, but people might need to choose more than one strategy to meet their needs (J. Berry, 2001; Schwartz & Zamboanga, 2008). People with multiple cultures might have to confront hard decisions to accept or to reject the scripted social roles of one or several groups (Deaux & Martin, 2003; Frable, 1993; Gudykunst, 1983; Matsumoto, 2007).

A substantial amount of research indicated the acculturation process relates to the interaction and adaptation among persons or groups with different backgrounds and experiences, but the focus has been on immigrant groups (J. Berry, 2001; Schwartz & Zamboanga, 2008). The acculturation strategies assimilation, integration, separation, and marginalization might cause distress to multicultural people (J. Berry, 2001; Tadmor et al., 2012). Assimilation refers to abandoning the cultural tradition and identifying only with the new culture, and integration refers to keeping the traditional culture (Tadmor et al., 2012). Separation refers to not accepting the new culture, and marginalization refers to avoiding identification with any culture (Chen et al., 2008; Qin, 2011; Rodríguez-García, 2010).

Song (2009) noted a multicultural person is able to understand more than one culture and to develop multiple identities for harmonizing. It is critical to understand inner identities to appreciate a multicultural society (Gavilán, 2010; Purdie-Vaughns & Eibach, 2008). To manage cultural intersections, it might be necessary to possess proper and self-advanced skills (Song, 2009). According to Campbell (2011), power could be a factor in social categorization that emotionally affects the experience of multicultural people.

Different findings included that several scholars do not include the multiethnic population in the literature, and according to Vivero and Jenkins (1999), the researchers might have three reasons. First, members of ethnically mixed backgrounds might be difficult to locate and study for the reason that they might have as different experiences as their ethnic combinations, they might not fit into a particular ethnic group, and they might not follow current groups' norms. Second, some might try to identify or self-classify as having only one ethic group. Third, some might have life experiences of being misunderstood, so they might try hard to adjust and hide their differences making them difficult to identify. Particularly, they might distrust and resist participating in a research study.

Other findings that emerged during the literature review are how scholars have addressed identity construction, diffusion, reception, and incorporation by influencing people with multiple cultures to mix behaviors. Some scholars have claimed human nature, individual differences, personality, identity, and intragroup and intergroup membership are influencers to mix behaviors (Buss, 2001; Deaux & Martin, 2003; Matsumoto, 2007). The "transmitted culture" (Buss, 2001, p. 974) concept that depicts transferring one idea from person to person included findings related to stereotypes that influence multicultural people to mix behaviors during social situations.

Matsumoto (2007) noted basic human nature, universal psychological processes, cultural influences, situations, social roles, personality, role identities, and experiences are some factors influencing people to mix behavior. Matsumoto also reported that the effects of culture necessitate to include the possible consequences of other sources to understand that some cultural differences developed from various other sources. Matsumoto indicated cultures and self-construal might influence people's behavior, for instance, an individualistic culture creates independent self-perception, whereas a collectivistic culture produces interdependent self-perception, and each self-perception might produce different types of behaviors (Alves et al., 2006; Friberg, 2009; Matsumoto, 2007).

The literature contained information about intra- and intergroup influences on mixing behaviors. In 1982, Tajfel discussed cognitive, evaluative, and emotional investment as fundamental components to achieve in- and out-group identification. These components work together; they are not separate (Tajfel, 1982; see also Ellemers et al., 2002; Hogg & Reid, 2006; Tajfel et al., 1964). Barreto et al. (2003) also discussed these components, indicating the involvement of thinking (cognitive) and the situation or opportunities that influence people to behave in certain ways (evaluative/strategic).

Cognitive component refers to knowing membership to a group, or self-definition, and self-categorization (Barreto et al., 2003; Tajfel, 1982; Verkuyten & de Wolf, 2002). The evaluative component refers to evaluating whether disclosing the identity is appropriate or sensitive to other people. The offensive component refers when disclosing an identity perceived as a threat by certain people or cultures, or affecting one's self-esteem (Barreto et al., 2003; Tajfel, 1982; Verkuyten & de Wolf, 2002). The emotional component refers to the investment in awareness (self-definition or self-categorization) and evaluation (self-esteem; Tajfel, 1982).

The literature examined revealed the influence of identity threat based on intra- and intergroup differences as influencing mixing behaviors. Two possible effects on people's identities are (a) when a social situation is likely to question the identity of a person and (b) when the disclosure of identity occurs within social situations. Experimental study outcomes indicated the evaluative group situation affected members' self-descriptions, acculturation, and in-group evaluations (Verkuyten & de Wolf, 2002). The literature review showed group membership as a strong factor that influences mixing behaviors. Research on in- and out-group problems with regard to acculturation indicated some attitudes are responses to the magnitude of ethnic minority groups wanting to retain their traditions, the value they place in such traditions, and the influences from the majority group (Verkuyten & de Wolf, 2002).

The terms identity, culture, gender, and multicultural used in the literature are complex terms used to define and to explain. Identity refers to the inner self. Identity also refers to a person's place and the meaning associated to social classifications such disability, ethnicity, gender, race, citizenship, class, religious affiliations, sexual orientation, and ability, among other classifications. Identity could also be an influence of individual's perspectives, ideas, and knowledge based on the connection between identity and experiences in life (McKenzie, 2011; Shen & Dumani, 2013).

Multicultural and cultural identities involve individuals as the process of association and describe culture as the communication among members of a group (Downie et al., 2006; Fiske, 2002; Oxford, 1977). People could have their own definition of identity based on environments, time, and situations (Gavilán, 2010). Walters and Auton-Cuff (2009) explained identity as the influence on defining the values, beliefs, and behavior of an individual and communicating with other people.

Throughout history, scholars have interchanged the terms multicultural, bicultural, and multiethnicity as referring to a person with multiple cultures (Briley et al., 2005; Pohlert, 2008). The theoretical and research interest related to identity development in race and ethnic minority groups strongly intensified in 1985. Scholars focused mainly on specific groups as African Americans, Asian Americans, Latinos, females, biracial individuals, sexual preference, immigrants, and people who are members of multiple minority groups (Vivero & Jenkins, 1999). Cohen (2009) gathered, organized, and categorized 164 definitions of culture with extensive or basic definitions. Fiske (2002) noted some intersecting, crosscutting, and interconnected cultural aspects could have negative effects in a person's life.

Research related to the term *multicultural* showed that sometimes researchers erroneously use the word *bicultural*. According to Briley et al. (2005), bicultural denotes the internalization of principles and traditions from two cultures. Several identity concepts are the foundation for psychological theories about multiple cultures focused on specific ages, racial or ethnic groups, or biracial backgrounds, but do not provide a multicultural perspective (Pohlert, 2008). Cramer and Plummer (2009) presented the intersection of race, gender, immigration status, language, disability, and economic status as factors influencing behaviors and affecting the life experiences of a person with multiple cultures. Cramer and Plummer (2009) indicated people with multiple suppressed identities face several challenges. Identity and culture might change, depending on the circumstances (Gavilán, 2010; Gómez et al., 2009; Hong et al., 2000).

Gender is also a difficult term to define, and many scholars interchanged the term sex with gender. Muehlenhard and Peterson (2011) discussed the research of numerous authors who offered several definitions of sex and gender and indicated scholars related sex and gender as society's categorizations as male and female. Some authors defined gender as related to cultural influences and sex as related to biology, and some made a distinction between gender and gender roles based on the lack of consensus (Muehlenhard & Peterson, 2011).

Different findings also provided arguments regarding the processes and procedures used to explore mixing behaviors. Many studies took place in laboratories using surveys or through other means. Matsumoto (2007) suggested acknowledging multiple and different sources of behaviors and noted the role a situation played in influencing behaviors might better serve an investigation of mixing behaviors. Brewer and Kramer (1985) suggested including social identity, categorization, rejection, and assimilation within the contact experience influencing a person to mix behaviors.

Several scholars suggested involving other components such as conformity, hyper-conformity, and the influence of information on behaviors when exploring the effects that influence mixing behaviors (Clandinin & Rosiek, 2007; see also Kim & Markus, 1999). Gudykunst (1983) recommended including the different analyses between low- and high-context cultures and within groups. Fiske (2002) suggested noting dissimilarities among people as individual differences not as culture differences.

Findings related to oppression indicated that the manifestation of any of the five faces of oppression elements as marginalization, powerlessness, cultural imperialism, exploitation, and violence represent oppression and is sufficient for describing a group as oppressed (Dubrosky, 2013; Young, 1990). There are different group and individual oppressions revealing different mixtures of these elements (Young, 1990; see also Kaltman et al., 2011). Young (1990) discussion and illustration made clear that people with multiple cultural identities might fit not just one, but all five conditions of oppression.

For example, according to Young (1990), many oppressed modern social movements experience cultural imperialism and other different oppression. Related to this analytic autoethnography focusing on disability, ethnicity, and gender some of the finding included that people with physical or mental disabilities might encounter oppression by marginalization and cultural imperialism. Women as a group might be exposed to gender-based exploitation, powerlessness, cultural imperialism, and violence. In the United States, many Blacks and Latinos might experience marginalization, and the members of these groups might experience all five forms of oppression (Young, 1990). The matrix of domination is a structure of different forms of oppression that might oppress people experiencing poverty, people with sex preferences, people of color, women, religious, and people overweight, the elderly, and people who look different from the established norm by the dominant culture (Collins, 1990; Staunces, 2003; Young, 1990).

Findings related to self-leadership indicated scholars focused on organizations, employees, or leading a group. The literature review related to mixing behaviors included self-presentation, self-esteem, self-views, self-perception, self-categorization, self-description, and so forth as influences to mixing behaviors for social situations (Bond, 1982; Leary & Allen, 2011; Verkuyten & de Wolf, 2002). Apprehension and ambiguity are stressors and have a strong effect on behaviors; self-leadership might offer guidance when multicultural people need to mix behaviors (Alves et al., 2006; Gudykunst, 1983; Matsumoto, 2007).

The perception of self-leadership might be different in collectivistic and individualistic cultures, as well as among individuals (Alves et al., 2006). Self-leadership could vary from individual centered to group centered and could vary from material-based to relational-based related to gender dimensions depending on a person's individual beliefs and background (Alves et al., 2006). People who use self-leadership might need to change or to adapt the strategy based on cultural contexts (Alves et al., 2006).

Qualitative analytic autoethnography is the study of self and is a form of qualitative research that mixes autobiographic and ethnographic methods (Doloriert & Sambrook, 2012; Jefferies, 2012; Maydell, 2010). Autoethnography includes researching, writing to self-reference, and cultural situations (Allen-Collinson, 2013; Berlak, 2005; Bochner, 2012; Chang, 2007, 2008; Denzin, 2014; Ellis, 2007; Fassett & Warren, 2007; Hamilton et al., 2008; Jupp, 2006; Kahl, 2011; Smith-Sullivan, 2008; Wall, 2006, 2008). Hamilton et al. (2008) indicated that in an autoethnography, the writer narrates personal experiences related to a larger situation associated to cultural concerns supported by academic research. Chang (2007) indicated that an autoethnography provides with groundwork to forming a cross-cultural partnership to accept others, even others opposing, in a society with multiple cultures. Qualitative analytic autoethnography was the appropriate study method to use when exploring why multicultural people might convert into cultural chameleons.

The literature reviewed indicated that social categorization might contribute to social stereotyping and prejudice. Multiple and intersecting identities could interlock and become inseparable. A person with multiple cultural identities (i.e., multiple social categorizations) might experience difficulties and complications when his or her cultures relate to another

81

culture and another identity (Salazar & Abrams, 2005; Shen & Dumani, 2013; Warner & Shields, 2013).

The findings included that some people representing marginalized social classifications not only might experience racism, sexism, ableism, heterosexism, and privilege over them, but also could experience negative information about them, avoidance, discrimination, and verbal and physical attacks (Collins, 1990; Dubrosky, 2013; Salazar & Abrams, 2005; Young, 1990).

Other findings involved identity as recurrent involving different stages for people with marginalized social categories. The stages included conformity, dissonance, resistance and immersion, introspection, and integrative awareness. Conformity referred to perceiving the majority culture as superior, and internalizing the values and negative messages about the self and the belonging group. Some scholars argued denial as necessary for some people's survival and sanity because of the continual oppression (Case & Hunter, 2012; Salazar & Abrams, 2005; Elsbach & Kramer, 1996; Garcia, 1981).

The dissonance stage results from an event that happened around the nation, the discrimination was directed toward the self or loved ones or the person met someone who challenged the negative set stereotypes. Resistance and immersion might take place when the person feels anger and shame of believing the stereotypes against a group, and expresses it as an injustice committed against the self and against members of the same group. Introspection is the external energy and attention becoming internal, in this stage the person might not be willing to continue giving something up in exchange for acceptance. In the integrative awareness stage, the person might experience inner security, autonomy, peace, and balance, and understands that oppression not only lessens the oppressed but also the oppressor (Flynn, 2012; Salazar & Abrams, 2005).

Numerous limitations emerged during the literature review for this research study. The limitations included finding a common agreement on the definition of culture, gender, ethnicity, identity, multiculturalism, and multicultural. The focus of the literature on self-leadership was on employment, employees' performance, and the acculturation process of immigration issues. Social situations root on social and public discourse and as intra- and intergroup issues (Gavilán, 2010; Purdie-Vaughns & Eibach, 2008).

Several researchers identified culture, gender, ethnicity, and multiculturalism in the United States as a political term for group categorizations, indicating the constant use of such term to soften tensions within ethnic matters and racial conflict (Qin, 2011). The difficulty of finding a common understanding and definition of culture, gender, ethnicity, multiculturalism, multicultural, and identity clearly resonated with the lack of research on individuals' identity to understand a multicultural person.

Significant gaps found within the literature review involved the interplay of individual differences in multicultural people or multicultural identity. For example, exploring people as ethnic or racial minority groups based on dissimilarities and studying in-group differences based on origin. The identities of immigrants with disabilities and social interactions, including intra- and intergroup demands or expectations, were an additional gap discovered within this literature review.

Other significant gaps found within the literature review included the lack of involving social classifications (e.g., gender, disability, and ethnicity) as cultures. The literature on multiple cultural identities identified multiple cultures as origins and traditions not as social classifications. Some of the literature focused for counselors included social classifications or categorizations as possible identities of a person and indicated the need for more inclusive frameworks to explore the experiences of people with multiple cultures, but the literature were limited (Salazar & Abrams, 2005).

Conclusion

The literature review involved exploring the aspects that might influence a multicultural person to become a cultural chameleon. The literature led to a deeper examination of the dynamics of gender, disability, and ethnicity and their intersection or multiple triangulations, including intra- and intergroup influences, depending on the cultural situation. The literature review indicated racial and ethnic theories or studies do not involve people as multicultural. The basis of the theories or studies was specific races, ethnic groups, or racial and ethnic groups, leaving other people or other groups invisible. Investigations related to mixing identities were also lacking, and researchers have not studied self-leadership strategy as a personal skill.

The purpose of the study was to explore why some multicultural people might turn into cultural chameleons to fit in or to adjust to a different culture. The qualitative analytic autoethnography involved exploring the intersection of disability, ethnicity, and gender to understand cultural chameleon behavior that some multicultural people might adopt as a method to respond to conflict and stresses while adjusting to a different culture. I developed a foundation of the reasons for mixing identities as a paradigm. This study might help people to understand cultural chameleon behavior and might add to research on the experiences of people described as unique (Badea et al., 2010; Leary & Allen, 2011) or as "solo" (Tajfel, 1982, p. 5; see also Tajfel et al., 1964).

Summary

This chapter contained a discussion on the reasons this study included the intersectionality theory complemented by the theory of multiple cultural identities and networks and social categorization framework as a guide to understand cultural chameleon behavior. A review of pertinent literature included the social situations and interactions of multicultural people and the possible influences of developing cultural chameleon behavior. Including the five faces of oppression, the matrix of oppression, and relevant discussion related to people with multiple cultures defined as social classifications. The literature review also involved the identity stages that a person with multiple social classifications might experience.

The literature review included a description of the relationship among gender, disability, and ethnicity; the connections to a multicultural person in numerous social situations; and the intersection of multiple cultures, including the perception of cultural intersection with the studied acculturation strategies. The review of the literature also included self-leadership as a strategy to manage stressful or conflicting intersections of cultures. Chapter 3 contains a description of the methodology for the qualitative analytic autoethnography that involved comparing my cultural experiences with the academic literature on disability, ethnicity, and gender to explore why some multicultural people might turn into cultural chameleons.

Chapter 3

Research Methods

The purpose of the study was to explore why some multicultural people might turn into cultural chameleons to fit in or to adjust to a different culture. The qualitative analytic autoethnography involved exploring the intersection of disability, ethnicity, and gender to understand cultural chameleon behavior that some multicultural people might adopt as a method to respond to conflict and stresses while adjusting to a different culture. Through ontological humility (Dillon, 2011; Pitts, 2005) and grounding this narrative to my own story, this study involved exploring one central question and two secondary questions:

R1: What influences some people with multiple cultures to turn into cultural chameleons?

R2: How do I behave as a cultural chameleon when my physical disability, my ethnicity, or my gender becomes my only attribute as a person?

R3: How and when do I perceive the need to behave as a cultural chameleon?

The focus of Chapter 3 is on the methodological approach I used to explore why multicultural people might turn into cultural chameleons. This chapter also includes the phases and procedures to collect and analyze data, and the measures of quality for this qualitative analytic autoethnography.

Methodology

The qualitative analytic autoethnography involved situating my personal cultural experiences within the larger academic literature on disability, ethnicity, and gender. I used intersectionality as a guide to understand cultural chameleon behavior. The selection of a qualitative research method and an analytic autoethnography research design was appropriate because qualitative research leads to an understanding of unfamiliar behaviors (Barbour, 2008; Pohlert, 2008; Sin, 2010), and analytic autoethnography involves analyzing and explaining personal cultural experiences (Allbon, 2012; Giampietro, 2008).

For the qualitative analytic autoethnography, I used the phenomenological methodology, and synthesized both the radical constructivist and social constructionist views. The idea of synthesizing both views aimed to integrate psychobiological, psycho-philosophical, and psycho-sociocultural truths to explore and comprehend the integral development of a person with multiple cultures (Jost & Kruglanski, 2002; W. Lui, 2009; see also J. Liu, 2011; Williams, 2005). Although essentialists support the idea of identity as

85

determined, fixed, and set from birth, and disagree with the concept of identity as fluid and changeable, studies on self-concept, social identity, group representation, attitudes as formations, communication, shared reality, and cultural psychology progressed incorporating constructionists concepts (Cantey, 2011; J. Liu, 2011; W. Lui, 2009; see also Jost & Kruglanski, 2002).

The radical or essentialist constructivist model, based on Vygotsky and Piaget's theories, suggest that knowledge and truth develop during childhood influenced by the life around the child, and by shared reality during social interactions (Cantey, 2011; Jost & Kruglanski, 2002; W. Lui, 2009; Shank, 2006). The essentialist view indicates self-representation, symbolic representation, and probability as the foundation of social psychology. Thus, people might have different information and understanding of central ideas and models, but could work together because each person's knowledge originates from the same social and cultural ideas and models (Jost & Kruglanski, 2002; Pearson, 2012; Shank, 2006).

The social constructionist suggests that human thinking and behavior relates to a particular context of history, culture, and ideology (e.g., Jost & Kruglanski, 2002; Muehlenhard & Peterson, 2011; Naples, 2009). The social constructionist paradigm indicates significant differences and similarities among people and recognizes that a meaning might change over time and across cultures. In other words, constructionists disagree that a set of experiences is the only true of an identity (Sherry, 2006).

In the constructionist perspective, validity moves from truth to useful; for example, scholars evaluate stories not for their accord with the studied life experience but more for how other people could use information for different purposes (Clandinin & Rosiek, 2007; Harrell & Bond, 2006). Social constructionist view, posits identity as fluid, accessible, instinctive, and shaped through daily interactions with others (Cantey, 2011; W. Lui, 2009; see also Ellis, 1991; Foster et al., 2006). The paradigm suggests considering the influence of each intersecting culture (e.g., disability, ethnicity, gender) as valid while seeking to understand the lived experience of identity (Cantey, 2011; Clandinin & Rosiek, 2007; see also Ellis, 1991; Jost & Kruglanski, 2002; Williams, 2005).

Appropriateness of a qualitative autoethnography. Self-narratives are prevalent in the arts and humanities (Anderson, 2006; Hamilton et al., 2008; Jefferies, 2012). A qualitative analytic autoethnography does not involve simply telling a story (Badley, 2014;

Chang, 2007, 2008; Walters & Auton-Cuff, 2009; see also Merryfeather, 2014). The study was an inquiry that involved exploring my perception of my own experiences as a person with multiple cultures, guiding me to perceive my personal, cultural, and theoretical experiences and enhancing knowledge related to identities and multiple cultures.

An association exists between my life's cultural events as an immigrant and as a woman using a wheelchair because of a physical disability and the content of this qualitative analytic autoethnography. This qualitative research study followed Ellis et al.'s (2011) discussion on a personal narrative inquiry as an autoethnography where the writer relates his or her personal story perceiving self as the phenomenon. In this case, I was the phenomenon to discuss because I represent multiple cultures or social classifications, and the narrative related to my personal cultural experiences. This narrative was, according to a narrative as an analysis, where the person tells the story of identity and acknowledges such identity within the narrative. Revealing my experiences related to cultures was a vital component of my autoethnography (Ellis & Bochner, 2000; Hamilton et al., 2008).

My reason for implementing a qualitative analytic autoethnography. The desire to understand my cultural experiences sociologically and the reasons that influence me to mix identities during social interactions drove my motivation to choose a qualitative analytic autoethnography. I wanted to understand why multicultural people might turn into cultural chameleons. Wall (2006) noted, "Ultimately, using self as subject is a way of acknowledging the self that was always there anyway and of exploring personal connections to our culture" (p. 11).

Using a research study that involved culturally exploring and unraveling the self in relation to others; exploring social phenomena encountered by some people; and involving data collection, analysis, and interpretation helped me to understand the reasons (Allen-Collinson, 2013; Maydell, 2010; McIlveen, 2008; Sariyant, 2002; Sin, 2010; C. Smith, 2005; Wall, 2006; see also Merryfeather, 2014). I wanted to share my cultural experiences, while at the same time, sharing my new learning using nontraditional research. I knew my life was not just a feature to reveal. Reading numerous autoethnographies in which the writers narrated and voiced diverse cultural experiences (e.g., Adams, 2011; Allen-Collinson, 2013; Burke, 2007; Cantey, 2011; Ellis, 2007; Ellis et al., 2008; Klinker & Todd, 2007; Linder, 2011; Merryfeather, 2014; Muncey, 2005; Pearson, 2012; Strolovitch, 2006; Stow, 2005; Tindongan, 2012; Voigts, 2009; see also Doloriert & Sambrook, 2012; Pearson, 2010) empowered me. I appreciated that an analytic autoethnography "says that what I know matters" (Wall, 2006, p. 3).

The next step was to choose the most appropriate research design to share my cultural experiences compared to the large academic literature on disability, ethnicity, and gender. I considered a narrative single-case study. According to Gomm, Hammersley, and Foster (2009), a single-case study originates in reality, enhances experiences, improves understanding, and could relate to the reader's experience. A narrative single-case study also provides openness, presents new or different perspectives, and includes a setting free of stress and pressure. Gomm et al. noted scholars generally use single-case studies in clinical settings and might conceal information based on client confidentiality.

The goal of a narrative single-case study is to help families, to improve or implement treatment, and for clinical interviews (Thyer, 2001). A narrative single-case study, therefore, would not be the appropriate method to explore why some multicultural people might turn into cultural chameleons or to understand cultural chameleons' behavior. The research study was not a case, treatment, or therapeutic process but involved the intersection of disability, gender, and ethnicity. I needed a research method that would allow me to explore my theme and to use intersectionality as a lens to understand behaviors; thus, qualitative analytic autoethnography was the most appropriate research method.

Qualitative research. Qualitative research involves the option to study how people perceive ideas, how they process information and make their choices, how they process their lives, and how to understand unreasonable behaviors. Pohlert (2008) noted qualitative research allows researchers to describe the complexity and the meaning of a person's life. Qualitative researchers strive to provide a deeper and more meaningful understanding of an explored topic (Sin, 2010). The purpose of the study was to explore why some multicultural people might turn into cultural chameleons to fit in or to adjust to a different culture. The qualitative analytic autoethnography involved exploring the intersection of disability, ethnicity, and gender to understand cultural chameleon behavior that some multicultural people might adopt as a method to respond to conflict and stresses while adjusting to a different culture.

The qualitative analytic autoethnography included methodologies that suited and enhanced the exploration of why a multicultural person might behave as a cultural chameleon. This study approach allowed me to share my personal cultural experiences in social interactions to explore possible factors that influence the behavior of mixing identities. The research study included opportunities for me to set the direction to explore why multicultural people might turn into cultural chameleons (Anderson, 2006; Ngunjiri et al., 2010; C. Smith, 2005).

The qualitative method helped to explore and reflect on my cultural experiences, my own internalization of adjusting to new and unfamiliar cultures, and my new self. The method allowed me to use a metaphor and its interconnections to explore and understand why some multicultural people might turn into a cultural chameleon and to understand cultural chameleon behavior. To provide a profound understanding of the reasons for adopting unfamiliar behaviors, the study included the narrative inquiry method because it is, according to Clandinin and Rosiek (2007), the foundation of human experiences that allows researchers to study stories, write, or explain personal experiences. B. Cole (2009) noted that a narrative could help break the silence of cultures that let oppression against ethnic minority groups continue.

Narrative inquiry. The qualitative analytic autoethnography included narrative inquiry as a primary tool to collect and to analyze data. According to Andrews, Squire, and Tamboukou (2008), narrative is the best way to study stories because it does not set the beginning or the end and it offers no rules on what to use, how to investigate the story, or where to find the stories to investigate (see also Chase, 2005; Trahar, 2009). The method permitted my own involvement in sharing, describing, and explaining my cultural experiences and giving a voice to some multicultural people behaving as cultural chameleons.

Researchers are interested in learning about the relationship between the researched and the research. The importance of narrative inquiry is growing (Andrews et al., 2008; Chase, 2005; B. Cole, 2009; Denzin, 2014; Ellis et al., 2008; Trahar, 2009). A narrative inquiry helped me to reflect on my personal experiences preventing negative attitudes or actions toward people around me. Ngunjiri et al. (2010) narrated the reasons for their decision to use a collaborative autoethnography to share their cultural experiences. They narrated the intersection of social identities as immigrant women of color in the American academy and noted their situatedness originated from lived opportunities and challenges. I related to their story because I am an immigrant and a woman of color. I empathized with their story, which intensified my curiosity on how I would approach the research study to narrate my own cultural experiences.

After reading Schneider's (2011) narrative autoethnography about disability and identity, I developed a profound empathy and felt encouraged to share my culture experiences by becoming an autoethnographer. I also read Voigts (2009) narration of her experience acquiring a disability, adjusting to her new self, and connecting her experience as an intercultural adjustment. Conlon (2009) shared her experience of her personal perception of identity development between her twin sister and herself. Harrison (2011) discussed some attitudes and beliefs of identity construction and language barriers among cultures. After reading these autoethnographies, I understood that a qualitative analytic autoethnography was the best study approach for the study because it allowed me to share different cultural encounters in diverse social situations. I felt fortunate to have the ability to share my cultural experiences in the same way as the autoethnographers I read had shared theirs. Their stories empowered me.

The purpose of the study was to explore why some multicultural people might turn into cultural chameleons to fit in or to adjust to a different culture. The qualitative analytic autoethnography involved exploring the intersection of disability, ethnicity, and gender to understand cultural chameleon behavior that some multicultural people might adopt as a method to respond to conflict and stresses while adjusting to a different culture. The qualitative analytic autoethnography included intersectionality as a guide to understand cultural chameleon behavior. Intersectionality and narrative inquiry helped to capture social relations and their challenges, the diversity of people's lives, and the methods people use for resistance (Chase, 2005; Naples, 2009). B. Cole (2009) noted intersectionality supports narratives and enables researchers to ask questions for exploration and to investigate interrelations. Combining intersectionality with narrative inquiry revealed the reasons that influence an unfamiliar behavior during social interactions intersected with disability, gender, and ethnicity.

Narrative inquiry was the method used to explore why a multicultural person might behave as a cultural chameleon, and connecting intersectionality with multiple cultural identities, interpersonal networks, and social categories was a lens used to help understand such behavior. The study included an emphasis on my cultural experiences compared to the larger academic literature on disability, gender, and ethnicity domains to support my narrative. Understanding these reasons was an essential component that served as a foundation for knowing how to collect and analyze data.

The qualitative analytic autoethnography included photographs taken over the course of my life to guide my narrative as an evocative moment rather than an accurate representation as discussed by Van House (2011). Van House also expressed that a particular past story could form from sensibly chosen memories, photographs, and collections because photos are permanent and effective images eliciting what human memory might not instantaneously recollect. Photo images might have the power to move into a person's past to see and understand what the person did not at the time (Van House, 2011). Although narrative inquiry was the dominant data collection technique for this qualitative analytic autoethnography, collecting personal notes, photos, academic journals, and self-observation provided support during my story's narration. The different data collection approaches for the autoethnography seemed appropriate to reach what Lorenz (2010) described as "making visible the invisible" (p. 220).

Analytic autoethnography data collection. The qualitative analytic autoethnography was not a description, a diary, or a set of journals; it was an exploration of my experiences with different cultures, and data supported and confirmed the truth of my story. To attain results from gathered data, Shank (2006) suggested maintaining communication between researcher and data. I analyzed personal documents as data for the analytic autoethnography. The external data included notes, photographs of me, academic journals, and pertinent data for the purpose of the study. I collected, stored, analyzed, and interpreted the data using NVivo10 qualitative research software and Zotero online software.

Data management took place using QSR International's NVivo10 because it provided tools to organize and analyze data. Finch (2012) explained NVivo allows researchers to classify data by recognizing trends or topics, indicating relationships, and revealing developments. Finch indicated NVivo10 allows researchers to categorize data by recognizing developments and themes within the data, in addition to providing access to information showing relationships.

I followed Shank's (2006) discussion on the steps to analyze data to provide authenticity, understanding, and significance of the information. McIlveen (2008) noted personal self-observation, self-reflection, recalling notable events, and external data are essential elements to an autoethnography. Shank's and McIlveen's discussions are significant because analyzing internal and external information is an important element of a qualitative analytic autoethnography.

Self-observation is a critical element for sharing cultural experiences, principally because it provides different types of information and helps notice reactions when responding or perceiving an event. Self-observation is the inner examination of personal intentions, feelings, thinking, expectations, and behaviors. Self-observation also helps to understand personal and other people's perceptions, including social and cultural relationships with others (Beitman & Soth, 2006; McIlveen, 2008). Data collection might involve journals; concise, reliable, and current culture information; and self-narrative responses to be aware of possible biases and assumptions when analyzing data (Oliver, 2010). Being self-reflective is not only part of an autoethnography but also a significant explanatory element (Hamilton et al., 2008; McIlveen, 2008).

Visual narrative is another method to collect data. Bach (2007) discussed a visual narrative as a method used to engage the mind and body as a process of exploring and interpreting the interaction between the storyteller and the environment involving feelings, doing, suffering, managing, and perceiving. The visual narrative allows researchers to link the past, present, and future within a story to build trust and rapport between the narrator and the participant (Bach, 2007). Mills, Durepos, and Wiebe (2010) discussed photo elicitation and photovoice as two ways for researchers to use a photograph to obtain a new perspective of social phenomena because the photograph situates people in the social situation and helps them to see things differently (see also Muncey, 2005).

Photo elicitation refers to eliciting information from the focused culture, and the researcher becomes a learner and listener from the storyteller (Mills et al., 2010). Photovoice communicates living in certain cultural environments in which the storyteller shares the experience that he or she could not explain using only words (Mills et al., 2010; see also Muncey, 2005). Baker and Wang (2006) discussed photovoice as a unique approach that brings to life particular experiences of adults and could provide a specific way to ask about the person's concerns. This method helps to supplement analytical data by allowing people to communicate their own experiences (Baker & Wang, 2006).

Wang (1999) discussed photovoice as an action research method that allows the development of communication related to the strengths and weaknesses within a community, permits people to address concerns, and could influence policy (Tindongan, 2012; Wang, 1999). The goal of the photovoice approach was to empower disadvantaged racial and ethnic minority group members by permitting the researcher to know daily interactions and to document and discuss people's experiences and needs (Wang, 1999; Weathers, 2012; see also Muncey, 2005). In Tindongan's (2012) study, for instance, the photovoice method helped participants to consider some concerns related to identity in which an interview might not provide the information that photovoice provided. In the qualitative analytic autoethnography, I used photovoice to analyze photographs related to my cultural experiences, and I used only photographs with my image and no other person or organization.

The photovoice analysis also used "multivocality" (Mizzi, 2010, p. 2) to provide me with a place to share and explain my cultural experiences, which on many occasions involved multiple and conflicting inner voices. Using multivocality, I articulated my cultural experiences based on my "personhood" (Morris, 1993, p. 143) and shared my own interpretations as a person with multiple cultures. Mizzi (2010) named these plural and contradictory inner voices as a researcher's "narrative voices" (p. 2). Mizzi (2010) also indicated these voices are a way to provide deeper understanding of possible unspoken researcher tensions within the story. Mizzi (2010) used multivocality to narrate racial, gender, and sexual identity and noted some identities connected and interacted with each other. Mizzi (2010) described narrative voices or multivocality as employee voice, safety voice, activist voice, educator voice, and so forth, depending on the inner conversation.

The photovoice analysis for the qualitative analytic autoethnography included a combination of Tindongan's (2012), Weathers's (2012) photo reflection method, and Mizzi's (2010) multivocality. Tindongan and Weathers indicated photo reflection helped their participants to think on what a photo represented for them and its significance. Mizzi's narrative voices helped Mizzi to narrate different inner feelings using multivocality in an autoethnography.

Using Mizzi's (2010) multivocality strategy for this study, I focused the narrative voices to my identity and background, my concerns, and my beliefs. The narrative voices emphasized my cultural experiences that stemmed from my disability, gender, and ethnicity for the qualitative analytic autoethnography. The identity and background narrative voices contained the *immigrant, advocate, activist, colleague, employee, woman, disability, Mexican,* and *city* native voices. The concerns and values narrative voices included *cultural sensitivity, safety, stereotype control, discouraging, attention, self-leadership,* and *mixing identities* narrative voices.

To help identifying between the reconstructed cultural experiences using photovoice and the scholarly reflection based on the academic literature, I used Spry (2001) and Fox (2014) concepts of ordering events in their work. Both, Spry and Fox, adapted from Geertz's (1988) distinction between the *Being There* and *Being Here* to organize their scholarly work. Fox adapted Geertz's concept in an autoethnographic account narrating his experiences living with obsessive-compulsive disorder (OCD). Spry adapted Geertz's idea to illustrate how autoethnographic performance method could be a defining feature to interpret culture through self-reflections and cultural diversions of identity.

Adapting the Being There and Being Here perceptions for this analytic autoethnography assisted me in converting a photograph into a postcard to mirror my cultural experiences with the academic literature. The concept also helped me to understand my cultural experiences, others, and myself during my social connections and my need to mix behaviors. I separated myself from those cultural experiences and used a critical, analytic, and interpretative lens allowing internalized feelings to emerge through each photograph by using photovoice methodology.

The collected pictures showed moments over the course of my life in Mexico City and in the United States and focused on the Labovian approach used for the study. Using multivocality, I narrated my thoughts during photo collection and described what was in the photo, what the picture meant to me, and what the image represented that I decided to use that specific picture instead of others. The reflection also indicated how I see my cultural experiences during social interactions, how each photo captured my feelings and reflections about my cultural experiences, and how the specific moment reflected my experience of mixing identities during social interactions.

First, after collecting and choosing the photographs for this study, I looked at each photo to initiate the reflection and interpretation of the image. Second, I wrote what was within the image, without assuming or interpreting the reasons I selected that specific photo; observing helped me to understand the emotions hidden within the picture. Third, I asked myself questions including who, what, where, when, why, and how I behaved after the social interaction. I answered these questions before interpreting and narrating my cultural experiences invisibly captured by the image.

Fourth, I wrote the narrative using the multivocality strategy based on the specific picture, and I indicated the event, the social situation, and the cultural experience. Fifth, I created a log, coded each picture, annotated text in the content column including the narrative voices used, and created links to other relevant data within my study using NVivo10 software. The information gathered through the selected pictures answered what, where, who, how, and why and used the multivocality approach related to my cross-cultural experiences.

NVivo10 software assists with exploring, manipulating, and interpreting data; provides a conceptual space for thinking; and facilitates space to allow the researcher to see things in different ways (Bassett, 2012). Bassett (2012) discussed critical interpretations when using NVivo software as a method to review data using different lenses or techniques to understand beyond comprehending and eliminating a biased view. Using Bassett's (2012) method of critical interpretation combined with the life story interview based on the Labovian approach and the multivocality strategy, NVivo software worked on self-observations and stories as well as data generated by interviews. The life story interview based on the Labovian approach guided the qualitative autoethnography during the exploration of self-observations and stories. The Labovian approach requires the interviewee to answer questions (see Appendix A), where I was both the interviewee and the interviewer.

Bassett (2011) also explained that NVivo software provides researchers with different ways of thinking and seeing, which could be an important way to observe an image while narrating its representation. According to Libby and Eibach (2011), when recalling the past and picturing the future, people use third-person imagery to contribute to the construction and maintenance of self-sense. Bassett indicated that by using and combining different functions of the software, the conceptual space becomes a mediated space for the research.

Based on Bassett's (2011) method of analyzing photographs imported into NVivo software, I selected a digital or scanned photo with my image, and I created a log with the necessary rows and columns. The rows and columns included region (if necessary), content, description, and related information. The rows had enough information to answer what, how, why, when, and who and contained pertinent narrative voices indicating the feelings, emotions, or challenges I encountered during the specific social interaction. I noted if I encountered the need to mix identities influenced by disability, gender, or ethnicity as the only attribute as a person or altogether. The rows included my narrative voices, indicating my inner conversation or conversations if my voices connected, intersected, or interfered with my cultural experience.

I created a code within the content row and coded it at a created node, or I created a new node if necessary to locate and analyze the narrative voices I used (e.g., based on my identity, background, concerns, and values). I linked the codes to the narrative voices content responding to why, where, how, when, and who and compared the coding of different images within the analytic autoethnography. NVivo10 software provided different methods to analyze qualitative data and helped to demonstrate the validity of findings (QSR International, 2013).

I took numerous NVivo10 trainings, webinars, and workshops to learn and to understand how to use NVivo10 software for the qualitative analytic autoethnography. The learning included attending *Using NVivo to Improve Research Team Collaboration, 5 Ways to Get More From Your Studies, Literature Reviews and NVivo, Work With Survey Results, NVivo Coding, NVivo10 Tutorial: What's New in NVivo10, NVivo as a Conceptual Space for Critical Interpretation, NVivo10 Tutorial: Get Up and Running With NVivo10, NVivo10 Text Search Queries, NVivo10 Coding Queries, NVivo10: Coding Sources to Classification Nodes*, and other pertinent and relevant trainings provided by QSR International.

The purpose of the study was to explore why some multicultural people might turn into cultural chameleons to fit in or to adjust to a different culture. The qualitative analytic autoethnography involved exploring the intersection of disability, ethnicity, and gender to understand cultural chameleon behavior that some multicultural people might adopt as a method to respond to conflict and stresses while adjusting to a different culture. The qualitative analytic autoethnography included NVivo10 qualitative research software to organize and analyze researched materials. According to QSR International (2013), NVivo10 imports, organizes, codes, records, provides coding queries, analyzes text, and uses visual tools. I imported digital photos and PDFs. I also used coding queries to test my ideas and explore the material. I applied text analysis and included Bassett's (2011, 2012) conceptual space method and Mizzi's (2010) multivocality approach to identify topics and to explore the use of narrative voices.

Creating codes and nodes for narrative voices using NVivo10 software features allowed me to measure the multivocality used within the narration of my cultural experiences. For example, NVivo10 helped to measure how I used my immigrant or mixing identity voice within my narration, and the frequency I used those inner voices. In addition, to indicate if the words used related to other inner voices as safety or self-leadership or any other voice, and how those voices linked within the autoethnography's content.

For the qualitative analytic autoethnography on exploring my cultural experiences, I was both the researcher and the researched. Given (2008) discussed the researcher's position as an instrument to create a comprehensible reliable depiction of the study based on what the researcher observed and experienced during the research. The researcher, according to Given, uses personal and professional skills, preparation, understanding, and knowledge to be the research instrument. For this autoethnography, I used my skills, training, knowledge, and background to explore and narrate my cultural experiences compared to the academic literature on disability, gender, and ethnicity.

Pompper (2010) indicated a researcher's identity could influence how the researched would respond to the study. For this autoethnography, I was the "cultural agent" (K. Berry & Warren, 2009, p. 603) of my own story in which I explored the domains of disability, gender, and ethnicity. Becoming a cultural agent also allowed me to speak from my heart to share my cultural experiences, my life challenges, and my desire to defend people like me and at the same time to protect myself, as Warren (2001) discussed in his autoethnography where he was the instrument of his own research. Given (2008) discussed observational research as a study method in which the researcher looks and listens to gather ideas of the world to learn about the phenomenon under study.

The data collection for this qualitative analytic autoethnography involved some of the key features proposed by Anderson (2006): "complete member researcher (CMR) status, analytic reflexivity, narrative visibility of the researcher's self, dialogue with informants beyond the self, and commitment to theoretical analysis" (p. 378; see also Pensoneau-Conway & Toyosaki, 2011). According to resources cited in Anderson (2006) and Ellis and Bochner (2000), there are two types of CMRs: opportunistic and convert. The opportunistic CMR refers to a researcher wanting to study a group because he or she is a member related to the group by birth; by unexpected circumstances (e.g., disability, sickness); or through professional, entertaining, or lifestyle activities. Convert CMRs obtain membership during research. This analytic autoethnography did not include a key feature dialogue with informants beyond the self, as proposed by Anderson, because this research study did not involve participants. This research study was an inner conversation that involved sharing my cultural experiences to explore why some people with multiple cultures might turn into

97

cultural chameleons. Based on the uniqueness of my culture experiences and their intersectionality, contacting other people encountering similar experiences was not achievable.

CMRs. Based on Anderson's (2006) definitions of group membership, I am an opportunistic CMR because I was born into two of the groups on which I conducted research, and I acquired membership to another group through disability. Although I did not conduct research with in-group members, it was necessary to specify that I am an opportunistic CMR because I wanted to conduct research within the disability, gender, and ethnicity groups. I was born in Mexico and I emigrated (ethnicity), I acquired my physical disability during my childhood (disability), and I am a woman (gender).

Data categories. Supporting my membership to those groups, I downloaded into NVivo10 software relevant categorized items such as personal photographs and proof of citizenship.

Analytic reflexivity of the self. According to Anderson (2006), analytic reflexivity involves a researcher's connection to the situation and data. The analysis of data also used a life story interview based on the Labovian approach and a visual narrative applying photovoice method.

A life story interview. Clandinin (2007) discussed a life story interview as a qualitative, ethnographic, and field research method to collect personal narratives revealing the life of a person and indicated that a life story interview using a narrative creates a powerful and original narrative inquiry approach (see also Chase, 2005). Anderson (2006) described two purposes to use for a life story as ideographic representing an individual or a personal story, and nomothetic relating to universal, collective, or social. "A life story may also revolve around an epiphanal event" (Chase, 2005, p. 652; Denzin, 2014). Clandinin (2007) argued that a life story interview is not about collecting, documenting, and categorizing data to be part of demographic statistics or based on research questions guiding the research. A life story interview is about what a person desires to share with others and the significance of the story (Clandinin, 2007).

The narrative inquiry involved using the Labovian approach, which included an abstract, an orientation, a complicating action, a result, an evaluation, and a coda (Andrews et al., 2008; see also Bamberg & Georgakopoulou, 2008). Narrators using the Labovian method provide a summary of the story; answer the questions who, when, and where the story happened; connect story events in chronological order, evaluate or justify sharing the story, provide the result, and go back to the beginning of the narration to tell that the story ended (Andrews et al., 2008; Bamberg & Georgakopoulou, 2008). This approach, according to Andrews et al. (2008), allows the narrator to identify critical narratives within the context, tells the detailed structure of an individual narrative, allows comparison, and is useful for certain forms of data and research studies.

Andrews et al. (2008) also contended some limitations when using the Labovian approach as a method determining the narrative's central, and challenging the narrator to maintain distinction between referential and evaluative sections. Although Andrews et al. presented an experiential approach for a narrative, the Labovian approach seemed appropriate for this qualitative analytic autoethnography because this research study involved comparing my cultural experiences with the larger academic literature on disability, gender, and ethnicity. The focus of the experiential approach is not in the event; rather, it provides insights into the personal experience narrative. The focus of this narrative inquiry was cultural events, the storyteller was the narrator, and the inquiry involved comparing cultural events, which Andrews et al. noted an experiential method does not allow.

Data categories. To achieve a powerful and original narrative inquiry using a life story interview (Clandinin, 2007), I used the Labovian approach to answer relevant questions based on abstract, orientation, complicating action, result, evaluation, and coda to guide the data collection for this study (see Appendix A).

Narrative visibility of the researcher's self. Anderson (2006) discussed the narrative visibility of the researcher's self as the writer incorporating his or her own feelings and experiences into the story. This incorporation makes the researcher visible within the narration (Anderson, 2006; Pompper, 2010; see also Chase, 2005; Denzin, 2014; Trahar, 2009).

Data categories. To achieve narrative visibility of myself within the story, I downloaded into NVivo10 software categorized data such as personal photographs, notes, journals, documents, and scanned documents relevant to the cultural event I was sharing.

Commitment to an analytic agenda. The key feature of data collection proposed by Anderson (2006) referred to using empirical data to explore social phenomena other than the data provided by the researcher. To achieve commitment to an analytic agenda, to provide a way to understand the social world of people representing multiple disadvantaged ethnic minority groups, and to explore their stigmatized experiences, I placed this study's topic within a social analytic context.

Data categories. Aiming to achieve commitment to an analytic agenda, I exported to NVivo10 software from Zotero the abstracts of the journals and dissertations used for the study on social situations, stigmatization, discrimination, or prejudice against people with disabilities, gender, and ethnic groups. The purpose of downloading the literature abstracts into NVivo10 software was to describe the methods used and the conclusions of research on mixing behaviors, to highlight important themes including intersectionality, and to document the areas needing further research. Some of the journals and dissertations included the following:

- Disability stereotypes: Nario-Redmond (2010) found that consensual knowledge between people with and without disabilities categorizes women and men with disabilities as dependent, inept, and sexually inactive. Related to gender stereotype, Nario-Redmond indicated some people classify women with disabilities as more dependent, and the differences among disabilities intensified with the grade of the disability. Stereotypes develop based on social categorizations of what people can see to define or perceive.

- Prejudice against people with disabilities: Park, Faulkner, and Schaller (2003) noted despite the improvements on disability issues, people often feel uncomfortable around individuals with physical disabilities. Park et al. indicated a disability not only stimulates pity, sympathy, and ambition to help but also provokes negative and antisocial effects, including disgust, anxiety, and judgments blaming the person for his or her disability. Park et al. noted people with physical disabilities encounter evasion when people without disabilities opt to mark greater interpersonal spaces when interrelating with individuals with disabilities.

- Racial and ethnic discrimination: D'Anna, Ponce, and Siegel (2010) indicated because of cultural, linguistic, and migratory experiences, the Latino or Latina population encounters unique discriminatory experiences and more stress responses. The study results reflected that Latinas experiencing discrimination had considerably negative consequences on emotional health. D'Anna et al. noted

100

people from Mexico encounter more struggles, discrimination, and acculturative pressures that increase the number of emotional and functional limitations.

- Gender, ethnicity, and disability: Rohmer and Louvet's (2009) study results reflected that disability is most noticeable because people described a person using a wheelchair as the disability more than his or her gender. People used the disability more often than ethnicity to describe a person in a wheelchair, and disability was more evident than gender when describing women. This comparison of disability with gender and ethnicity indicated people with disabilities who belong to an ethnic minority group are frequently reduced to their social categorization.

Data analysis and interpretation. Sources associated with social interaction, disability, gender, ethnicity, social influence, and intersectionality theory informed the data analysis process for the qualitative analytic autoethnography. I coded data both during and after data collection as an analytic approach (Saldaña, 2013). I changed all names and locations in this qualitative analytic autoethnography to preserve my family and friends' confidentiality. I used my name only as necessary to reflect my narrative, gender, and story. The data analysis process included an exploration of the effects encouraging some multicultural people to alternate behaviors and to turn into cultural chameleons. Intersectionality requires researchers to consider the whole person in the data analysis process, including social categorizations. Intersectionality has different effects on how people perceive an individual and how the individual behaves (Cramer & Plummer, 2009). Disability, gender, and ethnicity are categorizations that could intersect during social interactions.

The analysis of data included self-reflective and personal perceptions. In the case of an inquiry analysis, according to Shank (2006), the goal is the autoethnographer's situatedeness and the truth. Shank also noted there is no need for standardized methods to analyze data; analyzing data depends on the ethnographer's competence in clarifying data and expressing truth. For this qualitative analytic autoethnography, I used NVivo10 qualitative research software to organize and analyze my research materials.

According to QSR International (2013), NVivo10 imports, organizes, codes, records, provides code queries, analyzes text, and uses visual tools. I imported digital photos and PDFs. I also used coding queries to test my ideas and explored the material. I applied text analysis to identify topics and explored the use of language. I also created tables and figures to illustrate the outcome of my qualitative analytic autoethnography.

Analyzing narrative data. Values associated with culture, social influences, multiple cultures, disability, gender, and ethnicity provided information for the data analysis for the qualitative analytic autoethnography. A narrative implies situating different occurrences and events with enough details to make a story understandable. Some fundamental elements of analyzing narrative data include communicating, listening, organizing, and observing the information to detect diverse perceptions (Shank, 2006; see also Chase, 2005).

As the narrator of the analytic autoethnography, I was aware that many cultural stereotypes and assumptions exist about cultures. According to Shank (2006), learning how to follow collective perceptions and organizing the events are fundamental elements for a narrative because these elements tell if the information can form a story. Researchers need to be aware that stories support association, and the sequence of events might not form a story (Shank, 2006; see also Chase, 2005).

Codes and coding. Codes and coding were fundamental for data collection and analysis. Coding is what a title is to a book's central subject and functions as interpretative more than a specific science (Saldaña, 2013). Codes in qualitative research involve observations and processes to identify patterns and consistencies to generate data. According to Saldaña (2013), a code could be a word or short phrase symbolizing a cumulative, a significant, and either a captured or an evocative element from a segment based on language or visual data. Raw data can include field notes, archival data, art, reports, newspaper articles, journals, documents, literature, photographs, video, websites, and electronic communication (Given, 2008; Saldaña, 2013).

Saldaña (2013) explained the first set as the process of coding from a word, an entire sentence, a paragraph, or a page, including a group of images. The second coding set can originate from previous units, longer text, or a reconfiguration of codes already developed, and these labeled data are separated into groups, associations, or patterns to tell the story or to communicate conclusions (Given, 2008). According to Saldaña, there are 29 coding strategies for qualitative research, yet a review of coding strategies was beyond the scope of the study.

Based on the nature of the qualitative analytic autoethnography, it was appropriate to use a value coding strategy and coding filters to capture and label subjective perspectives (Saldaña, 2013) from academic literature, documents, and my narrative. One major theme was identity and the related categories were ethnicity, disability, and gender (e.g., category: identity; subcategory: ethnicity, disability, and gender; codes: social categorizations, stigma, discrimination, and prejudice).

Writing an autoethnography. The qualitative analytic autoethnography involved describing information and personal cultural impressions with the intention of providing truthful and accurate information. I wrote the analytic autoethnography using the concept of Being There… Being Here (Geertz, 1988; Fox, 2014; Spry, 2001; see also Coffey, 1999). I also used narrative inquiry and in first person. Narrative inquiry indicates that people could understand and give a meaning using stories (Chase, 2005; Trahar, 2009). According to Willis (2007), writing using first person is the best approach to discover biases that make the study subjective, because writing a story using third person results in a study that appears to be objective.

According to Spry (2001), autoethnography must avoid conventional writing. Autoethnography is stimulating story and theory that must engage emotionality and should not be a simply open diary of self-renewal. Ordinary writing might not transform or take readers into a motivating place to look upon their own identity development. "The researcher and text must make a persuasive argument, tell a good story, be a convincing "I-witness" (Spry, 2001, p. 713; see also Geertz, 1973; Haynes, 2011).

I wrote my personal and interpersonal cultural experiences using the Labovian life story interview, photovoice, CMR items, and commitment to theoretical analysis. I detailed my cultural experience position the narrative under Geertz's (1973) concept of Being There and compared my experience to the academic literature on disability, gender, and ethnicity positioned under Geertz's concept of Being Here. I aimed to make my cultural experiences meaningful and engaging to provoke a social change (Ellis et al., 2010; Jones et al., 2012; see also Barth, 2002; Yassour-Borochowitz, 2012).

Rigor in research. Although several qualitative researchers provided diverse models for rigor that included assumptions of ontological, epistemological, and methodological differences, rigor in research is essential (Ryan-Nicholls & Will, 2009; Sin, 2010). Numerous scholars have conducted qualitative research to explore complicated social phenomena requiring validity and reliability criteria to evaluate collected data (Sin, 2010). Linder (2011) noted scholars have the accountability to confirm the study is rigorous and ethical.

In the process of qualitative research, numerous concerns could result in uncertainty, including criteria for rigor. Rigor represents the agreement of consistent structures accepted by qualitative researchers regarding predictions and descriptions of the theory (Pereira, 2012; Ryan-Nicholls & Will, 2009). Rigor is essential for the study's evaluation, replication, error identification, and revision, as well as to refute the study if necessary (Ryan-Nicholls & Will, 2009; Sin, 2010).

Some scholars explained the data derived from qualitative study, after examination, describe or clarify experiences or help to understand a difficult phenomenon (Ryan-Nicholls & Will, 2009). For the purpose of this research, I implemented various criteria aligning with the theories of intersectionality and the cultural chameleon to ensure rigor, a commitment to trustworthiness, and authenticity related to my cultural experiences compared to the academic literature on disability, ethnicity, and gender.

Reliability, validity, transferability, and confirmability. In qualitative research, reliability, transferability, and validity are strategies for achieving rigor (Koch, 2006; Ryan-Nicholls & Will, 2009; Shenton, 2004). Thomas and Magilvy (2011) noted that professionals from different disciplines needed to build practice on the best evidence, with confidence and trust. For a qualitative analytic autoethnography, the rigor process is different. Ellis et al. (2011) inquired into the validity, reliability, and transferability of an autoethnography and indicated narrator's value context as truth. Ellis et al. also recognized that a truth could be different from person to person, depending on the topic, the type of writing, or the experience. Ellis et al. indicated it is not feasible to remember exactly how the person thought or lived such events. Specifically, the terms validity, transferability, and reliability, although part of qualitative research, are different for autoethnographers.

Reliability. Dependability and usability relate to reliability, which is when another researcher can make the same decisions as the researcher. Researchers explain a study's purpose; explain the reasons and methods used to select participants; discuss data collection methods and the time required; describe data analysis, interpretation, and presentation of study outcomes; and indicate the specific practices used to establish credibility (Koch, 2006; Shenton, 2004; Thomas & Magilvy, 2011). For autoethnographers, reliability means to demonstrate imagination was not the source of the story, it could happen, and the narrator is sharing a personal story (Ellis et al., 2011).

To establish reliability in this study, I synchronized and merged personal data into NVivo10 software. Data included tables, personal memos, data categories, links between events and data with links for external access, and instructions if necessary to accomplish auditability, as noted by Ryan-Nicholls and Will (2009). I also described the purpose of my autoethnography, my interest for exploring the topic, the reasons for not including participants, and a detailed description of the methods I used to collect data. I described any possible influences on me as the researcher and the specific methods I used to determine the applicability and truthfulness of the data, as suggested by Ryan-Nicholls and Will (2009).

Validity. Validity relates to credibility and entails the same concerns as reliability. To establish credibility in qualitative research, the researcher might review individual transcripts and find similarities among participants using strategies such as reflexivity, checking among participants, peer examination, or interviewing (Koch, 2006; Shenton, 2004; Thomas & Magilvy, 2011). In a qualitative analytic autoethnography, Ellis et al. (2011) noted validity stimulates readers to believe the story is real, credible, and possible. Other ways to establish the legitimacy of the story is to perceive its usefulness; offer ways to improve the lives of the author, the participants, or the readers; and improve communication among others. The reader establishes the legitimacy of the story. To reach validity in this study, I connected the narrative to sources such as pictures, videos, newspaper clips, and awards.

Transferability. Transferability indicates the ability to transfer research results or methods from one group of participants to another, achieved by providing a solid description of demographics and a study's limitations (Koch, 2006; Shenton, 2004; Thomas & Magilvy, 2011). For autoethnographers, transferability is nontraditional; readers test the story and determine if it shares something about the author or about known experiences. Transferability occurs when the autoethnographer enlightens cultural events unfamiliar to readers or when the readers can compare their lives to the life of the autoethnographer. Then readers could see differences and similarities within the author's experiences or by sensing that the story provided them with a new learning (Ellis et al., 2011). Autoethnographers have established transferability when the readers learn something new about people and cultures, feel identified, or sympathize with other people around them. To reach transferability, I presented cultural events that might be unfamiliar to readers, where they could see differences and similarities within my narrative.

Confirmability. Establishing reliability, validity, and transferability achieves confirmability. According to Thomas and Magilvy (2011), confirmability develops when the researcher leads the reader to sense trust in the credibility of the study's outcomes and its applicability. To reach confirmability, I achieved reliability, validity, and transferability through my narrative by sharing my cultural experiences based on my disability, ethnicity, and gender.

Researchers establish validity, reliability, and transferability of an autoethnography when their purpose is to stimulate readers' emotional experience, give a voice to the silent, expand reflection for readers and the narrator, and provide a credible story. An autoethnography is successful when the narrator is visible within the context and when the theme echoes with readers (Smith-Sullivan, 2008).

Summary

Chapter 3 contained a description of the methodology used for the study, including the research method and design appropriateness and the suitability of a qualitative analytic autoethnography to explore my personal culture experiences. The chapter included a description of the benefits, limitations, and methods selected to collect data; the analysis and interpretation of such data; and how I planned to write the autoethnography. Chapter 4 presents the findings to the data analysis presented within Chapter 3.

Chapter 4

Data Presentation and Analysis

The purpose of this qualitative analytic autoethnography was to explore why some multicultural people might turn into cultural chameleons to fit in or to adjust to a different culture. I used the narrative inquiry as the primary tool to collect and to analyze data. My narratives included a life story interview using the Labovian method and photovoice.

The data collection for this study also involved most of the key features of qualitative analytic autoethnography: CMR status, analytic reflexivity, narrative visibility of the researcher's self, dialogue with informants beyond the self, and commitment to theoretical analysis (Anderson, 2006). NVivo10 and Zotero software served to collect and store the study's data. NVivo10 software also served to manage, code, and analyze the data. Chapter 4 contains the thematic analytic procedure used for the qualitative analytic autoethnography.

I analyzed the data to develop emerging themes in terms of influences on mixing identities during social interactions as well as the need to turn into a cultural chameleon to fit-in and to adjust to a different culture. The presentation and analysis in Chapter 4 includes an explanation of the method of data analysis used to learn common themes. The results of the data analysis related directly to the research questions with supporting similarities and dissimilarities described using NVivo10 software. Chapter 5 contains the findings from Chapter 4 with interpretations based on the study's theoretical framework and review of literature.

Population Demographics

Presenting demographics as both the researcher and the researched, I was born in Mexico as able-bodied. At 2 years old, doctors diagnosed me with poliomyelitis. Today, I use a wheelchair for my self-sufficiency. In 1989, I emigrated from Mexico to the United States.

Data Collection

The narrative inquiry involved self-observation, self-narration, self-reflection, visual narrative, photo elicitation, and narrative voices. The narrative voices I used for identity and background were the immigrant, advocate, activist, colleague, employee, woman, disability, Mexican, and city native voices. The concerns and values narrative voices used were cultural sensitivity, safety, stereotype control, discouraging, attention, self-leadership, and mixing identities. Data management involved using QSR International's NVivo10 as a tool to organize and analyze data. The following were the steps in the data collection.

First, I looked in albums, binders, CDs, books, cabinets, drawers, and storage boxes for photographs, documents, journals, certificates, videos, artifacts, and any other items in my house that helped me recall something about my cultural experiences during social interactions. I asked my family, friends, and acquaintances to share photos that contained my image only if they had any available.

Second, I placed my findings in a designated box for scanning or photographing. The findings included photos, certificates, diplomas, award letters, and other important pieces. My immediate relatives provided some pictures and an old-fashioned 8-mm projector with a set of recorded film. I placed the pictures and the projector in the box with the other items.

Third, I searched my computer and an external drive for digital items including photographs, my website, information about my education, my small business, a local radio station broadcasting my name, and other digital items with relevant information for this analytic autoethnography. I created a folder and named it 4NVivo to save digital items I retrieved, and I created a backup copy on my external drive.

During data collection, I looked for data deficiency, redundancy, or irrelevancy. I collected an enormous amount of data. I began to organize the data I had collected and placed in the specific box before collecting any subsequent data.

Fourth, I organized the collected data by labeling each item with identifiers to provide information about the collection activities and data content; I also classified the data into groups. Chang (2008) suggested using primary and secondary identifiers, but to avoid breaching the confidentiality of my family, friends, organizations, or any other possible person or company indirectly involved, I mainly used primary identifiers. I only used secondary identifiers if the indicator did not reveal any private information. Finally, I logged the data using Microsoft Excel and saved it to my computer by naming the document Data Log.

In the beginning, I used the research tool Zotero as my personal research aide to save my research, including documents, websites, reports, and other items selected from the Internet. I created folders to separate and organize my search by saving the data while browsing the Internet, ProQuest and EBSCOhost databases, Sage Research Methods Online, Sage Publications, QSR International's NVivo10 qualitative research software, and other sources that could help with my data collection mainly through the University of Phoenix electronic library.

Zotero is an easy-to-use tool that provided the options to collect and organize research sources and to develop and cite references using the 6th edition of the *Publication Manual of the American Psychological Association* format, as required for the study (Zotero, n.d.). I also acquired the NVivo10 qualitative software to store, collect, and manage the study data. After I downloaded the software to my computer and learned the basics of its functionality, I began importing some academic literature from Zotero and from my computer to initiate self-learning on how to use the software and to create the necessary folders to store the appropriate data.

Research design takes careful planning and autoethnographic research is no different (Chang, 2008). The study involved more than recalling personal memories because it required, within the planning, explaining the reasons and the way I wanted to explore my own life, what I wanted to explore, and how I wanted to do it. The study also involved analyzing my cultural experiences from a researcher's perspective.

The analytic autoethnography was an exploration of my cultural experiences, and data supported and confirmed my story. I collected the data using the Labovian life story interview, photovoice, some key features of a qualitative analytic autoethnography, and relevant academic literature. Data collected included personal documents, media items, notes, photographs, and certificates.

A life story interview. The life story interview is a research method that enters into a person's life with the intent to understand it and comprehend how that person plays diverse roles in society (Atkinson, 1998). According to Atkinson (1998), a need exists for more women, members of different cultures, and members of underrepresented groups to voice their needs. The life story interview for this qualitative analytic autoethnography collected information from a woman who is a member of different cultures and various underrepresented groups. I answered the Labovian interview as the interviewee. I divided the Labovian questions into segments and labeled them as abstract, orientation, complicating action, result, evaluation, and coda, and I answered the questions. I named a folder DataSet_1 (see Appendix B).

Photovoice. I used a combination of photo reflection method for the photovoice analysis (Tindongan, 2012; Weathers, 2012) and "multivocality or narrative voices" (Mizzi,

109

2010, p. 2). I selected only pictures showing moments over the course of my early life in Mexico City and later in the United States. During the photo selection, I noted if I needed further data, if I collected sufficient data, and if I needed to trim and discard any data. The consciousness included being aware of repetitions, irrelevancy, and redundancy when collecting and organizing data (Chang, 2008).

I wrote my thoughts, feelings, and perceptions that emerged throughout the process using the narrative inquiry method with the photographs as a resource, also known as photo narrative (Clandinin, 2007; Radley & Taylor, 2003). The photo narrative included multivocality, which involved multiple and conflicting inner voices stemming from my disability, gender, and ethnicity. Mizzi's (2010) narrative voices facilitated explaining my cultural experiences articulated based on my "personhood" (Morris, 1993, p. 143) and provided an interpretation of the possible silent tensions within the story (see Appendix B). I created the folder DataSet_2.

CMR. The data collection also involved some of the key features in qualitative analytic autoethnography, including CMR status, analytic reflexivity, narrative visibility of the researcher's self, dialogue with informants beyond the self, and commitment to theoretical analysis proposed by Anderson (2006). To support my membership as a CMR, I included my birth certificate from Mexico and my citizenship certificate from the United States. I named the folder DataSet_3 (see Appendix D).

I included business plan classes and small business administration certificates I received upon completion of these courses. I downloaded related items including certificates of accomplishment from public speaking courses and feedback received as a motivational speaker. The flyers included information promoting my services providing written interpretations from English into Spanish, field peer-review services, and evidence of donations through my business to nonprofit organizations (see Appendix D). I created the folder DataSet_4.

Other items included information about my website, www.cecilialealcovey.com, which I exported using Zotero (see Appendix D). I named the folder DataSet_5. I also exported items related to my advocacy and activism, including an appreciation letter I received from local government, certificates as trainer-of-trainer, training grants advisory team, and strategic plan advisor. I also merged two Christmas cards I received from the White House, information about my past involvement as a member of the statewide disability council, information related to the work I have done nationally and internationally to end domestic violence, and a published article I wrote about disabilities and domestic violence (see Appendix D). I named the folder DataSet_6.

I also took pictures of four artifacts I selected to use: (a) a display at home, (b) a ping pong racquet I used when I played table tennis in Mexico, (c) the first hand control I had in my life, and (d) a postcard from Mexico (see Appendix D). I created a folder name DataSet_7. I merged information about my educational trajectory, such as certificates, diplomas, identification cards, newsletters, and newspaper article from both Mexico and the United States (see Appendix D). I created a folder named DataSet_8.

I included information about the awards I received as an Orgullo Hispano and the Beloved Woman of the Nations. Information related to scholarship granted to me by the League of United Latin American Citizens (LULAC), membership to the Phi Theta Kappa Honors Society, and thank-you cards I gathered (see Appendix D). I created the folder DataSet_9. I also photographed the crafts I have created by cross-stitching, embossing, crocheting, knitting, and making figures of ceramic. The tools I used as a computer technician and scanned identification cards from different organizations where I learned some of those skills (see Appendix D). I named the folder DataSet_10.

Commitment to theoretical analysis. To achieve the commitment to theoretical analysis feature, I downloaded to NVivo10 the abstracts of the journals and dissertations used for this study on social situations, stigmatization, discrimination, or prejudice against people with disabilities, gender, and ethnic groups. The purpose of downloading the literature abstracts was to describe the methods and conclusions of research on mixing behaviors and themes using intersectionality and to find areas for further research.

I downloaded relevant academic literature on disability, gender, ethnicity, mixing identities, and intersectionality to compare my cultural experiences. The disability folder contained journals discussing disability; race/ethnicity; gender; cultural oppression; acts of individual resistance; oppression of the different; impact and treatment; structural discrimination; stigma; and analysis of race, ethnicity, gender, and disability, among other relevant topics.

The ethnicity folder included journals discussing race, ethnicity, disability, intersections, interventions, psychology of immigration, and national and ethnic differences related to individualistic and collectivist cultures, among other themes. The gender folder

111

contained relevant information on racial/ethnic identities; gender role attitudes; multicultural counseling competencies; and intersections of dominant discourses on race, gender, and other identities, among other subjects.

The intersectionality folder contained journals on the effects of categorization, internal and external social identities, women and minorities, intersection within public health, and multiple social classifications, among other arguments. The mixing identities folder contained information on cultural homelessness, self-esteem, cross-cultural identities, cultures, behaviors, behaviors across cultures, and other related topics. I created the folder DataSet_11.

Data Analysis Process

The analysis of data included the life story interview based on the Labovian method (DataSet_1) and photovoice (DataSet_2). I also analyzed CMR items (DataSet_3 through DataSet_10) and the academic literature (DataSet_11). I coded data both during and after data collection as an analytic approach. The photovoice narratives helped me demonstrate honesty and impartiality while selecting cultural events and my responses during social interactions in which I encountered the need to mix behaviors.

Coding. Coding was fundamental for data collection and analysis. Coding the data was part of the active and interactive conversation between the researcher and the data. I coded using NVivo10, the Labovian life story interview, the photovoice narratives, the CMR items, and the academic literature abstracts. My initial coding ranged from a single word, to in vivo coding, to full sentences or paragraphs, to a specific area in a photograph.

To create the initial categories and nodes, I set NVivo10 to run a word-frequency query from the academic literature abstracts (DataSet_11) and selected the five first words to use with DataSet_11. The words were behavior, cultures, identity, people, and social. The nodes used from the academic literature were barriers, behaviors, discrimination, mixing, prejudice, social, classification, and stigma, shown in NVivo10.

Labovian method. I exported the answered Labovian life story interview to NVivo10 (see Appendix B). I used the nodes barriers, behaviors, discrimination, mixing, prejudice, social, classification, and stigma previously created using the academic literature. To find themes from the Labovian life story (DataSet_1), I set NVivo10 to run a word-frequency query. I set the properties window to (a) finding matches based on stemmed words, (b) search in text, (c) of selected items, (d) selected the Labovian folder, (e) selected the barriers node, (f) created by selected user (my name), (g) to display 150 most frequent words, with (h) minimum length of three, and clicked OK. Table 1 illustrates the results from the Labovian life story data coding process I followed using NVivo10 qualitative software. I followed the same process for each node (e.g., barriers, behavior, cultures, identity, people, and social).

Table 1

Labovian Life Story Data Coding Process

Category	Codes	Excerpts
Barriers	People	"I perceived that I was meeting angry people"
	Behaviors	(DataSet_1; Labovian_Abstract)
	Disability	
	Life	
	Cultural	
Behaviors	Behaviors	"I was an adult when I learned that I needed
	People	to mix behaviors to avoid rejection,
	Need	retaliation, and whatever comes with being
	Mixing	different" (DataSet_1; Labovian_Orientation)
	Self	
Discrimination	People	"I perceived myself as being where I wanted
	Need	to be before mixing behaviors, but if I had not
	Wheelchair	adopt such strategy I would be somewhere
	Behavior	else dominated by the angriness of many
	Cultural	cultures" (DataSet_1; Labovian_Coda)
Mixing	Behaviors	"I can say that mixing behaviors helped me to
	Mixing	overcome barriers built by people who, for
	People	some reason, have problems with people who
	Self	look different to them" (DataSet_1;
	Feel	Labovian_ComplicatingAction)
Prejudice	People	"During my first permanent job, someone told
	Disabilities	me that I was the "token" of the office. I was
	Need	somewhat proud when I heard her saying that
	Token	because I thought I was special" (DataSet_1;

	Wheelchair	Labovian_ ComplicatingAction)
Social classification	People Disability Social Classification Behaviors	"During my first weeks after I arrived to the Unites States, I noticed some behaviors that seemed strange to me but I thought it was my unfamiliarity to town" (DataSet_1; Labovian_Abstract)
Stigma	People Need Disability Avoid Aware	"Dominated by the senselessness against people who look different, dominated by people who need power and make others vulnerable, dominated by violence, and dominated by dependency and control" (DataSet_1; Labovian_Coda)

Photovoice. I exported the photographs and the photo narratives to NVivo10 (see Appendix C). I used the nodes barriers, behaviors, discrimination, mixing, prejudice, social, classification, and stigma previously created using the academic literature. Finding themes from the photovoice (DataSet_2), I set NVivo10 to run a word-frequency query. I set the properties window to (a) finding matches based on stemmed words, (b) search in text, (c) of selected items, (d) selected the photovoice folder, (e) selected the barriers node, (f) created by selected user (my name), (g) to display 150 most frequent words, with (h) minimum length of three, and clicked OK. Table 2 illustrates the results from the photovoice data coding process I followed using NVivo10 qualitative software. I followed the same process for each node (e.g., barriers, behavior, cultures, identity, people, and social).

CMR items. Table 3 illustrates the word-frequency query from the CMR artifacts (DataSet_3 to DataSet_11). The NVivo10 word-frequency query properties window was set to (a) finding matches based on stemmed words, (b) search in text, (c) of selected items, (d) selected DataSet_3 through DataSet_11 folders, (e) selected the folders containing the CMR artifacts, (f) created by selected user (my name), (g) to display 150 most frequent words, (h) with minimum length of three.

Table 2

Photovoice With Photo Narratives: Data Coding Process

Category	Codes	Excerpts
Barriers	Need	"I kept telling myself to move on from those
	Disability	thoughts" (DataSet_2; Photo30)
	Move	
	People	
	Cultures	
Behaviors	Move	"I resist to be one more statistic" (DataSet_2;
	Help	Photo19)
	Need	
	Avoid	
	Resist	
Discrimination	People	"I needed to adapt my needs to whatever I was
	Need	given" (DataSet_2; photo21)
	Disability	
	Moving	
	Box	
Mixing	Need	"I think that was the beginning of mixing
	Feel	identities" (DataSet_2; photo2
	Move	
	Mix	
	Cultures	
Prejudice	Move	"I noticed she kept looking away. She stared at
	Need	the wall" (DataSet_2; photo35)
	Expect	
	Look	
	People	
Social classification	People	"Living with multiple cultures in a difficult
	Need	environment" (DataSet_2; photo1)
	Disabilities	

	Cultures	
	Help	
Stigma	People	"They want to put me back on a box, but they do
	Disability	not know which box fits me well" (DataSet_2;
	Need	photo45)
	Box	
	Move	

Table 3

CMRs Items Data Coding Process

Category	Codes	Excerpts
Artifacts	Disabilities	"I do not belong to any box. I am free" (DataSet_7;
	Lost	Artifacts1)
	Box	
	Control	
	Difference	
Awards and	Education	"My challenges and achievements continue to motivate
honors	Award	me to persist and to use my education to better my own
	Community	life and advocate for the conditions within the Hispanic
	National	community, within people with disabilities, and for
	Opportunity	victims of domestic violence" (DataSet_9; LULAC)
Business	Inclusion	"…helping to build an inclusive and accessible
	Profession	community for all…" (DataSet_4; Do_BizSpeaker)
	Quality	
	Accessibility	
	Accurate	
Certificates	Accept	"I was told that in order for my other side of the family
	Family	to accept me, I had to have some type of similarity"
	Wannabe	(DataSet_3; Bday_Certificate)
	Achieved	
	Acted	

Education	Disability	"People at the exam offered me the test in Spanish but I
	People	was so mad at him that I took it in English" (DataSet_3;
	English	Certificate1_US)
	Class	
	College	
Hobbies	People	"Cross-stitched Sacred Heart. 50 colors. Beautiful
	Disability	work" (DataSet_10; Hobby3)
	Box	
	Believe	
	Feel	
Honors	Education	"National Scholarship Program" (DataSet_9;
	Award	LULAC_UOP_Thank you letter)
	Communities	
	National	
	Opportunity	
Web	Inclusion	"The language of diversity and inclusion as important
	Trainer	elements for change" (DataSet_6; Web)
	Accessibility	
	Change	
	Communication	

Commitment to theoretical analysis. Table 4 illustrates the word-frequency query from the commitment to theoretical analysis items (DataSet_11). I used the behavior, cultures, identity, people, and social categories previously created. I also used nodes on barriers, behaviors, discrimination, mixing, prejudice, social, classification, and stigma developed from the academic literature. The NVivo10 word-frequency query properties window was set to (a) finding matches based on stemmed words, (b) search in text, (c) of selected items, (d) selected DataSet_11 folder, (e) selected the behavior category, (f) selected the node barriers, (g) created by selected user (my name), and (h) to display 150 most frequent words, (i) with minimum length of three. I followed the same process for each category (e.g., behavior, cultures, identity, people, and social) and the node (e.g., behaviors, discrimination, mixing, prejudice, social, classification, and stigma).

Originated themes. This section indicates how I generated the themes for this study using the Labovian interview, photovoice, the CMR items, and the commitment to analytic agenda features keeping my visibility as the researcher within this analytic autoethnography (Anderson, 2006). The data analysis helped develop several themes. I searched for indigenous typologies or categories and meaningful words or terms with an unfamiliar sound or used in different ways within the coded data sets (Ryan & Bernard, 2003). Figure 1 shows the steps followed to originate the themes for the qualitative analytic autoethnography.

Table 4

Commitment to Theoretical Analysis Data Coding Process

Category	Codes	Excerpts
Behavior	Disability Group Cultural Ethnic Social	"People with a self-reported psychiatric disability and a self-reported comorbid physical disability faced more overall perceived discrimination/stigma (P = 0.04), than those with a psychiatric disability alone" (DataSet_11; Bahm & Forchuk, 2009, p. 63; imported notes).
Cultures	Cultural Ethnicity Disability Social Group	"Female immigrant workers encounter unique challenges in their work life transition to the host country environment, centering on factors such as ethnicity, gender, and cross-cultural adjustment" (DataSet_11; C. P. Chen & Asamoah, 2007, p. 67; imported notes).
Identity	Identity Social Research Intersections Ethnic	"Feminist and critical race theories offer the concept of intersectionality to describe analytic approaches that simultaneously consider the meaning and consequences of multiple categories of identity, difference, and disadvantage" (DataSet_11; E. Cole, 2009, p. 170; imported notes).
People	Disability Group Cultural Personal	"The BMA has called for a strategy of 'zero tolerance' towards discrimination against doctors in the NHS, after research has found that doctors' careers are being blocked on grounds of disability, ethnicity, sexuality, and gender"

	Social	(DataSet_11; Kmietowicz, 2004, p. 11; imported notes).
Social	Disability	"Findings support that identity and space is a fluid concept
	Cultural	shaped by social interactions" (DataSet_11; Cantey, 2011, p.
	Social	vii; imported notes)
	Group	
	Identity	

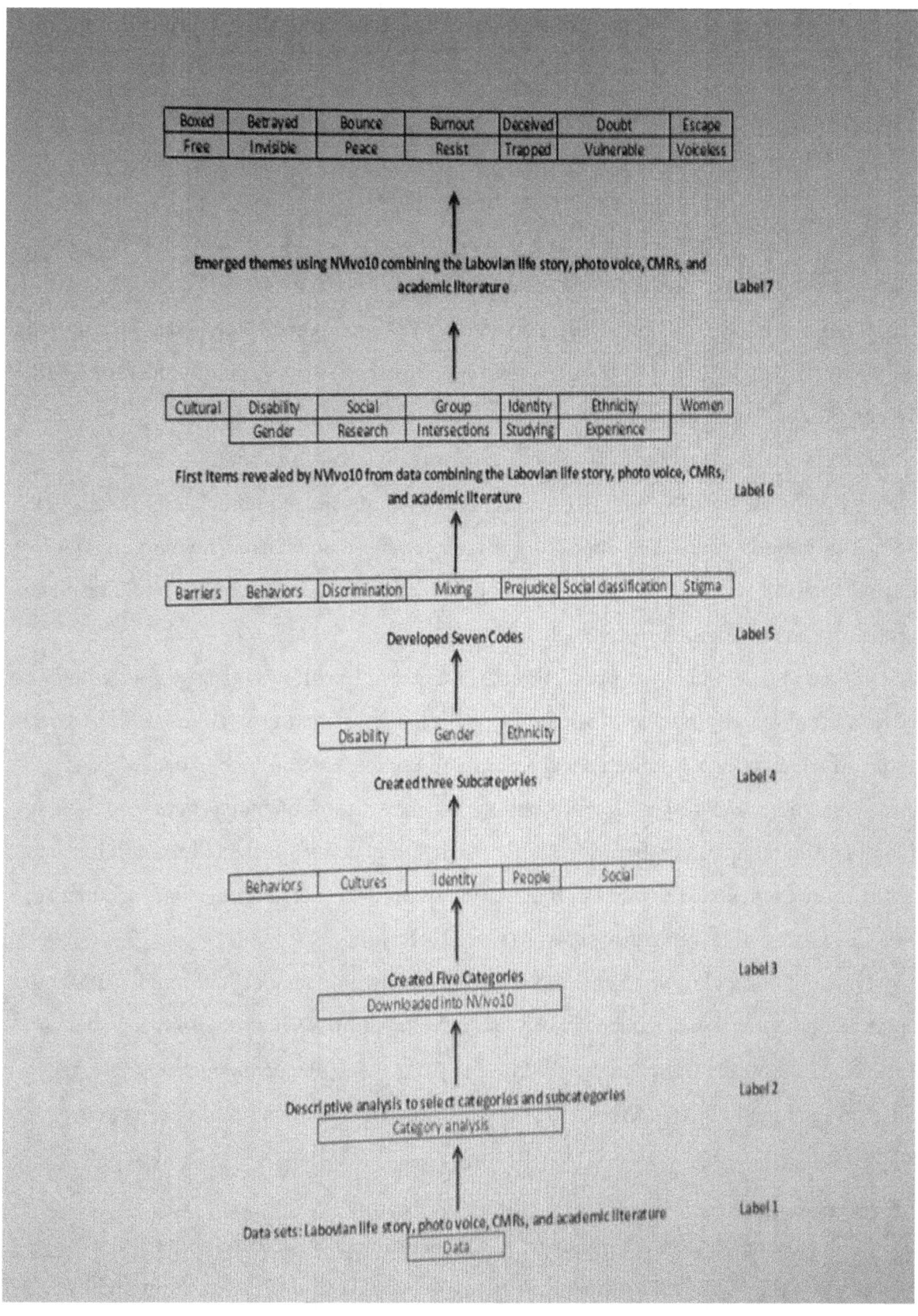

Boxed	Betrayed	Bounce	Burnout	Deceived	Doubt	Escape
Free	Invisible	Peace	Resist	Trapped	Vulnerable	Voiceless

Emerged themes using NVivo10 combining the Labovian life story, photo voice, CMRs, and academic literature   Label 7

Cultural	Disability	Social	Group	Identity	Ethnicity	Women
	Gender	Research	Intersections	Studying	Experience	

First items revealed by NVivo10 from data combining the Labovian life story, photo voice, CMRs, and academic literature   Label 6

Barriers	Behaviors	Discrimination	Mixing	Prejudice	Social classification	Stigma

Developed Seven Codes   Label 5

Disability	Gender	Ethnicity

Created three Subcategories   Label 4

Behaviors	Cultures	Identity	People	Social

Created Five Categories   Label 3

Downloaded into NVivo10

Descriptive analysis to select categories and subcategories   Label 2

Category analysis

Data sets: Labovian life story, photo voice, CMRs, and academic literature   Label 1

Data

Figure 1. The steps followed to originate the themes.

120

I also used a cross-sectional strategy to assess the themes within data sets without looking the time differences (McMillan & Schumacher, 2006). The analysis of the cross-sectional data involved comparing the differences among the frequency count of the themes within the data sets. The line chart was a useful tool that provided visual representation of the indigenous or silent words that emerged during coding.

The graph displayed the information as sequences of data themes connected by straight-line sections. To create cross-sectional analysis from the data sets coded, I used NVivo10 and Excel 2010. Using Excel, I created a workbook named Cross-sectional and ran a word-frequency query using NVivo10 with the Labovian life story, photovoice, the CMR items, and the academic literature.

The NVivo10 word-frequency query properties window was set to (a) finding matches based on stemmed words, (b) search in text, (c) of selected items, and (d) selected DataSet_1 through DataSet_11 folders, and (e) created by selected user (my name), (f) to display all frequent words, (g) with minimum length of three. I exported NVivo10 results to the cross-sectional workbook in Excel 2010.

In the cross-sectional workbook already created in Excel, I (a) created four columns (Labovian life story, photovoice, CMR items, and academic literature), (b) named the rows (boxed, betrayed, bounce, burnout, deceived, doubt, escape, free, invisible, peace, resist, trapped, vulnerable, and voiceless), (c) searched for the word frequency (count) provided by NVivo10 and entered the number in the appropriate Excel cell, (d) selected the columns and rows, (e) chose the insert tab from the Excel 2010 ribbon, (f) selected the charts section, (g) chose a line chart and layout charts, and (h) selected Layout 5.

The columns and rows or data table include data from DataSet_1 through DataSet_11. The plot area illustrates the frequency per word developed by NVivo10 within each data set. The line chart shows the found themes within the photovoice, the academic literature, the CMR items, and the Labovian life story. Figure 2 illustrates a cross-sectional analysis using Excel 2010.

Summary

In this chapter, I thematically detailed the data collection and analysis of my narratives using the Labovian method and photovoice to elicit information from photographs reflecting my experiences interacting with different cultures. I collected, stored, and managed data using NVivo10 qualitative research software. I created codes in NVivo10 and assigned them to relevant nodes revealed by the data.

I provided a thematic process of data collection including collection, organization, analysis, coding, and thematic analysis. I also detailed the thematic process of discovering themes by using NVivo10 software, created tables to illustrate the word frequencies, described the process used to develop appropriate themes, and provided a line chart to visualize the themes for the analytic autoethnography created by using Excel 2010. In this chapter, I also presented a thematic analysis using layering and interrelating themes to discover broader themes and information analyzed from the data. The thematic analysis helped to reach data saturation, which signified the end of data analysis.

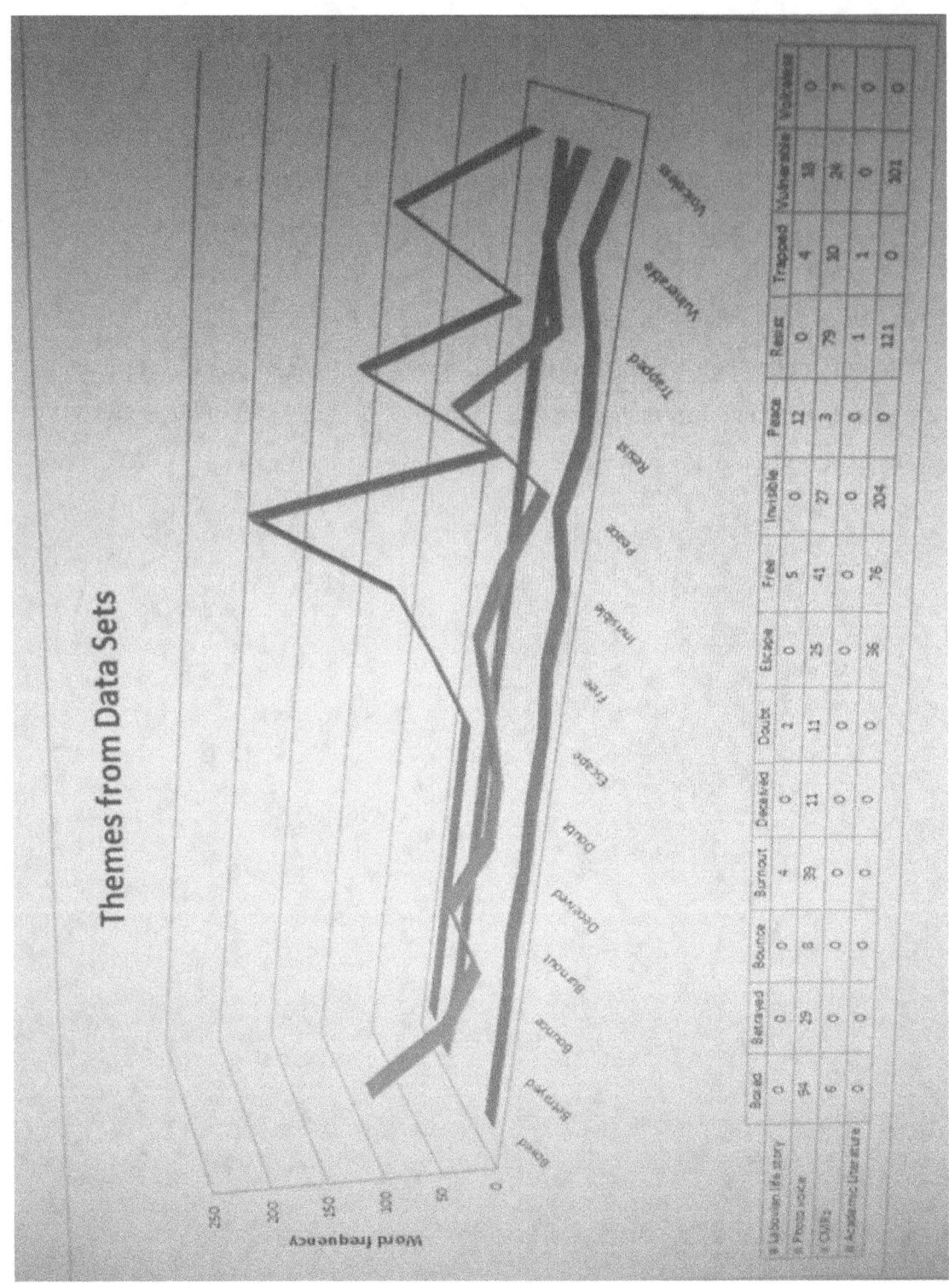

Figure 2. Graphical representation of a theme cross-sectional analysis among the Labovian life story, photovoice, CMR items, and commitment to an analytic agenda.

123

In Chapter 5, I will discuss the interpretation, personal findings, and themes discovered for the qualitative analytic autoethnography. The chapter will also contain an explanation of how my cultural experiences compared to the academic literature on disability, ethnicity, and gender. The comparison might provide a way to understand the reasons some people with multiple cultures might turn into cultural chameleons.

In this analytic autoethnography, I provided a more detailed description of the cultural experiences that a person with multiple social classifications might experience. When compared to the academic literature, I presented information illustrating how an inner self could perceive cultural experience (Dethloff, 2005). In Chapter 5, I will present the results as they relate to the conclusions and recommendations of this qualitative analytic autoethnography.

Chapter 5

Conclusions and Recommendations

The purpose of the qualitative analytic autoethnography was to explore why some multicultural people might turn into cultural chameleons to fit in or to adjust to a different culture. The study involved exploring the intersection of disability, ethnicity, and gender to understand a cultural chameleon behavior that some multicultural people might adopt as a method to respond to conflict and stresses while adjusting to a different culture. Chapter 4 contained the findings for the analytic autoethnography.

Chapter 5 includes the findings as they influenced the conclusions and recommendations related to turning into a cultural chameleon to fit in or to adjust to different cultures. I answered the research questions by providing the themes for each data set. Chapter 5 also includes a section on unanticipated or surprising findings. The chapter contains a discussion on the implications for education and education leadership and the limitations of the analytic autoethnography.

Chapter 5 contains a summary of the implications for professionals, the methodology used, and my reflections as the researcher. The chapter also contains recommendations for future research, a conclusion, and a summary. In this chapter, I focused on the new knowledge gained from the conclusions as they connected to my cultural experiences during social interactions.

Authenticity

A qualitative analytic autoethnography is distinctive and helps to draw from self-knowledge, where a personal biography interconnects to sociocultural situations and involves personal lives, identities, and feelings that connect to such intersections. The focus of the study was CMR status, analytic reflexivity, narrative visibility of the researcher, and assurance to academic investigation (Anderson, 2006). Because the focus of the analytic autoethnography was my cultural experiences, I collected data specifically for this research.

I analyzed the data using NVivo10 qualitative software and Excel 2010. I focused on the Labovian life story interview (see Appendices A and B) and photovoice (see Appendix C). The data helped me reveal common themes as they related to my cultural experiences as a person with multiple social classifications while mixing behaviors during social interactions to fit in or to adjust to a different culture. Sharing my cultural experiences compared to the academic literature on the disability, gender, and ethnicity domains might allow other people with multiple cultures an opportunity to reflect on their own behavior during social interactions, including developing an understanding of the challenges, difficulties, and successes associated with turning into a cultural chameleon.

Scholars have conducted limited studies on why some people with multiple cultures might turn into cultural chameleons to fit in or to adjust to a different culture. It was essential to explore the behavior of mixing identities from the perspective of a multicultural person to enhance understanding of the complexities of cultural chameleon behavior. Exploring oneself within a social perspective, in this case a person with multiple underprivileged cultures, provided a rich perspective about the inner self and the silent forces behind the decision to mix identities during social interactions.

Using personal narratives permits understanding the self and comprehending cultural intersections and might invite the reader into the narrator's life to reflect, comprehend, and bring their own experiences (Carrico, 2010; Ellis et al., 2011; Holman Jones et al., 2013). The life story interview allows looking at a life as a whole from an individual perspective, where the person tells his or her own story in her or his own words, recognizing the significance of personal truth from a biased perspective (Clandinin, 2007). I did not review, discuss, or collect any data, perspectives, ideas, or settings from any other people with multiple cultures.

Findings

I organized the research and communicated the findings and results using an analytic autoethnography approach and the intersectionality, multiple cultural identities, and social categorization theories as combined conceptual framework. In this section, I discuss the results of my study from my position as a person with multiple social classifications focused on disability, gender, and ethnicity. I also discuss the gap in the research and the way my study helps close the gap. The outcomes allow me to explore conclusions and recommendations that might provide information to other people with multiple cultures or to anyone motivated to learn and improve cultural perspectives.

I present the findings in relation to the research questions. I also integrate the self-reflection encountered as the researcher and researched within the process of this analytic autoethnography (Carrico, 2010; Struthers, 2012). The response to each research question follows based on the data collected and thematic analysis using the Labovian life story, photovoice, and CMR items and from the commitment to theoretical analysis.

Research questions and answers. The research questions for this qualitative analytical autoethnography were as follows:

R1: What influences people with multiple cultures to turn into cultural chameleons?

R2: How do I behave as a cultural chameleon when my physical disability, my ethnicity, or my gender becomes my only attribute as a person?

R3: How and when do I perceive the need to behave as a cultural chameleon?

The data provided several insights to these questions, and some links for multicultural education, including counseling and social service providers to consider in their work. In the following sections, I answered the research questions, discussed the findings, and compared those events with the academic literature. Specifically, 14 themes emerged from DataSet_1 through DataSet_11 as follows:

1. The Labovian life story (DataSet_1): burnout, doubt, free, peace, trapped, and vulnerable

2. Photovoice (DataSet_2): boxed, betrayed, bounce, burnout, deceived, doubt, escape, free, invisible, peace, resist, trapped, vulnerable, and voiceless

3. CMR items (DataSet_3 through DataSet_10): boxed, resist, and trapped

4. Commitment to theoretical analysis (DataSet_11): escape, free, invisible, resist, and vulnerable

Discussion. According to the literature review in Chapter 2, for this analytic autoethnography, negotiating multiple cultures might cause conflicts and stress for some multicultural people (Downie et al., 2006; Lynam & Cowley, 2007; Rodríguez-García, 2010; see also Adam et al., 2010). Although there was valuable literature within which researchers explore ethnic and racial minorities as whole groups (Mich & Keillor, 2011; Qin, 2011), current literature did not contain any investigations into why some multicultural people might turn into cultural chameleons to fit in or to adjust to a different culture (Downie et al., 2006; Ungvari et al., 2000).

The analytic autoethnography comprised examining and relating my cultural experiences to the larger academic literature on disability, ethnicity, and gender to explore the factors leading to cultural chameleon behavior. This study could serve as a reference point for understanding cultural chameleon behavior and the effects when cultures, as social classifications, intersect. The findings added to the limited body of literature on multicultural people and provided insight into the importance and influence of assumptions, negative attitudes, norms, and expectations on turning into a cultural chameleon.

The Labovian life story interview, photovoice, CMR items, and commitment to theoretical analysis data sets served as the data for the study. These methods became a way to describe cultural experiences during social situations to fit in or to adjust to a different culture. Using these methods, I was able to document various aspects of my cultural experiences that could help scholars, educators, and other people with multiple cultures, including other people interested in understanding the dimensions of turning into a cultural chameleon. The following sections contain a discussion of the specific findings from answering the research questions.

Being there. Pretending. *She was beautiful, elegant, tall, happy, and well educated. She could have been a front page model for any popular magazine. She had the face, the body, and the style. She spoke three languages or more, studied and traveled around the world hiding. Her father did not want anybody to know that she existed and that he had a beautiful daughter. A daughter who walked awkward helped by two metal orthopedic canes. Two canes to support her stumbling body, but challenged her tripping arms by the tremors Cerebral Palsy could cause. Until he could not afford to hide her abroad any longer, he traded her disappearing for alcohol.*

I was the opposite of her. I had high school and a short-term degree. I was not a good prospect for a magazine's model or newspaper. I was short, overweighed, in a wheelchair, spoke only one language, and lived with my mother and my brothers. Some in my family loved me, some did not love me; some in her family loved her, some did not love her. We were so different but at the same time so similar connected to a single perception of disability between two different individuals.

We were classmates in elementary school, a school designed for disabled and abnormal people, as the school's banner exhibited. We met when she was 18, and I was 12 years old. We were classmates for a couple years and stopped seeing each other for many years. Until someone told me, she was panhandling inside the subway next to my shoe-shining spot.

I tried to approach her to say hi, to hug her, but she refused talking to me. I intended several times, but as soon as she saw me approaching her spot she ran as much as she could. She knew the subway's stairs would stop me. More than once, she only walked a few steps and turned her back on me. People stared at us. Some even stopped walking and turned around to observe how my wheels attempted to reach her orthopedic flying canes. We were like an everyday novelty or a funny passage to watch, to laugh, or to inspire. People staring, whispering, and laughing was usual for us.

One day, she decided to approach my spot, and talk to me. I saw that beautiful woman stumbling, trying to walk toward me. Her canes looked like they were trying to knockout people around her; they seemed as flying out of her arms, but the canes' bracelets hold themselves secured to her arms. She was nervous and excited; the cerebral palsy made her looked anxious. She did not want me to see her economic condition, but knowing that I was cleaning shoes on the streets made her confident that I was not going to reject or judge her. We were the same; we could not embarrass each other.

We reestablished our friendship, and one day, we became the "transformers", as we jokingly called ourselves to make our survival strategies less uncomfortable and less embarrassing. She was from an affluent and well-educated defeated family; I was from the other side labeled as poor and ignorant. She begged for money at different subways every day in the morning and afternoon while I shoe shined on the other side. In the evenings, after my shoe shining work, she whistled to let me know we were ready to leave, to pack my show-shining chair and my equipment.

Every evening, I got into her beat up car driven by her drugged up husband. He was as tall as Herman Monster –I remember– overweight, and always high. One overdose made him act as if he were drugged up all the time. He got as high as cocaine took him but he could not come back down, as I was told. His traveling between reality and fantasy never ended. Some people, who did not know him, thought he had a mental disability causing him to drool and shake, but since he belong to a wealthy family, wealthy people looked at him as one of them, away and ignored, but still one of them. My people were afraid of him.

In the car, we changed clothes, and we transformed from less to worse. I removed my shoe shining uniform, and she changed to a torn blouse while her husband looked at the sky laughing and talking to himself. After transforming, we were ready to walk the wealthiest streets in Mexico City, begging for money in Polanco, Reforma, or Lomas de Chapultepec.

One day, we decided to have a fashion show to raise more money for the wealthy among the rich. We all knew that such money was for us to survive, including the models, the host, and many others involved. The show was in an elegant and expensive restaurant where only wealthy people assisted. Some parts of the restaurant were dark, darker than normal in purpose, then people would not be able to see and recognize the famous actors and actresses dinning there. Other areas were beautifully bright where people could show their expensive vivid clothes and jewelry, making them more dazzling and astonishing with the light reflecting the precious gems.

The models were her sister and her sister's friends, and her mother was the organizer and host. The models were wealthy beautiful teens, who knew us, but they wanted to play our game as long as they got a VCR and a newer TV. Her mother got some money too, including cases of alcohol. They were struggling. Her father passed away leaving them bankrupted, losing what they had, and what they did not have. They were struggling more than I was because they had to pretend they were still "one of them".

Before the fashion show day, we went to different beauty salons to have our faces, hair, and nails done; aiming to look like one of them –at no charge. My sweater, or I should say her mother's very expensive sweater, had a hole in the back. A large shredded rounded hole that nobody could see as long as I did not move out of my wheelchair. The wheelchair's back seat was wide enough to cover the immense perforation. My hands, my arms, were duty but covered by the sweater long sleeves. I could not remove the ink, oil, and other stings that are done by cleaning shoes. If I had removed my sweater, people could see my hard work cleaning someone else's mess.

I acted my part, as she acted hers, and everybody else. The teens looked beautiful. The elegance shined on them, and the older women watching the show bought every single piece of clothing the teens modeled. That night, after the show, we did not have to walk the streets. We already had pleaded with the fashion show. We could go back to our homes and rest for next day's journey. That night, during the fashion show, I grasped that her panhandling was to support herself, her husband, her mother, her sister, and her gorgeous house. A house located in one of the wealthiest places in Mexico City –Polanco.

One occasion, she was ill and told her husband to ask me to visit her, at her home. A Spanish style mansion, with swimming pool, with gorgeous and large paintings hanging on the garage's walls; walls covered with green and purple vines, roses, and many other flowers. The garage was inside the house divided by a wall made with colorful plants between the garage and the first living room. The paintings were astonishing. I touched one of them, as she asked me to do, and I could feel the buttons of the uniform the man in the painting wore. The painting was a soldier and touching the picture, I could feel his face, eyes, and uniform, just like a 3D picture today. These types of paintings were all over her house.

She asked her housekeeper to give me something to eat, but the housekeeper whispered something in her ear. She laughed and told her that I knew what hunger meant. It was OK for her to say that there was nothing to offer me but water. Her reality was that I knew about starvation, but my reality was different, I did not know about hunger, I was not hungry, but I was not wealthy nor I needed to pretend being one. I lacked luxury, and I had an assumed worse disability; hence, I had to be hungry.

Being there. Fucking Mexican. *He called me asking for help. The team needed only one more person to complete some grant requirements. I only needed to pretend I was playing, although I never played tennis and, it was not my forte. I could not even hit one ball, but it was OK, I did not care, I was helping my American colleagues with disabilities. I was so proud of being able to help them.*

After the game she wheeled toward me, I straighten my hand to shake hers but she refused. Involuntary, I said, "Well, I think I need a cigarette" and she added, "I am not sharing my cigarettes with a loser… fucking Mexican!" She called me fucking Mexican! That hurt! I was surprised!

I kept thinking that I needed to go home; it hurt! I wanted to escape! I wanted to put my wheelchair in front of hers and say, "Hey you fucking Whitty, do you know that I had the gold medal in tennis table in Mexico? I was one, I am one, of the best basketball players. I can kick your little White butt! Come on let us play, and I will show you how good a fucking Mexican can be!!" I said nothing. I smiled.

I started questioning if my team did it in purpose. I kept wondering, "Did he call me asking for my help knowing? Did he call me to mockery me but not the others, the Whites? I am the only Mexican, immigrant! Do they think I am a fucking Mexican too?" I asked myself if my personality or my looks reflect vulnerability attracting aggressors, "Or just people in wheelchairs have to attack each other. I do not attack people. I think my skin color as brown is the issue because how could they tell that I am from Mexico, I could be from el Salvador or any other place from South America", I thought.

I smiled. I did not speak enough English to respond to her insults. I did not know what to say. I would say nothing. I just wanted to help my colleagues.

I thought not to assist them anymore. I did not wish to be called a name or something else, but I did it again. When one of them asked me to oppose to a change during a board meeting. I did it, and I lost again. Nobody called me names at loud, but if eyes could kill, I would be dead right there. I just wanted to fit in, I wanted to be part of the group, to integrate, but after a few disempowering experiences I did not care anymore. I did not want to be part of their group, White.

Being here. Research question 1. Research Question 1 was as follows: What influences people with multiple cultures to turn into cultural chameleons? With regard to the influences on turning into a cultural chameleon, I presented the themes that emerged in DataSet_1 through DataSet_11. As such, the themes *burnout, resist,* and *doubt* provided more insights into turning into a cultural chameleon during social interactions. Based on the literature review and combining intersectionality with multiple cultural identities, and the

132

interpersonal networks and social categories conceptual as framework, I theorize the themes in the following paragraphs.

Theme 1: Burnout. The first theme to emerge was *burnout.* Burnout is a consequence of experiencing stressful situations for a long time. The literature indicated stressful situations might involve emotional and physical exhaustion, tension, apathy, and mental fatigue (Ekstedt & Fagerberg, 2005; Grant & Campbell, 2007; Tyrrell, 2010). The study's themes showed that I encountered an inaccurate burnout diagnosis based on feeling like a "fish-out-of-water" (Chang, 2008, p. 74). I remember I related such a feeling to a cultural disconnection, but it prompted a suicidal risk sign for a mental health professional and ended on a diagnosis of burnout for excessive school debt. The basis for this diagnosis could have been influenced by the many existing research on student, teacher, and school administration burnout.

Stressful situations and feeling like a fish out of water might relate to the burnout theme that emerged within the data. The academic literature helped me to understand this phenomenon. I had access to academic journals and autoethnographies discussing negotiating spaces, antiracist stories, disabilities, identities, disadvantaged groups, gender, age, and intersectionality, among others.

Accessing these educational materials gave me a sense of understanding the relationship between cultural influences and human behavior (Burke, 2007; Cantey, 2011; Klinker & Todd, 2007; Linder, 2011; Strolovitch, 2006; Tindongan, 2012; Voigts, 2009). Journals, books, school material, and my personal experiences all provided a way to increase my knowledge on burnout (Carrola, Yu, Sass, & Lee, 2012; Pines, 2004; Mann-Feder & Savicki, 2003; Mungo, 1981; Pines, Neal, Hammer, & Ickeson, 2011). The analytic autoethnography provided me the means to claim reflexive agency in my connections with others in same circumstances, but different backgrounds (Alexander, 2014; Anderson, 2006; Spry, 2001). Yet, differences exist between this analytic autoethnography and the academic literature.

Returning to the theory of intersectionality enhanced with multiple cultural identities, and the interpersonal networks and social categories and comparing it with this study and the academic literature, intersecting factors might influence the occurrence of burnout that leads

133

to turning into a cultural chameleon. People might not perceived burnout as different within people with one or multiple cultures. The intersecting factors relate to disability, gender, and ethnicity evolving within those social classifications when brought together (Best et al., 2011; Hae Yeon & Ferree, 2010).

The difference found between this study and previous studies was that burnout is not only a work-related diagnosis but also culture-related. Researchers mostly study burnout within work-related stress or job burnout (Pines et al., 2011; Thunman, 2012); limited studies related to adult attachment styles (Pines, 2004), and scarce research related to couples burnout connected to work-related burnout (Pines et al., 2011). Mann-Feder and Savicki (2003) found notable differences between cultures and burnout, but still focused on work. Alarcon, Edwards, and Menke (2011) discussed demands and lack of support leading to burnout in students.

Pines et al. (2011) found a connection between culture and burnout but focused on couples burnout and work-related stress. Shinhwan (2006) related burnout to perfectionism, overconscientious, or narcissism but focused on pastoral work. Although Farber (2000) discussed some type of burnout in a changing culture and mentioned *disillusioned burnout,* which relates to cultural burnout, Farber focused on work-related stress. Mungo (1981) also studied culture shock related to burnout but focused on work-related stress.

Little information exists on the events leading to such social diagnosis. The work-related stress diagnosis and disease might also have other concerns such as emotional fatigue; feeling drained and tired; treating other people as objects; and feeling inept, unproductive, and inadequate (Lau et al., 2005; Pines et al., 2011). The themes showed that these concerns might relate to the feelings of culture-related burnout.

An Autoethnographic text discloses the true inner self when connecting with others in the contest of exploring lived experience (Ellis, 2008; Spry, 2001; Warren, 2009). Writing an autoethnography accurately helped me to analyze, realize, and understand the reality of some people, including my own. In the transforming stage, I realized that we were two disabled begging for money on the streets, which is all that we were. Nothing less nothing more, just nothing.

In the insulting Mexican stage, writing the autoethnography and comparing with the academic literature, I grasped we were two disabled women playing sports. One with more power than the other, with the more accepted skin color, owning her territory and her place to belong. I was in the other side. I internalized her words and attitudes toward my social classifications.

Limited perspectives relate cultural differences, demographics, well-being, behavior, and social interactions to burnout (Ekstedt & Fagerberg, 2005; Etzion, 1984; Pines et al., 2011). Friberg (2009) offered an unfamiliar perspective of how burnout developed as a contemporary social diagnosis and disease. According to Friberg, Freudenberger, who fathered the concept of burnout, worked around the clock and alternated his identity every day (i.e., from role model to patients' perspective), which led to Freudenberger's emotional collapse.

Related to influence to turn into a cultural chameleon, burnout might stem from the constant identity interchange based on the cultural intersection and possibly lead to emotional collapse (Friberg, 2009). Alarcon et al. (2011) discussed society demands and a lack of support for people with multiple cultures. Based on my analysis, I proposed negative behaviors toward people with multiple social classifications are a critical stress factor behind the high number of mental exhaustion diagnoses. Emotional collapse might not refer only to work-related burnout.

For instance, the themes revealed for this study indicated that some people with multiple cultures are encouraged to feel motivated, inspired, and determined to strive for the apparently same opportunities for citizens. Later, the same people face expectations to behave the way dominant cultures define those behaviors, that is, who behave accordingly based on their membership to racial and minority groups.

Congruent with the literature on intersectionality, such experience might affect the "psychological lives of those who are different" (Campbell, 2011, p. 30). The study also provided evidence that the lack of competence regarding multicultural mental health services (Carrola et al., 2012; Chao, 2012; Harrell & Bond, 2006) could lead to a misdiagnosis of a misperception of work-related issues rather than an emotional collapse resulting from constantly switching cultural identities.

The analytic autoethnography required my visibility, participation, and being reflexive involved in the text (Anderson, 2006). The requisite allowed me to disclose and to incorporate my cultural experiences, feelings, and emotions into the study. I was part of the phenomena being studied (Ellis, 2008). The autoethnographic requisite allowed me to explain analytic insights while narrating my experiences and feelings as well as those of others (Anderson, 2006).

In conclusion, burnout might be an influencer and a possible consequence of behaving as a cultural chameleon. The outcomes from this analytic autoethnography might have a distinctive significance for previous studies on burnout as a work-related contemporary disease and social diagnosis. This finding indicated burnout might develop as a consequence of constantly switching identities trying to fit in or to adjust to a different culture leading to emotional collapse (see Friberg, 2009), in addition to society's expectations, demands, and lack of knowledgeable support (see Alarcon et al., 2011). Some multicultural people might enter into the workforce as an already burned out cultural chameleon interconnected to culture burnout, in which the individual with culture-related burnout might receive a misdiagnosis of work-related diagnosis. While writing this conclusion, the emotional collapse theme emerged as an influencer to turning into a cultural chameleon.

Another discovery was the lack of studies on disability, gender, and ethnicity as intersecting factors. Several researchers have explored disability, race, and ethnicity, but not gender. The next theme to emerge was *resist*. The themes *escape* and *bounce* appeared related to the theme *resist*; hence, I included these themes in this section as well.

Theme 2: Resist. The second theme of significance was *resist*. Scholars have discussed three major acculturation strategies: cultural incorporation, cultural resistance, and cultural shift. Cultural incorporation refers to the adaptation of traditions from the majority and minority groups or blending cultures or integration. Cultural resistance relates to the rejection of traditions from the majority group or separator. Cultural shift refers to replacing traditions of the minority group with the traditions from the majority group or assimilation (J. Berry, 2001, 2005; Torres & Rollock, 2009).

J. Berry (2001, 2005) noted a marginalizer is a person who does not want to be, or resists being, associated with either a home culture or a host culture. Orbe and Drummond

(2009) also discussed resist as "resisting the status quo" (p. 447). The data illustrated that I resisted adapting to the cultural identities or identity markers assigned to me based on my gender, disability, and ethnicity.

The autoethnography method provides a place where the writer posits the experiences and spreads them in a place where people can read and interpret them. A place where the writer involves the content written by self or others with a commitment to challenge, change, embrace, and interrogate researcher's own beliefs with a desire to better understand the self and others within a specific sociocultural context. "In an autoethnography self *is* the other" (Spry, 2001, p. 716; see also Alexander, 2014; Anderson, 2006; Warren, 2009).

The analytic autoethnography allowed me to reflect and to understand my relations with others and the norms around me (Alexander, 2014; Anderson, 2006; Spry, 2001). I resist the status quo, and I resist the inflexible social categorizations in the United States. The themes indicated that I resist choosing a label to describe myself, or a label I believe I belong, or where I do not fit in based on my other intersected social classifications (Orbe & Drummond, 2009). I turn into a cultural chameleon to *escape* from being *bounced* among social classifications and their limitations because I *resist* being divided among the classifications I represent.

This finding from analytic autoethnography was in agreement with Orbe and Drummond's (2009) explanation that implementing racial and ethnic labels of a characteristic does not work to eliminate racism. Each label creates another label and adds another perception. The intersection among labels might lead people with multiple cultures to feel confused (Moore & Barker, 2012).

Based on the data for the study, people with multiple cultures might encounter what I have labeled as an intersectional "culture cycle" (Markus, 2013, p. 15; see also Cramer & Plummer, 2009), where disability, gender, and ethnicity might become one whole culture. Once again, the reduced association, the other, the unique individual, and the solo become the label establishing differences (Badea et al., 2010; James & Wu, 2006; Leary & Allen, 2011; Rohmer & Louvet, 2009; Tajfel, 1982; see also Ellemers et al., 2002). In the intersectional culture cycle, gender, disability, and ethnicity intersected in different ways depending on the multicultural person's positionality (Alexander, 2014; Naples, 2009). As such, I have

137

resisted framing my social classifications as my identity, one by one or all together. As Alexander (2014) conferred:

> Social difference that can be qualified not only as those qualities that mark someone outside the perceived social norm, but social difference as a self-knowing perceptual awareness when one comes to recognize how their difference affects the social response to them. (p. 2)

To summarize, people with multiple cultures might feel forced to acculturate, although they cannot find a chance to initiate an enculturation process. Some people with multiple cultures might engage in acculturation to one culture but *resist* acculturating to the others by turning into a cultural chameleon. The themes revealed that I wanted to integrate to my new cultures, but I might have faced what Lyttle et al. (2011) described as a "unique universalized or multicultural perspective as well as greater cognitive differentiation" (p. 689). My way to resist was by turning into a cultural chameleon as a way to escape from being bounced among social categorizations.

Therefore, the findings in the study conflicted with those from previous studies on acculturation strategies. The focus of the strategies studied and presented (cultural incorporation, cultural resistance, and cultural shift) was groups and cultures as a whole. For instance, those researchers explored immigrants incorporating, resisting, or changing cultures but did not investigate how the intersection of social classifications (or designated cultures such as disabilities, gender, and other ethnicities) might affect integration, marginalization, separation, and assimilation to a culture.

The findings in the study might supplement previous studies. These studies could include research demonstrating the need to explore and investigate cultures within cultures, including the intersection of cultures when the social classifications are brought together (e.g., Bodenhausen, 2010; Frost, 2011; McDonald et al.,2007; Rudmin, 2003; Ruwanpura, 2008; Ward, 2008). The analytic autoethnography contradicted some studies on culture strategies. This contradiction was grounded on the lack of differentiation or inclusion between social classifications as cultures and common cultures (e.g., J. Berry, 2001; Chen et al., 2008; Mich & Keillor, 2011; Schwartz & Zamboanga, 2008). The outcomes from the study support the need to explore the apparent interrelation between interpersonal and emotional sensitivity (Lyttle et al., 2011) that affects the emotions and sensitivity of others.

The themes showed that in some cultural experiences, a physical disability might be a salience within able-bodied people but not within people with disabilities. If a person with multiple cultures who has a visible disability interacts with other people with disabilities, the silent evidence might be the ethnicity representation. Multicultural people with disabilities might encounter additional difficulties based on the disability and their ethnic minority group's identities (McDonald et al., 2007; Molina, 2006; Ruwanpura, 2008; Voigts, 2009). These difficulties might also involve rejection within the dominant culture of people with disabilities (e.g., dominant culture members with disabilities). An immigrant with disabilities might not be welcome to join the culture of Americans with disabilities. The next theme of significance discussed is *doubt.*

Theme 3: Doubt. The final theme of significance for Research Question 1 was *doubt.* Doubt might relate to uncertainty, distrust, and insecurity about something or someone (Doubt, n.d.). As the theme indicated, I doubted the content of some social conversations, the person, the person's words, and the situation. Merriam-Webster's online dictionary indicated doubt (Doubt, n.d.) means to be uncertain about (something), to believe that (something) might not be true or is unlikely, or to have no confidence in (someone or something). Some multicultural people might experience *uncertainty* toward people and the situation, *distrust* people and the situation, and might feel *insecure* about people and the situation. People with multiple cultures might struggle to *trust* people or the situation or both.

Beliefs, uncertainty, and anxiety shape the meaning of cultural background (Matsumoto, 2007). The doubt theme indicated the adaptation to a new culture relating beliefs, uncertainty, and anxiety might intersect with the social classification of a person with multiple cultures. The intersection could increase the ways people differentiate against others in different forms based on the combination of their social classifications or their individual characteristics (Goward, as cited in Cramer & Plummer, 2009).

Congruent with the literature on intersectionality, "multiple social identities intersect in complex ways to show social inequality" (Bowleg, 2012, p. 1269; see also Frost, 2011; McDonald et al., 2007; Warner & Brown, 2010). People with multiple cultures might

139

experience "cultural uncertainty" (Hoersting & Jenkins, 2011, p. 19) or doubt based on the cultural intersection spanning within the culture cycle (Markus, 2013), or what I have labeled the *intersectional culture cycle*.

In the process of writing autoethnography, the engaged conversation with the self, encourages the autoethnographer to question personal beliefs from inside out and from outside in. Spry (2001) wrote, "to interrogate the political and ideological contexts and power relations between self and other, and self *as* other" (p. 716; see also Butz, 2010; Denshire, 2014; Fox, 2014). An autoethnographer writing with and against a belief or profession might initiate understanding representations of power within relationships, friends, clients, colleagues, and social relationships including social responsibilities (Denshire, 2014).

Grounded on my personal cultural experiences and supported by the commitment to theoretical agenda, the adaptation to a new culture relating beliefs, uncertainty, and anxiety could intersect with a person's social classifications (Bowleg, 2012; Hoersting & Jenkins, 2011). My analysis indicated that doubt, uncertainty, and distrust could develop from cultural experiences. For instance, the themes for this study indicated that I fully trusted cultural interactions. Later, I confronted unexpected responses (e.g., comments such as "there is always something" or "a chip on your shoulder"), negative attitudes, inexplicable reactions, and expectations based on racial and minority groups' status.

Writing an autoethnography is different from self-representing during daily activities. The autoethnographer becomes self-conscious and reflexive making sure to produce academic knowledge. The autoethnographer also focuses on understanding and embodying social situations or relationships beyond the self (Butz, 2010). Becoming self-conscious, reflexive, concerned to understand and to place myself in my own cultural situation I understood the unexpected experiences influenced me to begin doubting the truthfulness and honesty of cultural interactions.

The process of generating a self for the autoethnographer at the same time of generating a self for the others required me to incorporate not only my own cultural experiences, but also my feelings and emotions into my analyses (Butz, 2010). The incorporation allowed me to comprehend that I hesitated to speak up, to share, to disclose, or even to join social interactions. I turned into a cultural chameleon to avoid being affected by the surprising interactions.

The literature indicated that social classifications or categorizations or social locations designate the "positionalities of people . . . and construct the social value that is assigned to individuals according to various components" (Harley et al., 2002, p. 216; see also Alexander, 2014; Frost, 2011). The theme exposed that this positionality might lead to doubt, uncertainty, and issues believing in some multicultural people. Multicultural people might have a concern about their positionality within cultural interactions based on the chosen social classification by other people. Spry (2001) wrote, "…performing autoethnography provides space for the living, experiencing, and researching body to be seen and felt" (p. 720) as it provided for me.

The theme also indicated that some people, as members of racial and minority groups, might experience being "reduced to their category membership" (Rohmer & Louvet, 2009, p. 80; see also Alexander, 2014) or becoming the "'other'" (James & Wu, 2006, p. 3), the "unique individual" (Badea et al., 2010, p. 24; see also Leary & Allen, 2011) or the "solo" (Tajfel, 1982, p. 5). An autoethnography offers a critical method emphasizing that self-representation cannot be extremely self-centered, but in order to write the social experience, the autoethnographer must situate him or herself in relation to projected readers (Butz, 2010). The critical method helped me to acknowledge the known including that the lessened association, the other, the unique individual, and the solo might become the background of doubt, uncertainty, and issues believing, as it became mine, as "certain people seem to get positioned as not only different but also troublesome and, in some instances, marginalized" (Staunces, 2003, p. 101). As such, this analytic autoethnography showed that doubt, uncertainty, and issues believing might be critical influencers to behave as a cultural chameleon.

The findings from this analytic autoethnography were in accord with some of the previous findings in the literature in which doubt develops when adapting to a new culture intersecting with the person's social classifications (Bowleg, 2012; Hoersting & Jenkins, 2011). The themes confirmed Matsumoto's (2007) discussion on beliefs, uncertainty, and anxiety shaping the meaning of cultural background. This confirmation is grounded on the

141

illustration that doubt developed based on people's perceptions and expectations that originated on the stereotypes of my cultural backgrounds.

Being there. Multiple cultures. Roughly, two years after I immigrated to America I was learning English, and I thought that learning sign language at the same time would be helpful. I encountered my position as a multicultural person when I met with a disability service provider. The consultation lasted more than 45 minutes, but this is what glued to my brain from the meeting

> *...a woman in a wheelchair who emigrated from Mexico cannot learn sign language because of her physical limitations and strong accent. More opportunities will develop when she attends the English as second language (ESL) program. The local Latino or Hispanics services will provide her with relevant information...*

There, I learned something that struck my truth. The awareness not only gave me goosebumps but also located me in an unknown personal authenticity. I became aware that being multicultural was an issue.

About the same time, I needed to learn English. I needed to communicate with people other than Spanish speakers —my family. I signed up to take classes in the mornings, afternoons, and evenings, and when I did not have classes, a mentor was assigned to me. It took me about two or three months to communicate in English, limited, but I did not need an interpreter.

A local newspaper and a local organization providing services to people with disabilities noticed my determination and invited me to be part of a disability awareness program. A newspaper and a governmental agency preparing a documentary interviewed me and videotaped my regular day activities with other people with disabilities.

Being there. It is unfair for Americans with disabilities. I was told I was the dumb there, but brilliant here. A woman, a friend or boss, arrived at my apartment with a newspaper in her hand and tossed it on my table saying, "Did you see this shit?" I asked "What shit? Do not you think this is good?" She responded, "No. This is bullshit! They picture you as an idiot, ignorant idiot, coming from Mexico. They said you were just dumb there, but coming here, you have become a brilliant star! Smart, intelligent, an example, an inspiration… full of shit!"

"I do not read that… Is what they meant? You know my English is limited, I do not get their main point" I said. "Well, you will understand what you want to understand even if the article was in Spanish. That is called "ego!" I would call them and complaint about it. Because it is not fair for the disabled Americans! That is ridiculous!!" she shouted.

She was angry. That article boiled her soul on fire, and she was fuming. I still do not know why. I think she mentioned all my social classifications, but my name. She also said, other than immigrant and disabled, from Mexico I guess she meant Mexican. She added some more like dumb, brilliant, star, smart, intelligent, an example, inspiration…!

I was helping her to set up appointments for her business. I worked at home making phone calls inviting people to listen to her presentation. She was beautiful, smart, well educated, and determined to get what she wanted. She told me that her dad was African American and her mother Hispanic.

I felt desolated because I did not know how to handle the new culture and my new self. I could not voice how difficult the adjustment to America life was, and I did not know whom I could go to for support. When I thought about asking other immigrants or Mexicans, I got no answers, and some responses exuded more pain. When I thought to ask to other people with disabilities, I became worried that I could be taken as trashing my people or risking to show weakness.

I did not know how to veil my feelings. After she left I cried and cried, and then the same day I went to my English class, and my teacher tried to show the newspaper to my classmates. I asked him not to do it. I was so deeply hurt. I cried again with my teacher. During a break, I cried again with some classmates. "What is going on? What is happening?" I kept asking myself. I was not used to it. I did not know what to do. I thought it was the American way, but I did not like it.

I did not understand why or how the newspaper article would affect Americans with disabilities. Why couldn't I be an inspiration or motivation just because I was from another country? After this experience, although I cried so much, I did not let people see the newspaper article or a documentary that was broadcasted later. I did veil my progress. I was humble but afraid of being hurt again.

Being there. Be aware. *When I shared the behavior and comments about the newspaper article with some of my classmates during our break, their comments puzzled me even more. I remember listening to their conversation in Spanish:*

Creo que estas confundida. Estas pensando en lo que tú "amiga" o "jefa" te

dijo. Creo que está equivocada, a lo mejor celosa... envidia. Lo único que

quiero decirte es que debes de tener en cuenta de que aquí tú peor enemigo

son los Mexicanos, los Chicanos, y claro los mixtos (I think you are confused.

You are thinking about what your "friend" or "boss" told you. I think she is

wrong, perhaps jealous... envious. The only thing I want to tell you is that you

must be aware that your worst enemy here are Mexicans, Chicanas, and of

course, mixed).

Her comment seemed out of place because she was from Mexico as well, and I could not grasp what she meant. Another classmate interrupted her saying, "¡Los mixtos son malos! ¡Están enojados con cualquiera que se les ponga al frente! ¡Aguas!" (Mixed are bad! They are angry with anyone who steps in front of them! Watch out!)" My other classmate continued saying, "Eres nueva aquí, en América y estas luchando fuerte. No escuches. ¡Los Mexicanos le echan tierra a los mismos Mexicanos! ¡Solo acuérdate! (You are new here, in America, and you are working hard. Do not listen. Mexicans pour dirt over Mexicans! Remember that!)"

I listened to their words, but I doubted what they were saying because, in my perception, it was impossible that a woman so smart, educated, and pretty, would be jealous of me. After such experience with the newspaper article, when the documentary was released and aired I did not show it to anyone. If people saw it on the news or somewhere else was OK but I did not show it nor discussed it, I felt disempowered and afraid of the possible comments or responses. My family watched it on the local news, but I did not discuss it –I did suppress it.

After analyzing the comments, something saddened deep inside of me. I understood the strange people's behavior I could not understand. It was not my feelings of melancholy,

144

lonely, sadness, or needed to go back home —my country. It was not me; something unfamiliar was happening around me, in my new environment. I perceived that I was meeting angry people. I was entering into a hostile culture, an unknown territory.

__Being there. There is always something.__ I drove to an office, 15 miles from home, to sign a contract as freelancer. Chatting with the contractor she happily and proudly told me that she was promoted and she had an opening. As if she was insinuating to hire me, suddenly she mentioned, "Umm, I do not know, so many skills ...but there is always something." First, I did not understand her comments because I was not interested in her opened position, and she did not offer it to me directly. I was not sure about her comment, but my docile and submissive other responded, "Yes. There is always something. I am thinking to see a mental health provider because ...there is always something."

I was not even sure what her comments meant, but it felt as if a bucket of ice-cold water ran all over my body. While driving home, my thoughts were about my disappointment for trusting. It felt grief. I blamed myself. It hurt deep, very deep inside. I trusted her. I thought I could share my cultural experiences with her and be safe. I should not have said anything.

"Did she bring this up as an excuse, not to hire me?" I kept asking myself, but I did not want to work with them! I was not asking for a job. "I do not trust my experiences with many people, but after this I will not trust anyone! I promise!" I told myself over and over. I began making excuses, finding reasons to deviate my reality. I thought my disappointment was because she was White able-body woman, and I expected her to be better than many. She was a woman just like me, but that did not matter, "...there is always something".

People use my experiences against me or as a reason for retaliation. I made a mistake trusting her. My thoughts became a war of words. I had many voices in my head telling me "there is always something", "see? I told you not to trust!" "cannot trust anybody!"

"If a mental health professional diagnosed me with burnout, what can I expect from other people? I need to make sure that I do not disclose or share any experience. This type of people may diagnose me as crazy. I do not have anything to defend myself. She meant it,

145

and she may be right based on her cultural beliefs, and she is White and able-bodied. What can I expect?" Kept bouncing in my mind.

Being here. Research question 2. Research Question 2 was as follows: How do I behave as a cultural chameleon when my physical disability, my ethnicity, or my gender becomes my only attribute as a person? In the following paragraphs, I briefly explain *invisible (voiceless)* as the revealed theme of my behavior.

Theme 1: Invisible. The theme that emerged was *invisible.* According to Rohmer and Louvet (2009), disability is the most silent evidence in perceptions of people with visible physical disabilities. People describe individuals in a wheelchair by their disability, not by their gender or ethnicity. Rohmer and Louvet suggested disability projection is defined socially. The data showed that some people describe individuals with multiple cultures by their disability, not by their gender or ethnicity.

This theme indicated that some people with multiple cultures might experience feeling voiceless or invisible and silenced because of who they are and significantly perceptible as part of the others (Higgins, 2010; Jones et al., 2012). The data indicated cross-cultural women with disabilities might be invisible in different sectors in society (Cheng, 2009; Higgins, 2010). This theme also showed staring is not only bothersome but also a common behavior toward people with disabilities. Hansen and Philo (2007) noted people's stares are "often averted if the disabled person does try to make eye contact, alongside a pitying attitude towards someone's 'imperfect' control of their bodily movements" (p. 497).

Writing an analytic autoethnography, the descriptions strive to connect across the space between the inside and outside or the self and the other (Butz, 2010). According to Butz (2010) the outside setting or the other, influence the representations of the inside or the self. The autoethnographic representation helped me to follow the themes for this study indicating that I observe people's body language when interacting with me.

I smile if I notice some differences emerging based on my disability, gender, or ethnicity. I continue the interaction or I move on, depending on the situation and my personal needs to be there or not. If I notice that the person or persons stare at my wheelchair, including the wheels, seat, footrest, and position, and ignore the person sitting on the wheelchair, I smile and kindly move on.

According to Hansen and Philo (2007), people with disabilities also experience people patting them on the head when the disability becomes their only attribute as a person. The theme showed that my behavior when patting occurs is to become invisible, passive, and maintain quiet. The theme also showed that smiling is the way I become invisible.

Numerous scholars in the literature reviewed discussed smiling as a way to influence emotional processing and to communicate intentions based on the situation. Ochs, Niewiadomski, Brunet, and Pelachaud (2012) discussed smiling as a facial expression that represents amusement, politeness, and embarrassment. Kunz, Prkachin, and Lautenbacher (2013) discussed smiling as "enjoyment, dominance, and affiliative smiles" (p. 1). The enjoyment smile could represent happiness, the dominance smile could represent dominant social status or control, and the affiliative smile could represent positive social purposes and create social connections (Kunz et al., 2013).

Scholars also described smiling as a behavior for social signal transmission, as an emotionally salient social impulse to differentiate the self and the other, and as a way to signal intentions (Ochs et al., 2012; Schilbach, Eickhoff, Mojzisch, & Vogeley, 2008; Smith & Schyns, 2009). Some other scholars noted smiling could be a signal of submission, lower status, or cooperation, but also a mild aggression. Mild aggression manipulates the perception of the other or others as a means to control the situation (Burton et al., 2011; Kunz et al., 2013).

Although the study is still in process, Botella et al. (2012) indicated smiling could be a coping tool. The coping strategy could help regulate or manage emotions in people facing high levels of stress. The themes for this analytic autoethnography illustrated some people with multiple cultures might smile to swerve negative perceptions before entering to the inner self, and to disarm the other person.

I am aware, based on some of my cultural interactions, that a smile's intensity could irritate another person or persons. Therefore, this study was in accord with Kunz et al.'s (2013) suggestion for more research on the impact of smiling on the observer. Although Kunz et al.'s study related to smiling during pain, the analytic autoethnography indicated a need for more research on smiling during emotional pain.

147

Burton et al. (2011) noted "deliberate smiles could play a role in the regulation of hierarchical relationships" (p. 34). Burton et al.'s discussion might relate to the reasons I behave as invisible when my ethnicity, disability, or gender becomes my only attribute as a person. I might smile to regulate or to avoid social classifications within a categorized relationship perception (Burton et al., 2011).

I am aware, as the revealed themes illustrated, that I choose how and when to behave as a cultural chameleon when my disability, gender, or ethnicity is my only attribute. I can be me or I do not have to be, but people do not overlook my disability. My wheelchair does not hide the aspect of who I am.

I also understand that behaving as a cultural chameleon is somewhat of a privilege that I have, but at the same time it is a fake way of living, experiencing, and enjoying. When I am interacting with people within the majority groups, themes showed that my origin or ethnicity takes precedence and becomes my only attribute as a person. I behave as a cultural chameleon by smiling, a nice and subtle smile.

In sum, smiling is a tool for me to become invisible when one of my social classifications becomes my only attribute as a person. Smiling also helps me to control social situations and to manipulate the other's perception related to the racial and ethnic minority groups I represent. The present analytic autoethnography indicated deliberate gentle smiling could be an effective tool to influence social situations.

Being there. Embarrassment. *I wanted to open my own business. I wanted the freedom of working from home, planning my own time with my deadlines. I wanted to be an independent worker, a free spirit. I was OK as a hired employee, with my space, fair responsibilities and doing the advocacy and activism, I love to do, but I was missing something –I needed a change.*

I was invited to sell insurance for a large company. Because of my English as Second Language (ESL), I struggled to pass the license test. After trying a couple of times, I got my license in the mail and a mentor was assigned to me. I had a good friend playing as my mentor, but I needed someone recognized and qualified by the company as my official mentor, and then one was assigned to me. I was told that I would be an asset for my new mentor because he was very successful and needed some help with the Latino community. He

148

needed someone who spoke Spanish and understood the culture. I thought that the "token me" was a perfect match. I could help my new mentor not only speaking Spanish to outreach the Latino or Hispanic communities, but also I could help him empathizing with some people because I had a physical disability.

I agreed that I was an asset to my new mentor's group and the company. I planned to make my token label work benefiting my new group, my new mentor, and myself. I had the skills and the determination to make a fantastic income.

One evening, my new mentor called me requesting to meet next afternoon to talk about my new position and responsibilities. We agreed to meet at a coffee shop in a large local casino. I was excited! Next day, I arrived at the casino's coffee shop a few minutes earlier. My purpose of arriving earlier was to find a comfortable table where I could accommodate my wheelchair without moving people around asking them to make some space for me.

Few minutes later, I saw a handsome White man, dressed in shorts and a t-shirt walking toward me. He looked like a movie star, the perfect profile of a Caucasian male. He said hi, introduced himself, and placed much insurance material on the table. After explaining the material, he said, "Cecilia, well, I hope you understand that I cannot take you with my clients. I do not know what they would think about me taking someone like you, you know, in a wheelchair, with me. You are on your own. Good luck to you." His words felt like ice cubes sliding down all over my body. I did not know what to say, and I did not know how to react, I did not expect anything similar, and I responded, "Yes. I understand, and I thank you for your honesty. Good luck to you too."

I could not yell discrimination right there in front of the casino's clients, employees and whoever else was there. I could not do anything because my social classifications against a White male would work against me. I could even get deportation if I step into a jail. Filing a lawsuit against him was not an option either because it was my word against his. I would win nothing, but I would lose all –I kept thinking.

When I went back home, I cried and cried, I felt sad, and I questioned my reaction, but I was in my home, and nobody could see how much such action hurt me. I could not work with the group any longer. I could not motivate myself to sell their product, I lost faith and trust in them, I had to move on in peace. I knew that not only I could file a formal complaint against the entire company, but I also knew I could bring the worst to my life in addition to losing the case.

Being there. Your own people. *I finished training to become employed, but the person in charge said, "The only place I can locate you is in a factory. You have no skills, and you do not speak English enough to get a job in an office. I cannot find jobs with your limited qualifications. If you want to work in an office go and talk to business or organizations run by your own people and ask them to hire you." My own people? Who were my own people? Disabled? Immigrants? Latinos? Hispanics? Women? My family? My dogs? Freaks?*

I thought that, since it was my first job officially in the USA, a factory would be perfect for me! Her words discouraged me to the point that I could not see myself working in an office. I graciously thanked her and left. Next day, I applied for a job on my own with the local school district. I was interviewed, and the same day, in my way back home, I received a phone call offering me the position I had applied. Were they my own people? I got a job and a well-paid job!

I kept thinking, for a long time if that happens to everybody here. Was her comment "your own" a common suggestion for people with disabilities? Were my skills as a bilingual, tech savvy and a good worker not enough? I had the skills, the knowledge, the willing, and my God's blessings, besides the tokenism I represented.

Being here. Research question 3. Research Question 3 was as follows: How and when do I perceive the need to behave as a cultural chameleon? When people's body language makes me feel *boxed, trapped,* and *vulnerable* during social interactions, I perceive the need to turn into a cultural chameleon. The following section served to present concisely the boxed theme as revealed by data sets.

Theme 1: Boxed. The first significant theme was boxed. This theme showed that some people with multiple cultures who feel boxed might turn into a cultural chameleon. The dialectic box, boxed, or boxed-in related to social classifications representing a person confined to a place with no opportunities, with limitation to do what they want to do or to have what they want to have. The metaphor might also describe the positionality of a person with multiple social classifications as boxed, boxed-in, or limited to perform outside of his or her designated box.

The theme revealed some multiracial Americans refuse to be boxed into one racial classification and support different sources of their racial identities. Including people whose identities reflect two different races, racial and ethnic combinations, family identification, physical appearance, friends, and relations with extended family members. Some people "resist any racialized labels other than human race" (Orbe & Drummond, 2009, p. 441).

The boxed theme also revealed that some people with multiple cultures resist others boxing them into one classification (e.g., racial, ethnicity, disability, gender, native or foreign-born) or into many simultaneously. Rohmer and Louvet (2009) noted, "Persons with disability, belonging to a minority and socially devalued group in western cultures, are often reduced to their category membership" (p. 80). The category membership for this analytic autoethnography is more than one membership and category, and that includes ethnicity, gender, and disability. As such, some people with multiple cultures might refuse to allow others to box them. The next theme of significance is *trapped.*

Theme 2: Trapped. The second theme that emerged was trapped. The data sets also revealed the theme trapped is an influencer to turning into a cultural chameleon. The theme revealed that some people with multiple cultures might turn into cultural chameleons because they feel trapped by their social classifications (see Wong, 2010). Some people with multiple cultures might feel trapped by cultural norms and fear related to a social classification intersecting with other categorizations (see Cramer & Plummer, 2009).

Numerous people with multiple cultures might feel trapped within the tokenism experiences, for instance, sense as especially noticeable, isolated, or trapped in pleasing stereotypes (Danaher & Branscombe, 2010). Some multicultural people might feel trapped, powerless, and isolated related to feeling shame (see Rondero & Mendoza, 2011). As such, some people with multiple cultures might turn into a cultural chameleon because they feel trapped between their social categorizations and the intersectional culture cycle. The next theme of significance is *vulnerable.*

Theme 3: Vulnerable. The final theme that emerged was vulnerable. This theme indicated that assuming a group's lack of power and the dominance this might represent

151

makes marginalized groups vulnerable (Hyers & Hyers, 2008). The entire person and the elements surroundings such person could be felt as vulnerable because those elements are culture (Stamm et al., 2004). The theme also revealed the combination of social classifications and the intersection of those same cultures might make a person vulnerable to discrimination.

For instance, the cycle of gender, disability, and ethnicity, including the intersectional discrimination among the disability, gender, and ethnicity revolving in an endless intersectional culture cycle. Immigrants, Latinos, Latinas, and women are vulnerable populations (Ojeda & Bergstresser, 2008). Nario-Redmond (2010) also indicated people characterize women with disabilities as vulnerable, socially ignored, and deprived.

As such, some people with multiple cultures might be more vulnerable to pressures from each social classification and the cycle the classifications might represent (e.g., racial and ethnic minority groups). The intersectionality of those classifications might increase multicultural people's feelings of vulnerability and intensify others' perception of vulnerability. The intersectionality of those classifications' increasing vulnerability might influence a person with multiple cultures to turn into a cultural chameleon.

The acculturation categories indicated that bicultural people who keep their native cultures and acquire some characteristics of the new culture are more vulnerable to pressures from both the native and the new cultures (Rudmin, 2003). The themes in the study showed some people with multiple cultures might encounter pressures from native and new cultures making them more vulnerable, as Rudmin (2003) discussed. I felt vulnerable during social interactions and turned into a cultural chameleon. I was not sure what classification was going to be stronger than the others were or when or how quickly a switch could happen that would increase my feelings or perceptions of vulnerability.

The results of the study were consistent with previous studies on vulnerability influences related to native and new cultures, including perceiving gender, disability, and ethnicity as the most vulnerable populations. The sensitivity of vulnerability based on cultural representation might unintentionally influence the perceptions, expectations, and judgments of people identified as belonging to different social classifications. The following section contains the surprising findings.

Being there. You do not belong here. *During my masters' graduation ceremony, I was among graduates, wearing my graduation gown like every graduated, and I "parked" on the hallway next to the graduates' seats waiting to hear my name. I made sure to lock my wheelchair to avoid sliding down the corridor. Suddenly, I felt someone grabbing my wheelchair's back handles and felt like my wheelchair shook. I immediately smiled thinking it was a friend or someone who knew me and wanted to congratulate me on my accomplishment.*

I turned my face to greet the person, but I did not know her. The woman kept trying to push or pull my chair saying, "Mom, you need to move, this is not your place. You do not belong here mom." She kept trying to push my wheelchair, but it was locked. I told her that I was graduating, and soon they would call my name. I could not leave the corridor, and that particular space was designated to me by the university's administration.

She kept telling me that I did not belong there and I needed to move. At the same time she was forcing my wheelchair to move. Until a graduate next to me stood up and asked her to leave because I was part of the group and I was not going to leave. The woman left, and the graduate looked at me as if she were saying, "WTF?"

I wrote a letter and mailed it to the administration's office telling what happened, and I recommended sensitivity training for employees. The company did not answer to my letter, meaning they ignored my compliant and my request. I took the risk of mailing the written letter because I was "forced" by a friend to do it. She said to do it, or she would do it and knowing her, she could get me in trouble. I moved on and left the company alone hoping the letter raised some awareness because what the employee did was wrong and emotionally disturbed not only me but also a witness.

I could not even image what could have happened if either the employee took me away or if I reacted and complained right there in the middle of the ceremony. My assumptions were that I would be arrested for some reason, and the employee would be in the right arguing that my wheelchair obstructed the emergency pathway of some people. I would lose either way. I only thought she wanted to congratulate me on my achievement.

Being there. Ill-fated icon. *After we had graduated from high school, my team of classmates and I planned attending the UNAM (Universidad Autónoma de México) together.*

153

My father denied any type of support for me to attend UNAM, and then my classmates, and I took different paths. They continued their education as doctors and attorneys, and I attended a short career as a computer programmer.

Few years later, I needed to make some income to support my family and myself, but the discrimination, multiple and varied, pushed me to find odd jobs for women. I became the first woman with and without disabilities to work as a shoe shining in Mexico –the entire country not just in the City. Becoming the first shoe shiner, I believed, I opened doors for various women with or without disabilities to become economic independent, but it came with its own story of a difference of treatment.

My mother, one older sibling, and I supplicated and bought out the union's leader to allow me joining the shoe shiners group, but I had an intense restriction. I was banned to attend any meetings, reunions, or anything that required being present, including stepping into the office to pay my fees. The leader sent a "special" group to collect the required fees to pay for my spot. He stated that it was embarrassing for him, and for the group of shoe shiners to have a "wheelchaired invalid one" in the group. The wheelchair embarrassed him or them. According to him, if people saw me as part of the shoe shiners, the group could lose reputation, business, and allies. I was a bad icon for the group.

Few months later, during the day, I did the shoe shining and at night, I panhandled pleading for money with a group of friends with different disabilities. When I asked for money, I did not tell people that I needed the money to support my family or that I could not get a job as a computer programmer. People saw the wheelchair and assumed whatever they wanted to think.

I had the education, the wiliness, the desire, and I had the wheelchair too. I did not need to explain anything because people saw the wheelchair and assumed whatever they believed. The discrimination against people with disabilities in Mexico stopped my opportunities for employment and more education.

Being there. Fire drill or fired. *In one place I worked; there was a fire drill. I requested to be exempt because of my disability. The office manager told me that I had to participate. I asked if presenting an ADA request would help me not being part of the drill, but she answered that the ADA did not exist in that office, and if I wanted my job, I had to*

154

participate. She was laughing and singing, I think even dancing, and I overlooked her discriminative behavior.

I was concerned because the office was in the third floor. I looked in eBay for something that could help me and found an emergency evacuation chair –I ordered the special chair over 100 pounds made with metal. I learned to use it and brought it to the office. A week after I brought the chair, the office manager decided to have a fire drill. She had two of my coworkers helping me going down on the fire escape stairs with the super thick special chair. Two months later, she had them to do it again but this time she changed the "helpers." They struggled as much as I was embarrassed.

Several incidents happened to me, and I witnessed some, or the person shared with me the impacting experience lived. I could not handle working there, and I opted for leaving. A few months after I resigned such position, I was hired to work on an office in the third floor also.

In order to enter the new job building, I had to talk to security officers. When I talked to them, I offered to bring my "special" chair. They looked at me with their eyes wide opened and said, "What are you talking about? A special chair? For what?" I told them about my experience with the fire drill in my previous employer, and they were surprised. "No Cecilia. That is against the ADA! They put your life at risk and the life of your coworkers helping you! Wow!"

I said and thought the same thing, "Wow!" I missed that one. I did not show my truth feelings about doing the fire drill; it tore my heart. I bought a special chair to comply with her demands in order for me to keep my job. I could not handle witnessing and ignoring so much discrimination against a large group of White women and a small group of a powerless minority including myself.

I feel I need to apologize to some White women who helped me for letting the office manager using me to disempower them. I was not part of her discriminative behavior. I should have stopped her, but I did not do anything. I think her intimidating behavior scared me as well. After talking to the security officers I realized that I could file a lawsuit against based on the ADA violation. I was not sure if I could prove the discrimination if my former coworkers did not want to testify in fear to losing their "super" job.

155

Being here. Surprising findings. The themes *free, peace, betrayed,* and *deceived* were surprising results. These themes were a revelation lighting a dark tunnel throughout many years of my life. Although I lived and felt those emotions, I did not relate them as influences to mix behaviors during my social interactions. In the following paragraphs, I will attempt to explain the meaning of the revealed themes based on my personal cultural experiences compared to the literature review for this study. I will also provide the lived cultural intersection and a brief description of the reasons the themes were a personal revelation.

The literature review indicated that the United States is rapidly becoming ethnically and culturally diverse as quick as society constructs more groups with racial and ethnic minority classifications. Researchers at the Centers for Disease Control and Prevention (2014) reported, "According to the 2010 U.S. Census, approximately 36.3 percent of the population currently belongs to a racial or ethnic minority group" (para. 1). Despite the myth of equality that indicates people are equal and have the same rights and opportunities, people with multiple social classifications within the growing racial and ethnic minority groups face innumerable cultural challenges. The themes revealed in the data sets showed that I am part of those groups.

Theme 1: Free. The first unexpected finding was *free.* I was not sure what free meant related to cultural chameleon behavior. According to the reviewed literature, members of racial and ethnic minority groups usually encounter various types of oppression. Although there is a concept that members of racial and ethnic minority groups are able to choose between their native cultures or to assimilate to a new or a majority culture, their choice does not affect their freedom. The choice can cause pain, sorrow, and discomfort, but they are free to decide because minority groups have the same degree of freedom as majority groups (see Wong, 2010).

Several people assume that immigrants, either groups or individuals, have the opportunity to choose how they want to participate with different cultures. The basis of the assumption is the assimilation, separation, integration, and marginalization strategies for immigrants to participate within society (J. Berry, 2001, 2005; see also Hogg & Reid, 2006). There, I found the meaning of free as a theme for this study, and I contend that this concept does not include racial and ethnic minority groups representing multiple social classifications such as gender, disability, and ethnicity as a whole. I do not belong to any of the "Berry boxes" (Ward, 2008, p. 106).

The basis of my argument was the concept that people with multiple cultures might face dominance by more than one majority culture and the intersectionality that multiple cultures represent. The themes revealed integration was a strong impediment within different dominant majority cultures. Numerous people expect assimilating and transforming to be the same as to a native-born citizen within a short period (see Wong, 2010). These expectations become demands, although some people are not willing to give up their native culture to integrate because someone or something forced them to move into a new culture.

The themes revealed people with multiple cultures related to gender, ethnicity, and disability might not have the desire to assimilate or integrate into a new culture. Some multicultural people based on the rejection and unacceptance involving their social classifications might separate and marginalize to be free from social classification impositions. The marginalization, separation, rejection, unacceptance, and outcast labels could be the high costs that multicultural people might experience to feel free from the repercussions of social classifications. Freedom for some people with multiple social classifications might be a state of mind (Cantey, 2011). The next significant theme is *peace*.

Theme 2: Peace. The second surprising theme was peace. I had the same question as I had for the theme *free.* According to the reviewed literature, several people with multiple cultures might want peace within themselves, within their communities, and within cultures that constantly reject people with multiple social classifications. As such, some multicultural people might turn into cultural chameleons while looking for peace of mind, a sense of self-worth, and something to tell themselves who they are. Turning into a cultural chameleon might also signify creating a place for their identity while conserving the characteristics of self.

Themes 3 and 4: Betrayal and deception. The third and fourth themes of significance were *betrayed* (betrayal) and *deceived* (deception). These themes clarified my continuing struggle for understanding the reasons I turned into a cultural chameleon. The literature review indicated social identity concerns supersede satisfying individual needs. The

157

literature also revealed that group membership is essential for people to understand who they are and to obtain psychological benefits from identifying with social groups (Badea et al., 2010). The themes showed the groups to which I thought I belonged did not accept me. I felt someone or something had rejected me, thereby *betraying* my trust.

One reason for my feelings of betrayal and deception, based on the themes revealed, could relate to the negative history on disabilities endorsing discrimination and marginalization (Esmail et al., 2009; Loewen & Pollard, 2010). Many people without disabilities tend to patronize, pity, and treat people with disabilities differently or ignore them (Coleman & Croake, 1987; Stone, 2005). People with disabilities might face rejection or discrimination if they do not behave as scripted (Ramey, 2007; Rembis, 2010; Voigts, 2009).

To have an association with people with disabilities or with the accommodations some disabilities might require is stigmatizing. Even other people with disabilities have used this strategy in an attempt to repel discrimination. Rosemarie Garland Thomson noted, "Disabled people also often avoid and stereotype one another in attempting to normalize their own social identity" (Baynton, 2001, p. 51).

Other reasons that developed my emotions of betrayal and deception could include that I felt like people declared a cultural war against me, described as *a language barrier; you are angry at your tokenism; if you do not like it, you know what to do; there is always something;* or *a chip on your shoulder.* The study themes showed that I entered into a new culture where I perceived and noticed much anger against me that transformed into enmity.

Through the academic literature and the themes revealed, I realized the division of humility, solidarity, and respect among majority groups. Society leaves minority groups to their manipulated destiny (Bostdorff, 2004; Dunbar, 2006; Lawson, 2008; McMahon et al., 2004; Zaykowski, 2010). I recognized that, although my social classifications represent many ethnic minority groups, I did not belong to any group.

I was able to compare that I emigrated from a culture where culture does not exist if an individual does not meet the common definition of normality (Baynton, 2001; Cheng, 2009). I was aware of the normality perception and I emigrated with it, thinking it could be the same everywhere. I ended up encountering a culture where the solo, the unique, the useless, and the other exists (Badea et al., 2010; James & Wu, 2006; Leary & Allen, 2011; Rohmer & Louvet, 2009; Sherr & Montesino, 2009; Tajfel, 1982), including normality.

The themes and the literature review helped me to understand that I entered a culture filled with revolving hostility or an intersectional culture enmity cycle against certain groups (Perlmutter, 2006; Wortley, 2003) in a never-ending cycle (Bostdorff, 2004; Dunbar, 2006; Lawson, 2008; McMahon et al., 2004; Zaykowski, 2010). I felt relieved when I understood that such behavior was not specifically against me. The behavior was about the social classifications I represent and the message those classifications convey.

The themes and the literature helped me accept and embrace my existence based on the notion that this is who I am and meant to be. The autoethnographies I read encouraged me to live aloud with dignity and pride about who I am. I deserve to be visible, voice my concerns, and create a difference while living with dignity and visibility (see Blanchard, 2012; Cantey, 2011; Schneider, 2011; Voigts, 2009).

General Discussion

The purpose of this analytic autoethnography was to explore why some multicultural people might turn into cultural chameleons to fit in or to adjust to a different culture. The study involved exploring the intersection of disability, ethnicity, and gender to understand a cultural chameleon's behavior. I drew conclusions from the Labovian life story, photovoice, CMR items, and commitment to an analytic agenda as data sources collected and analyzed using NVivo10 qualitative software.

Themes that emerged from the study were burnout, bounce, escape, resist, and doubt to answer Research Question 1; invisible and voiceless to answer Research Question 2; and boxed, trapped, and vulnerable to answer Research Question 3. The emerged themes free, peace, betrayed, and deceived were surprising results. Specifically, the data revealed themes of persistent and prevalent barriers for racial and ethnic minority groups (Simpson, 2010; Song, 2009; Torres & Rollock, 2009).

As an intersectional approach would help to predict, problems are framed in different ways, which affect people with multiple cultures (Campbell, 2011; Naples, 2009; Tadmor et al., 2012; Ward, 2008). Some people with multiple cultures might turn into a cultural chameleon to protect themselves from those problems. The focus of the study was on the factors of disability, gender, and ethnicity, and intersectionality as a framework. The study also provided evidence to support the idea that culture should not be understood or research solely as whole group identity. The results of Research Question 1 were as follows:

- Burnout might be an influencer and a consequence of turning into a cultural chameleon.

- Burnout might develop as consequence of switching identities leading to emotional collapse.

- Some multicultural people might experience burnout before entering the workforce.

- Burnout might relate to culture.

- Culture-related burnout might be wrongly compared to work-related stress.

- The need exists to explore emotional collapse as an influencer to turning into a cultural chameleon.

- The need exists to include social classifications in explorations of identity, behavior, and acculturation strategies.

- The need exists to include intersectionality to explore what happens when all social classifications are brought together.

- The need exists to explore interpersonal and emotional sensitivity when investigating acculturation strategies, social classifications, and the perceptions of others.

The results of Research Question 2 indicated a need to explore (a) the negative effects of behaving as a cultural chameleon, (b) the impact that smiling might have on the observer (Kunz et al., 2013), and (c) the effects of smiling during emotional pain. The results of Research Question 3 revealed a need to explore the intersection within a culture cycle, which I labeled an *intersectional culture cycle*. The results from surprising themes indicated a need to explore how the intersection of cultures intensifies anger or dislike among groups and individuals, which I labeled an *intersectional culture enmity cycle*.

Taken together, the outcomes of the analytic autoethnography were consistent, which indicated some people with multiple cultures might strive for positive social interactions and take other people's perceptions into consideration (Hansen & Philo, 2007; Schneider, 2011;

Scott, 2012). The analysis was different from a solely cultural perspective and from a solely intersectional perspective. The findings from the analytic autoethnography indicated both cultures and intersectionality are likely to be influential when someone turns into a cultural chameleon.

Researchers could explore social classifications, intersectionality, emotional collapse, and the effects of cultural chameleon behavior individually. The revealed themes for the study provided profound insights into a cultural chameleon's behavior. Future researchers could attempt to establish some way to explore such behavior. The exploration could include the conditions under which the effect intensifies or fades within people with multiple social classifications (Chartrand & Bargh, 1999).

Researching frame switching based on the different types and needs of mixing behaviors would be difficult. This analytic autoethnography echoed Luna et al.'s (2008) suggestions to explore different populations of bicultural switching types. Such research could include participants with multiple cultures, not only two cultures, to provide a more complete exploration. The findings in the analytic autoethnography reiterated Chartrand and Bargh's (1999) suggestion to study cultural chameleon behavior and its effects on social behavior, on the individual, and on the group.

This study questioned Tadmor et al. (2012) indicating that marginal people, although show low levels of identification with cultures, achieve more. Tadmor et al. contended the marginalized might be individualists or people who choose their own expectations. The themes showed that some people with multiple cultures who behave as cultural chameleons might marginalize themselves to avoid more culture interactions without considering themselves as individualist or collectivist. For instance, the emerged themes indicated the researched as reaching and achieving in different aspects throughout her life, but the researched is a collectivist not an individualist. Future researchers could explore the differences and similarities between collectivists and individualists, and the reasons to opt for marginalization among some people with multiple cultures.

The analytic autoethnography included important contributions to the literature on cultural chameleon behavior, intersectionality and social classifications, disability, gender, and ethnicity. Other contributions included distinguishing burnout as work-related or culture-

161

related and determining the intersection inside a culture cycle (Markus, 2013), which I labeled an intersectional culture cycle. This study also contributed to the literature on cultural intersection enmity, which I labeled an intersectional culture enmity cycle. The study contributed to a more complete understanding of the reasons some people with multiple cultures might turn into cultural chameleons. These contributions could influence future directions in research on multiple cultures, including using autoethnography as a research methodology.

Implications for Scholars

According to Linder (2011), intersectionality theory challenges researchers to consider the whole person in their work. Realizing that multiple social classifications intersect when bringing social classification together is important to understand the effects of power (Best et al., 2011; Hae Yeon & Ferree, 2010; Naples, 2009). The data in the study supported the importance of intersectionality and its importance when turning into a cultural chameleon. The themes revealed provided examples of the ways cultural experiences intersect and form a social interaction.

The focus of much of the literature on intersectionality was on the intersections of multiple racial and ethnic minorities or marginalized groups (Best et al., 2011; Hae Yeon & Ferree, 2010; Linder, 2011). This study involved exploring the intersections of majority and minority groups' perceptions related to cultural chameleon behavior. The contribution might help understand the ways some people with multiple cultures could make sense of the reasons to turn into a cultural chameleon.

Implications for Educational Leadership

Educational leaders encounter different challenges. The challenges involve multicultural communities, student needs, curriculum and instruction, and program development and evaluation. The challenges also include educator readiness and personal and staff development, among other responsibilities.

As the results of the study show, the need exists for more research to improve people's knowledge and skills to understand cultures and multicultural communities. It is the responsibility of educational leaders to provide multicultural training and education for any staff involved with student learning and activities. Educational leaders are also responsible for implementing and improving multicultural education. Multicultural education involves researching, exploring, and investigating how cultural, social, and cognitive matters influence students and their families.

Limitations of Study

I encountered some of the limitations discussed in Chapter 1 within the qualitative analytic autoethnography. The first limitation was that, as an autoethnography, the study would have the potential for personal bias. The purpose of the study was to explore why some multicultural people might turn into cultural chameleons to fit in or to adjust to a different culture. Fulfilling the purpose of the study involved incorporating my cultural experiences, thoughts, reflections, and self-observations to collect data using the Labovian method and photovoice. The focus of my story was on a woman who used a wheelchair and who emigrated from Mexico as a young adult.

Researcher Reflections

I began the study with a strong belief that I mixed identities because I had a goal in mind, which allowed my self-leadership to lead me to achieve what I wanted in life. I also thought I was so afraid of making waves or upsetting people that I opted to suppress my own identities. My experiences as a woman with a physical disability formed my beliefs as a natural consequence of my disability experience over the past 47 years.

This exploration led me to explore emotions that I did not know existed. Part of the research tested or questioned my beliefs as I collected, analyzed, and drew conclusions about the data from my own perspective. Another part of the research was a revelation that lit a dark tunnel in my life. I never thought that, through this journey, I would discover so much about myself and simultaneously benefit from those findings. I now understand the reasons I mix behaviors during social interactions to fit in or to adjust to a different culture.

Writing my cultural experiences during social interactions, and the intersectionality influencing those interactions, has been the most difficult yet satisfying effort I have encountered. I wanted to share my story to help make a difference in the life of one or more people. I wanted to give voice to people with multiple cultures who encounter challenges. This research has been an empowering learning experience.

Writing an autoethnography involved developing not only a different skill researching but also a new perspective on how to look at an individual's world, including my own. Wall (2006) discussed the benefits of writing an autoethnography and asked, "How much more promise could it hold for people far more marginalized than I?" (p. 3). My own experience indicated an autoethnography reaches marginalized people and goes beyond reaching people wondering about culture interactions. Autoethnographies help people to find possible reasons for marginalization. This study gave me the voice I had searched for a long time to find the answer that nobody else could find.

By conducting an analytic autoethnography, I had the opportunity to uncover my social interactions and cultural experiences for the reader and for myself. This revelation aimed to increase understanding of why some people with multiple cultures might mix behaviors during social interactions. At the end, I could have indicated what I intend to do through this study. I know now that collecting and analyzing data allowed me to come "out of the shadows and into the study" (Smith-Sullivan, 2008, p. 26) by discovering the reasons why I turned into a cultural chameleon.

I understand the main objective of traditional research is to educate, inform, and bring positive change. The primary objective of an autoethnography is to provide a tool to help and be helped by someone who has the experience of *been there* and *done that* (Smith-Sullivan, 2008). *Been there, done that* provides the experience and background necessary to understand situations and events a person with multiple social classification might go through in his or her life.

After I listened a man saying, "I turn into a cultural chameleon because I cannot behave gay everyplace I go" (personal communication, September 22, 2013), confirmed the benefits of an autoethnography. Writing an autoethnography helped me develop empathy for others and understand that someone else might be experiencing similar or different but interconnected events. Writing an autoethnography reveals that help is available, that people are not alone. Someone else might be looking for the same answers I just found.

An autoethnography could also be a wake-up call. As I explored the collected data and elicited information from the photographs, I realized I had not forgotten those negative cultural experiences where I had to mix identities. I did not know I had internalized the encounters and developed a bubble around me to protect my inner self and at the same time to isolate myself.

This autoethnography helped me to discover that I felt threatened by my new culture, which was an unfamiliar territory where I did not know where to go. I was uncertain how to behave to protect myself from the animosity around me. I tried to become invisible. I blamed my disability and myself. I found a voice expressing the challenges I have encountered.

Struthers (2012) stated, "I did shed tears as I type my recollection of how I addressed a long standing emotional tension" (p. 125). I had difficulties listening to my voice inside the narrative voices that emerged during social interactions (Ribbens & Edwards, 1998). I continued to allow myself to discover aspects that I was not aware of and did not anticipate.

I let the new information and themes emerge. I wanted to understand my own place and my actions or reactions during social interactions. I wanted to explore the possible causes and solutions. I wanted to find a way to be me again without imagining what could happen if I speak up and disclose my inner feelings.

Writing an autoethnography allowed me to discover, to be aware, and to take action. Writing an autoethnography made me feel safe to say, do, and share without sensing the need to mix identities to protect myself. Now I know I am aware, have enough information, and feel safe to turn my life around to the direction I want it to be.

Through this journey, I have learned a lot that I needed to learn. I learned what I did not want to learn. I also learned what I did not want to realize I had already learned. The new learning and by refreshing of what I already knew were awakening tools for self-empowerment.

Writing an autoethnography is "easier said than done" (Wall, 2008, p. 38). Anderson (2006) discussed the influence of writing on the writer who invests too much time researching or neglects daily life activities and family obligations. I spent hours, every day, for several months, searching and reading journals related to my cultural experiences. The more information I found and read, the more I comprehended that external influences are stronger than my one persona. Investing a lot of time researching and neglecting daily life activities and family obligations helped me answer many questions.

Smith-Sullivan (2008) and Wall (2008) explained an autoethnography could bring internal and external challenges for the author, making the process a difficult journey. I faced the challenges to accept the memories that emerged when recollecting my cultural events. Reading the literature helped to voice my feelings of surprised, relived, disappointed, glad, questioned, or appreciative of my inner self.

Wall (2008) noted identity and self-understanding could lead to anxiety. Hamilton et al. (2008) indicated an autoethnographer's situatedeness could develop some challenges. I believe that is what I experienced, but I relaxed and kept going. The learning was more interesting than continuing to live in darkness.

In Chapter 1, I mentioned being aware of scholars' discussion on the possible limitations of writing an autoethnography. I indicated that many explanations were relevant to my personal narrative, and I understood the need to maintain distance from other factors that could divert my attention, for example, my advocacy, activism, and beliefs. I thought these factors could interfere when validating academic data because they played a strong role in my cultural experiences. In the end, these factors had nothing to do with my investigation. I was disarmed. I placed myself to the new information as honest and visible as I could to receive, understand, and process the new information.

The analytic autoethnographies and the literature I reviewed lacked consistency on how to approach the research design. I went different directions trying to follow one methodology route. Struthers (2012) encountered similar difficulties and noted, "the lack of established definition of concepts related to analytic autoethnography did not assist me as researcher to be able to visualize a methodology pathway" (p. 124). I continued to find my own route.

I also learned that my experiences were not far from the experiences of other autoethnographers. Blanchard (2012), Struthers (2012), Wall (2006, 2008), and many other doctoral candidates encountered their own challenges writing or presenting their study. My challenges helped me to realize that being the researcher, the researched, the data collector, the narrator, the data analyst, the writer, and so forth, including working alone, means an autoethnographer turns into a skillful multitasking researcher.

My learning also included using the qualitative research software NVivo10. I learned that NVivo10 is powerful, useful, interesting, and exciting software. The challenge was my inexperience using the software. I took several trainings online and practiced, but I realized I needed more time to process and practice how to use the software to its full potential. I learned that practice and proficiency are essential to use NVivo10 to its full capacity.

I also learned there is a gap in research of writing from an actual person with multiple cultures sharing his or her cultural interactions to fitting in or to adjust. In my analytical autoethnography, I initiated the goal of closing such gap. I learned that an autoethnographic work is a highly promising form of inquiry (Wall, 2006, 2008). I learned that persistence, motivation, faith, hope, and self-leadership were critical to start, to continue, and to finish this journey. In sum, I learned that I am making a difference in my own life, hoping to reach others to give them a sense of relief as well.

Recommendations for Future Research

This qualitative analytical autoethnography consisted exclusively of my cultural experiences during social interactions to fit in or to adjust to a culture. I found answers to my research questions concerning cultural chameleon behavior and the factors influencing me to adopt mixing behaviors. For this study, being the researcher and the researched provided the opportunity to think, to consider, and to add valuable elements to the research. My recommendations for future research are as follows.

First, I recommend using self-studies, life stories, or autoethnographies, as they are important to understand cultural and personal characteristics of fitting in and adjusting to a different culture. Second, the outcome of the analytic autoethnography indicated the need for discussion and exploration of the issues of multiple cultures and their intersection. Third, the outcome of the study also indicated the need to discuss and explore adopting behaviors and the influencers to mix those behaviors during social interactions.

Fourth, the outcome of this study also indicated the need to discuss and explore burnout related to cultural chameleon behavior and the health risks and consequences. Fifth, I recommend conducting a study exploring marriages between people with multiple cultures and members of a dominant culture, including how the intersection of majority with minority cultures might influence a person to turn into a cultural chameleon. Sixth, I recommended exploring what people with multiple cultures consider their support system.

Seventh, the results of this analytic autoethnography indicated the need for discussion and exploration related to using metaphors and emotional collapse (e.g., feeling like a fish out of water, there is always something, and ni de aquí ni de allá [neither from here nor there]). The exploration could involve investigating the metaphor's connection to turning into a cultural chameleon. The eighth recommendation is to explore what research means for people with multiple social classifications. Giving voice to an invisible group could improve disciplines such as multicultural studies; disability studies; and cultural, multicultural, and rehabilitation psychology (Voigts, 2009).

The ninth recommendation is to conduct autoethnography to examine the meaning and influence of verbal and nonverbal messages that might develop within the learning setting including a classroom. Numerous sociocultural issues might exist in a learning environment. In order to determine the existing problems Kahl (2011) proposed conducting and connecting autoethnography with critical communication instruction.

Based on the findings of this qualitative analytic autoethnography an autoethnographic writing could be a positive tool for practical scholarship bridging the critical communication pedagogy gap from ideology to praxis (Kahl, 2011). I echo Kahl (2011) contending the need to identify social locations as race, class, gender, sexual orientation, and disability within a classroom. Including identifying racism perpetuated by whiteness, and oppression and marginalization of women. After doing autoethnography, instructors could move to critical communication pedagogy as Kahl discussed (see also Hendrix et al., 2003).

When instructors moved to critical communication, they share goals, chat about learning, and create action. This process, according to Kahl (2011), allows the instructor to foster communication, to work toward oppression-free setting, and to reduce hegemony. Next, teachers learn and familiarize the link between micro-level interactions and macro-level structures, which involve hegemonic hierarchies in the learning environment and hegemonic social hierarchies in the educational system. Using autoethnography to reflect on sociocultural problems and implementing the autoethnography findings to create change might provide different opportunities for instructors to become better teachers, to empower their students, and to create a change within the learning environments and within the educational system.

Conclusion

The purpose of this dissertation was to explore why some people with multiple cultures might turn into a cultural chameleon to fit in or to adjust to a different culture. Using an analytic autoethnography and intersectionality as framework shown to be unlimited, useful, and helpful, both theoretically and practically. The incorporation of an analytic autoethnography and intersectionality allowed an exploration into the nature of the experience and the impact of social classifications on people with multiple cultures.

This time of researching, collecting, and analyzing data was a journey of discovery. I learned the importance of intersectionality and social classifications and the effects both might have on people with multiple social classifications. Finding themes throughout the data sets had a real and lasting effect on me. Understanding the reasons I turned into a cultural chameleon motivated me to share with people who might be in similar situations.

Summary

Chapter 5 contained the authenticity of the analytic autoethnography, the findings, the answers to the research questions, and the surprising findings. The chapter also included the explored implications and directions for future research based on the study. Specifically, I highlighted the importance of understanding the reasons some multicultural people might turn into cultural chameleons during social interactions. I described the importance of understanding the intersection that a culture cycle might have within social classifications. I also presented a general discussion based on the research questions.

In terms of implications for scholarship, I presented the connections of the study to the intersectionality theory and highlighted the need for scholars to include intersectionality in research. I also presented implications for educational leadership and remarked upon the responsibilities an education leader has relating to multicultural education, its effects, and its needs. I provided research reflections, the limitations I encountered, a conclusion, and a summary.

References

Acharya, P. (2010). Ethnicity and prejudice: A historical shift. *Dhaulagiri: Journal of Sociology & Anthropology, 4,* 85-98. doi:10.3126/dsaj.v4i0.4514

Adams, T. E. (2011). *Narrating the closet: An autoethnography of same-sex attraction.* Walnut Creek, CA: Left Coast Press.

Adams, T. E., & Jones, S. H. (2011). Telling stories: Reflexivity, queer theory, and autoethnography. *Cultural Studies ↔ Critical Methodologies, 11,* 108–116. doi:10.1177/1532708611401329

Adam, H., Shirako, A., & Maddux, W. W. (2010). Cultural variance in the interpersonal effects of anger in negotiations. *Psychological Science, 21,* 882–889. doi:10.1177/0956797610370755

Alarcon, G., Edwards, J., & Menke, L. (2011). Student burnout and engagement: A test of the conservation of resources theory. *Journal of Psychology, 145,* 211-227. doi:10.1080/00223980.2011.555432

Aldarondo, F. (2001). Racial and ethnic identity models and their application: Counseling biracial individuals. *Journal of Mental Health Counseling, 23,* 238-255. http://www.amhca.org

Alexander, B. K. (2014). Bodies yearning on the borders of becoming a performative reflection on three embodied axes of social difference. *Qualitative Inquiry,* 1-10. doi:10.1177/1077800414545231

Allbon, C. (2012). "Down the rabbit hole" – "curiouser and curiouser": Using autoethnography as a mode of writing to re-call, re-tell and re-veal bodily embodiment as self-reflective. *Journal of Organizational Ethnography, 1,* 62-71. doi:10.1108/20466741211220660

Allen-Collinson, J. (2013). Autoethnography as the engagement of self/other, self/culture, self/politics, selves/futures. In S. Holman Jones, T. E. Adams & C. Ellis (Eds.), Handbook of Autoethnography (pp. 281-299). Walnut Creek, CA: Left Coast Press.

Alves, J. C., Lovelace, K. J., Manz, C. C., Matsypura, D., Toyasaki, F., & Ke, K. (2006). A cross-cultural perspective of self-leadership. *Journal of Managerial Psychology, 4,* 338-359. doi:10.1108/02683940610663123

170

American Psychological Association. (2003). Guidelines on multicultural education, training, research, practice, and organizational change for psychologists. *American Psychologist, 58,* 377-402. doi:10.1037/0003-066X.58.5.377

Anastasiou, D., & Kauffman, J. M. (2013). The social model of disability: Dichotomy between impairment and disability. *Journal of Medicine & Philosophy, 38,* 441-459. doi:10.1093/jmp/jht026

Anderson, L. (2006). Analytic autoethnography. *Journal of Contemporary Ethnography, 35,* 373-395. doi:10.1177/0891241605280449

Andrews, M., Squire, C., & Tamboukou, M. (2008). *Doing narrative research.* Thousand Oaks, CA: Sage. doi:10.4135/9780857024992

Applegate, J. S. (1990). Theory, culture, and behavior: Object relations in context. *Child & Adolescent Social Work Journal, 7,* 85-100. doi:10.1007/BF00757647

Arvidsson, S., Bergman, S., Arvidsson, B., Fridlund, B., & Tops, A. (2011). Experiences of health-promoting self-care in people living with rheumatic diseases. *Journal of Advanced Nursing, 67,* 1264-1272. doi:10.1111/j.1365-2648.2010.05585.x

Asdornnithee, S. (2010). When a Five wants to grow: Using autoethnography to examine inner changes through the eyes of the Enneagram. *Enneagram Journal, 3,* 87–104. Available from http://www.internationalenneagram.org

Atkinson, R. (Ed.). (1998). *The life story interview.* Thousand Oaks, CA: Sage. doi:10.4135/9781412986205

Atkinson, P. (2006). Rescuing autoethnography. *Journal of Contemporary Ethnography, 35,* 400–404. doi:10.1177/0891241606286980

Bach, H. (2007). Chapter 11 composing a visual narrative inquiry. In D. Jean Clandinin (Ed.), *Handbook of narrative inquiry: Mapping a methodology* (pp. 280-308). Thousand Oaks, CA: Sage. doi:10.4135/9781452226552.n11

Badea, C., Jetten, J., Czukor, G., & Askevis-Leherpeux, F. (2010). The bases of identification: When optimal distinctiveness needs face social identity threat. *British Journal of Social Psychology, 49(Part 1),* 21-41. doi:10.1348/000712608X397665

Badley, G. F. (2014). Hunting roaches a sort of academic life. *Qualitative Inquiry, 20,* 981–989. doi:10.1177/1077800413505548

Bahm, A., & Forchuk, C. (2009). Interlocking oppressions: The effect of a comorbid physical disability on perceived stigma and discrimination among mental health consumers in Canada. *Health & Social Care in the Community, 17,* 63-70. doi:10.1111/j.1365-2524.2008.00799.x

Baker, T. A., & Wang, C. C. (2006). Photovoice: Use of a participatory action research method to explore the chronic pain experience in older adults. *Qualitative Health Research, 16,* 1405-1413. doi:10.1177/1049732306294118

Bamberg, M., & Georgakopoulou, A. (2008). Small stories as a new perspective in narrative and identity analysis. *Text & Talk, 28,* 377–396. doi:10.1515/TEXT.2008.018

Bampi, L., Guilhem, D., & Alves, E. (2010). Social model: A new approach of the disability theme. *Revista Latino-Americana De Enfermagem (RLAE), 18,* 816-823. doi:S0104-11692010000400022

Barbour, R. (2008). *Introducing qualitative research.* Thousand Oaks, CA: Sage. doi:10.4135/9780857029034

Barnartt, S. N. (1996). Disability culture or disability consciousness? *Journal of Disability Policy Studies, 7,* 1-19. doi:10.1177/104420739600700201

Barnett, B. (2007). Theories and research on the intersections of race, gender, and class inequalities: From Lenski's Status Inconsistency to Collins' Matrix of Domination and Beyond, 1954 to present. *Conference Papers -- American Sociological Association,* 1-28. Available from http://www.asanet.org

Barth, F. (2002). An anthropology of knowledge. *Current Anthropology, 43,* 1–18. doi:10.1086/324131

Barreto, M., & Ellemers, N. (2000). You can't always do what you want: Social identity and self-presentational determinants of the choice to work for a low-status group. *Society for Personality and Social Psychology, 26,* 891-906. doi:10.1177/01461672002610001

Barreto, M., & Ellemers, N. (2002). The impact of respect versus neglect of self-identities on identification and group loyalty. *Personality and Social Psychology Bulletin, 28,* 629-639. doi:10.1177/0146167202288007

Barreto, M., & Ellemers, N. (2003). The effects of being categorised: The interplay between internal and external social identities. *European Review of Social Psychology, 14,* 139-170. doi:10.1080/10463280340000045

Barreto, M., Ellemers, N., Spears, R., & Shahinper, K. (2003). Who wants to know? The effect of audience on identity expression among minority group members. *British Journal of Social Psychology, 42,* 299-318. doi:10.1348/014466603322127265

Bassett, R. (2011). 27 visual conceptualization opportunities with qualitative data analysis software. In E. Margolis & L. Pauwels (Eds.), *The SAGE handbook visual research methods* (pp. 530-547). London, England: Sage. doi:10.4135/9781446268278.n27

Bassett, R. (2012). NVivo as conceptual space for critical interpretation: The use of analysis techniques with Nvivo Software. Retrieved from http://explore.qsrinternational.com

Baynton, D. C. (2001). Disability and the justification of inequality in American history. In P. K. Longmore & L. Umansky (Eds.), *The new disability history: American perspectives* (pp. 33-57). New York: New York University Press.

Bazerman, M. H., Tenbrunsel, A. E., & Wade-Benzoni, K. (1998). Negotiating with yourself and losing: Making decisions with competing internal preferences. *Academy of Management Review, 23,* 225-241. doi:10.5465/AMR.1998.533224

Beitman, B. D., & Soth, A. M. (2006). Activation of self-observation: A core process among the psychotherapies. *Journal of Psychotherapy Integration, 16,* 383-397. doi:10.1037/1053-0479.16.4.383

Benet-Martínez, V., & Haritatos, J. (2005). Bicultural identity integration (BII): Components and psychosocial antecedents. *Journal of Personality, 73,* 1015–1049. doi:10.1111/j.1467-6494.2005.00337.x

Berg, J. A. (2010). Race, class, gender, and social space: Using an intersectional approach to study immigration attitudes. *The Sociological Quarterly, 51,* 278-302. doi:10.1111/j.1533-8525.2010.01172.x

173

Berger, L. (2001). Inside out: Narrative autoethnography as a path toward rapport. *Qualitative Inquiry, 7,* 504–518. doi:10.1177/107780040100700407

Berlak, A. C. (2005). Confrontation and pedagogy: Cultural secrets, trauma, and emotion in antioppressive pedagogies. In M. Boler (Ed.), *Democratic dialogue in education: Troubling speech, disturbing silence* (pp. 123–144). New York: Peter Lang Publishing.

Berry, J. W. (2001). A psychology of immigration. *Journal of Social Issues, 57,* 615-631. doi:10.1111/0022-4537.00231

Berry, J. W. (2005). Acculturation: Living successfully in two cultures. *International Journal of Intercultural Relations, 29,* 697-712. doi:10.1016/j.ijintrel.2005.07.013

Berry, K., & Warren, J. T. (2009). Cultural studies and the politics of representation: Experience, subjectivity, research. *Cultural Studies/Critical Methodologies, 9,* 597-607. doi:10.1177/1532708609337894

Best, R., Edelman, L. B., Krieger, L., & Eliason, S. R. (2011). Multiple disadvantages: An empirical test of intersectionality theory in EEO litigation. *Law & Society Review, 45,* 991-1025. doi:10.1111/j.1540-5893.2011.00463.x

Betancourt, H., & López, S. R. (1993). The study of culture, ethnicity, and race in American psychology. *American Psychologist, 48,* 629-637. doi:10.1037/0003-066X.48.6.629

Bhabha, H. K. (1994). *The location of culture.* New York, NY: Routledge

Blanchard, J. A. (2012). *Critical love praxis in a middle school classroom: Exploring the struggles, outcomes, and possibilities of loving practice through critical practitioner action research and autoethnography* (Doctoral dissertation). Available from ProQuest Dissertations and Theses database. (UMI No. 3534117)

Bochner, A. P. (2010). Resisting the mystification of narrative inquiry: Unmasking the real conflict between story analysts and storytellers. *Sociology of Health & Illness, 32,* 662–665. doi:10.1111/j.1467-9566.2010.01240_2.x

Bochner, A. P. (2012). On first-person narrative scholarship: Autoethnography as acts of meaning. *Narrative Inquiry, 22,* 155–164. doi 10.1075/ni.22.1.10boc

Bodenhausen, G. V. (2010). Diversity in the person, diversity in the group: Challenges of identity complexity for social perception and social interaction. *European Journal of Social Psychology, 40,* 1-16. doi:10.1002/ejsp.647

Bond, C. F., Jr. (1982). Social facilitation: A self-presentational view. *Journal of Personality & Social Psychology, 42,* 1042-1050. doi:10.1037/0022-3514.42.6.1042

Boss, A. D., & Sims, H. P., Jr. (2008). Everyone fails! Using emotion regulation and self-leadership for recovery. *Journal of Managerial Psychology, 23,* 135-150. doi:10.1108/02683940810850781

Bostdorff, D. M. (2004). The internet rhetoric of the Ku Klux Klan: A case study in web site community building run amok. *Communication Studies, 55,* 340-361. Retrieved from http://associationdatabase.com/aws/CSCA/pt/sp/journal

Botella, C., Mira, A., Garcia-Palacios, A., Quero, S., Navarro, M. V., Riera López Del Amo, A., . . . Baños, R. M. (2012). Smiling is fun: A coping with stress and emotion regulation program. *Interactive Media Institute and IOS Press, 181,* 123-127. doi:10.3233/978-1-61499-121-2-123

Boufoy-Bastick, B. (2004). Auto-interviewing, auto-ethnography and critical incident methodology for eliciting a self-conceptualised worldview. *Forum: Qualitative Social Research, 5,* 1-13. Retrieved from http://www.qualitative-research.net/fqs/

Bowleg, L. (2008). When Black + lesbian + woman ≠ Black lesbian woman: The methodological challenges of qualitative and quantitative intersectionality research. *Sex Roles, 59,* 312–325. doi:10.1007/s11199-008-9400-z

Bowleg, L. (2012). The problem with the phrase women and minorities: Intersectionality- an important theoretical framework for public health. *American Journal of Public Health, 102,* 1267-1273. doi:10.2105/AJPH.2012.300750

Boyle, M., & Parry, K. (2007). Telling the whole story: The case for organizational autoethnography. *Culture & Organization, 13,* 185-190. doi:10.1080/14759550701486480

Brewer, M. B., & Kramer, R. M. (1985). The psychology of intergroup attitudes and behavior. *Annual Review of Psychology, 36,* 219-243. doi:10.1146/annurev.ps.36.020185.001251

Brewer, M. B., & Gardner, W. (1996). Who is this "we"? Levels of collective identity and self representations. *Journal of Personality and Social Psychology, 71,* 83-93. doi:10.1037/0022-3514.71.1.83

Briley, D. A., Morris, M. W., & Simonson, I. (2005). Cultural chameleons: Biculturals, conformity motives, and decision making. *Journal of Consumer Psychology, 15,* 351-362. doi:10.1207/s15327663jcp1504_9

Brooks, T. W., & Redlin, M. (2009). Occupational aspirations, rural to urban migration, and intersectionality: A comparison of White, Black, and Hispanic male and female group chances for leaving rural counties. *Southern Rural Sociology, 24,* 130–152. Retrieved from http://www.ag.auburn.edu

Browne, I., & Misra, J. (2003). The intersection of gender and race in the labor market. *Annual Review of Sociology, 29,* 487-513. doi:10.1146/annurev.soc.29.010202.100016

Brown, M. (2012). Gender and sexuality I: Intersectional anxieties. *Progress in Human Geography, 36,* 541-550. doi:10.1177/0309132511420973

Buchanan, N. T., Bergman, M. E., Bruce, T. A., Woods, K. C., & Lichty, L. L. (2009). Unique and joint effects of sexual and racial harassment on college students' well-being. *Basic & Applied Social Psychology, 31,* 267-285. doi:10.1080/01973530903058532

Burke, D. (2007). *An autoethnography of whiteness* (Doctoral dissertation). Available from ProQuest Dissertations and Theses database. (UMI No. 3268278)

Burnier, D. (2006). Encounters with the self in social science research: A political scientist looks at autoethnography. *Journal of Contemporary Ethnography, 35,* 410-418. doi:10.1177/0891241606286982

Burton, L., Bolt, N., Hadjikyriacou, D., Silton, N., Kilgallen, C., & Allimant, J. (2011). Relationships of smiling and flirtation to aggression and 2D:4D, a prenatal androgen index. *Evolutionary Psychology, 9,* 28-37. Retrieved from http://www.epjournal.net/wp-content/uploads/EP09028037.pdf

Buss, D. (2001). Human nature and culture: An evolutionary psychological perspective. *Journal of Personality, 69,* 955-978. doi:10.1111/1467-6494.696171

Butz, D. (2010). Autoethnography as sensibility. In D. DeLyser, S. Herbert, S. Aitken, M. Crang, & L. McDowell (Eds.), *The SAGE handbook of qualitative geography.* (pp. 138-156). London: SAGE Publications Ltd. doi:10.4135/9780857021090.n10

Campbell, D. B. (2011). Oppression of the different: Impact and treatment. *International Journal of Applied Psychoanalytic Studies, 8,* 28-47. doi:10.1002/aps.274

Cann, C. N., & DeMeulenaere, E. J. (2012). Critical co-constructed autoethnography. *Cultural Studies <=> Critical Methodologies,12,* 146-158. doi:10.1177/1532708611435214

Cantey, N. I. (2011). *Negotiating space: Women of African descent managing multiple marginalized identities* (Doctoral dissertation). Available from ProQuest Dissertations and Theses database. (UMI No. 3480335)

Carrico, H. (2010). *Working to improve literacy learning for all students through school leadership: An analytic autoethnography* (Doctoral dissertation). Available from ProQuest Dissertations and Theses database. (UMI No. 3399040)

Carrola, P. A., Yu, K., Sass, D. A., & Lee, S. (2012). Measurement invariance of the counselor burnout inventory across cultures: A comparison of U.S. and Korean counselors. *Measurement & Evaluation In Counseling & Development, 45,* 227-244. doi:10.1177/0748175612447630

Case, A., & Hunter, C. (2012). Counterspaces: A unit of analysis for understanding the role of settings in marginalized individuals' adaptive responses to oppression. *American Journal of Community Psychology, 50,* 257–270. doi:10.1007/s10464-012-9497-7

Centers for Disease Control and Prevention. (2014). Racial & ethnic minority populations. Retrieved from http://www.cdc.gov/minorityhealth/populations /remp.html

Chang, H. (2007). Autoethnography: Raising cultural consciousness of self and others. In G. Walford (Ed.), *Methodological Developments in Ethnography (Studies in Educational Ethnography, Volume 12)* (pp. 207-221). doi:10.1016/S1529-210X(06)12012-4

Chang, H. (2008). *Autoethnography as method.* Walnut Creek, CA: Left Coast Press.

Chao, R. C.-L. (2012). Racial/ethnic identity, gender-role attitudes, and multicultural counseling competence: The role of multicultural counseling training. *Journal of Counseling & Development, 90,* 35-44. doi:10.1111/j.1556-6676.2012.00006.x

Chao, G. T., & Moon, H. (2005). The cultural mosaic: A metatheory for understanding the complexity of culture. *Journal of Applied Psychology, 90*, 1128–1140. doi:10.1037/0021-9010.90.6.1128

Chao, M. M., Chen, J., Roisman, G. I., & Hong, Y.-Y. (2007). Essentializing race: Implications for bicultural individuals' cognition and physiological reactivity. *Psychological Science, 18*, 341–348. doi:10.1111/j.1467-9280.2007.01901.x

Chao, G. T., O'Leary-Kelly, A. M., Wolf, S., Klein, H. J., & Gardner, P. D. (1994). Organizational socialization: Its content and consequences. *Journal of Applied Psychology, 79*, 730–743. doi:10.1037/0021-9010.79.5.730

Chartrand, T. L., & Bargh, J. A. (1999). The chameleon effect: The perception–behavior link and social interaction. *Journal of Personality and Social Psychology, 76*, 893-910. doi:10.1037/0022-3514.76.6.893

Chase, S. E. (2005). Narrative inquiry: Multiple lenses, approaches, voices. In N.K. Denzin, & Y. S. Lincoln (Eds.), *The Sage Handbook of Qualitative Research* (3rd ed., pp. 651-695). Thousand Oaks, CA: Sage.

Chatman, J. A., & Flynn, F. J. (2001). The influence of demographic heterogeneity on the emergence and consequences of cooperative norms in work teams. *Academy of Management Journal, 44*, 956–974. doi:10.2307/3069440

Chen, C. P., & Asamoah, A. (2007). Vocational psychology of immigrant women: Special issues and practical implications. *Baltic Journal of Psychology, 8*, 67-75. Retrieved from http://www.lu.lv/apgads/izdevumi/elektroniskie-izdevumi/

Chen, S., Benet-Martínez, V., & Harris Bond, M. (2008). Bicultural identity, bilingualism, and psychological adjustment in multicultural societies: Immigration-based and globalization-based acculturation. *Journal of Personality, 76*, 803-838. doi:10.1111/j.1467-6494.2008.00505.x

Cheng, R. P. (2009). Sociological theories of disability, gender, and sexuality: A review of the literature. *Journal of Human Behavior in the Social Environment, 19*, 112-122. doi:10.1080/10911350802631651

Cheryan, S., & Monin, B. (2005). Where are you really from?: Asian Americans and identity denial. *Journal of Personality and Social Psychology, 89,* 717–730. doi:10.1037/0022-3514.89.5.717

Chiao, J. Y., Harada, T., Komeda, H., Zhang, L., Mano, Y., Saito, D., . . . Iidaka, T. (2010). Dynamic cultural influences on neural representations of the self. *Journal of Cognitive Neuroscience, 22,* 1-11. doi:10.1162/jocn.2009.21192

Chiu, C.-Y., Gelfand, M. J., Yamagishi, T., Shteynberg, G., & Wan, C. (2010). Intersubjective culture: The role of intersubjective perceptions in cross-cultural research. *Perspectives on Psychological Science, 5,* 482–493. doi:10.1177/1745691610375562

Chohan, S. K. (2010). Whispering selves and reflective transformation in the internal dialogue of teachers and students. *Journal of Invitational Theory and Practice, 16,* 10-28. Retrieved from ERIC database. (EJ942555)

Ciol, M. A., Shumway-Cook, A., Hoffman, J. M., Yorkston, K. M., Dudgeon, B. J., & Chan, L. (2008). Minority disparities in disability between Medicare beneficiaries. *Journal of the American Geriatrics Society, 56,* 444-453. doi:10.1111/j.1532-5415.2007.01570.x

Claidière, N., Bowler, M., & Whiten, A. (2012). Evidence for weak or linear conformity but not for hyper-conformity in an everyday social learning context. *Plos One, 7,* 1-8. doi:10.1371/journal.pone.0030970

Clandinin, D. (2007). *Handbook of narrative inquiry: Mapping a methodology.* Thousand Oaks, CA: Sage. doi:10.4135/9781452226552

Clandinin, D., & Rosiek, J. (2007). Mapping a landscape of narrative inquiry: Borderland spaces and tensions. In D. J. Clandinin (Ed.), *Handbook of narrative inquiry: Mapping a methodology* (pp. 35-77). Thousand Oaks, CA: Sage. doi:10.4135/9781452226552.n2

Coffey, A. (Ed.). (1999). *The ethnographic self.* London, England: SAGE Publications Ltd. doi:10.4135/9780857020048

Cohen, A. B. (2009). Many forms of culture. *American Psychologist, 64,* 194-204. doi:10.1037/a0015308

Cohen, E. (2010). Anthropology of knowledge. *Journal of the Royal Anthropological Institute, 16,* S193-S202. doi:10.1111/j.1467-9655.2010.01617.x

Cohen, D., & Gunz, A. (2002). As seen by the other . . . : Perspectives on the self in the memories and emotional perceptions of Easterners and Westerners. *Psychological Science, 13,* 55–59. Available from http://www.jstor.org/stable/40063695 .

Cojocaru, S. L. (2013). *Between self-identification and wholeheartedness: A critical study of personal autonomy* (Doctoral dissertation). Available from ProQuest Dissertations and Theses database. (UMI No. 3529015)

Cole, B. (2009). Gender, narratives and intersectionality: Can personal experience approaches to research contribute to "undoing gender"? *International Review of Education/Internationale Zeitschrift Für Erziehungswissenschaft, 55,* 561-578. doi:10.1007/s11159-009-9140-5

Cole, E. R. (2009). Intersectional and research in psychology. *American Psychologist, 64,* 170-180. doi:10.1037/a0014564

Coleman, R. L., & Croake, J. W. (1987). Organ inferiority and measured overcompensation. *Individual Psychology: The Journal of Adlerian Theory, Research & Practice, 43,* 364-369. Retrieved from http://utpress.utexas.edu /index.php/journals/journal-of-individual-psychology

Collins, P. H. (1990). Black feminist thought in the matrix of domination. In P. Hill-Collins (Ed.), *Black Feminist Thought: Knowledge, Consciousness, and the Politics of Empowerment* (pp. 221-238). Boston: Unwin Hyman

Collins, P. (2001). Like one of the family: Race, ethnicity, and the paradox of US national identity. *Ethnic & Racial Studies, 24,* 3-28. doi:10.1080/01419870020006525

Conlon, J. L. (2009). *One-whole or one-half: A case study of an identical twin's exploration of personal identity through family perceptions* (Doctoral dissertation). Available from ProQuest Dissertations and Theses database. (UMI No. 304905192)

Constantine, M. G. (2002). The intersection of race, ethnicity, gender, and social class in counseling: Examining selves in cultural contexts. *Journal of Multicultural Counseling & Development, 30,* 210-215. doi:10.1002/j.2161-1912.2002.tb00520.x

Cook, J. E., Purdie-Vaughns, V., Garcia, J., & Cohen, G. L. (2012). Chronic threat and contingent belonging: Protective benefits of values affirmation on identity development. *Journal of Personality & Social Psychology, 102,* 479-496. doi:10.1037/a0026312

Corrigan, P., & Matthews, A. (2003). Stigma and disclosure: Implications for coming out of the closet. *Journal of Mental Health, 12,* 235-248. doi:10.1080/0963823031000118221

Couser, T. G. (2005). Disability and (auto)ethnography: Riding (and writing) the bus with my sister. *Journal of Contemporary Ethnography, 34,* 121-142. doi:10.1177/0891241604272089

Cox, N., Vanden Berghe, W., Dewaele, A., & Vincke, J. (2010). Acculturation strategies and mental health in gay, lesbian, and bisexual youth. *Journal of Youth & Adolescence, 39,* 1199-1210. doi:10.1007/s10964-009-9435-7

Creamer, D. (2012). Disability theology. *Religion Compass, 6,* 339-346. doi:10.1111/j.1749-8171.2012.00366.x

Cramer, E. P., Gilson, S. F., & DePoy, E. (2003). Women with disabilities & experiences of abuse. *Journal of Human Behavior In The Social Environment, 7,* 183-199. doi:10.1300/J137v7n03_11

Cramer, E. P., & Plummer, S. (2009). People of color with disabilities: Intersectional as a framework for analyzing intimate partner violence in social, historical, and political contexts. *Journal of Aggression, Maltreatment & Trauma, 18,* 162-181. doi:10.1080/10926770802675635

Crawford, L. (1996). Personal ethnography. *Communication Monographs, 63,* 158-170. doi:10.1080/03637759609376384

Crisp, R. J., & Hewstone, M. (2001). Multiple categorization and implicit intergroup bias: Differential category dominance and the positive–negative asymmetry effect. *European Journal of Social Psychology, 31,* 45–62. Available from doi:10.1002/ejsp.31

Curral, L., & Marques-Quinteiro, P. (2009). Self-leadership and work role innovation: Testing a mediation model with goal orientation and work motivation. *Revista de*

Psicologia del Trabajo y de las Organizaciones, 25, 165-176. doi:10.4321/S1576-59622009000200006

Cutforth, N. (2013). The journey of a community-engaged scholar: An Autoethnography. *Quest, 65,* 14–30. doi:10.1080/00336297.2012.727369

Danaher, K., & Branscombe, N. R. (2010). Maintaining the system with tokenism: Bolstering individual mobility beliefs and identification with a discriminatory organization. *British Journal of Social Psychology, 49,* 343-362. doi:10.1348/014466609X457530

D'Anna, L., Ponce, N., & Siegel, J. (2010). Racial and ethnic health disparities: Evidence of discrimination's effects across the SEP spectrum... socioeconomic position. *Ethnicity & Health, 15,* 121-143. doi:10.1080/13557850903490298

Deaux, K., & Martin, D. (2003). Interpersonal networks and social categories: Specifying levels of context in identity processes. *Social Psychology Quarterly, 66,* 101–117. doi:10.2307/1519842

Delgado, R. (2011). Rodrigo's reconsideration: Intersectionality and the future of critical race theory. *Iowa Law Review, 96,* 1247-1288.

Demos, V., & Lemelle, J. J. (2006). Introduction: Race, gender, and class for what? *Race, Gender & Class, 13,* 4-15. Available from http://www.suno.edu

Denshire, S. (2014). On auto-ethnography. *Current Sociology, 62,* 831–850. doi:10.1177/0011392114533339

Denzin, N. K. (Ed.). (2003). *Performance ethnography.* Thousand Oaks, CA: SAGE Publications, Inc. doi:10.4135/9781412985390

Denzin, N. K. (2013). Performing methodologies. *Qualitative Social Work, 12,* 389–394. doi:10.1177/1473325013493533

Denzin, N. K. (2014). *Interpretative autoethnography (2nd Ed.)* [Kindle DX Version]. Thousand Oaks, CA: Sage. Available from Amazon.com

Denzin, N. K., & Lincoln, Y. S. (Eds.). (2002). *The qualitative inquiry reader.* Thousand Oaks, CA: SAGE Publications, Inc. doi:10.4135/9781412986267

Dethloff, C. H. (2005). *A principal in transition: An autoethnography* (Doctoral dissertation). Available from ProQuest Dissertations and Theses database. (UMI No. 3246462)

Devlieger, P. J., & Albrecht, G. L. (2000). Your experience is not my experience: The concept and experience of disability on Chicago's near West Side. *Journal of Disability Policy Studies Summer, 11,* 51-60. doi: 10.1177/104420730001100115

Dietz-Uhler, B., & Murrell, A. (1998). Effects of social identity and threat on self-esteem and group attributions. *Group Dynamics: Theory, Research, and Practice, 2,* 24-35. doi:10.1037/1089-2699.2.1.24

Dickerson, P. (2000). 'But I'm different to them': Constructing contrasts between self and others in talk-in-interaction. *The British Journal of Social Psychology, 39,* 381-398. doi:10.1348/014466600164552

Dillon, L. (2011). Writing the self: The emergence of a dialogic space. *Narrative Inquiry, 21,* 213-237. doi:10.1075/ni.21.2.03dil

D'Intino, R. S., Goldsby, M. G., Houghton, J. D., & Neck, C. P. (2007). Self-leadership: A process for entrepreneurial success. *Journal of Leadership & Organizational Studies, 13,* 105-120. Retrieved from http://www.baker.edu

Doloriert, C., & Sambrook, S. (2009). Ethical confessions of the "I" of autoethnography: The student's dilemma. *Qualitative Research in Organizations and Management: An International Journal, 1,* 27-45. doi:10.1108/17465640910951435

Doloriert, C., & Sambrook, S. (2012). Organisational autoethnography. *Journal of Organizational Ethnography, 1,* 83-95. doi:10.1108/20466741211220688

Doubt. (n.d.). In *Merriam-Webster's online dictionary.* Retrieved from http://www.merriam-webster.com/dictionary/doubt

Downie, M., Mageau, G. A., Koestner, R., & Liodden, T. (2006). On the risk of being a cultural chameleon: Variations in collective self-esteem across social interactions. *Cultural Diversity & Ethnic Minority Psychology, 12,* 527-540. doi:10.1037/1099-9809.12.3527

Duarte, F. (2007). Using autoethnography in the scholarship of teaching and learning: Reflective practice from 'the other side of the mirror'. International Journal for the Scholarship of Teaching and Learning, 1, 1-11. Retrieved from http://www.georgiasouthern.edu/ijsotl

Dubrosky, R. (2013). Iris Young's five faces of oppression applied to nursing. *Nursing Forum, 48,* 205-210. doi:10.1111/nuf.12027

Dutta, U. (2014). The long way home the vicissitudes of belonging and otherness in Northeast India. *Qualitative Inquiry,* 1-12. doi:10.1177/1077800414542703

Dunbar, E. (2006). Race, gender, and sexual orientation in hate crime victimization: Identity politics or identity risk? *Violence and Victims, 21,* 323-337. doi:10.1891/088667006780644604

Dyson, M. (2007). My story in a profession of stories: Auto ethnography: An empowering methodology for educators. *Australian Journal of Teacher Education, 32,* 36-48. doi:10.14221/ajte.2007v32n1.3

Ekstedt, M., & Fagerberg, I. (2005). Lived experiences of the time preceding burnout. *Journal of Advanced Nursing, 49,* 59-67. doi:10.1111/j.1365-2648.2004.03264.x

Elsbach, K. D., & Kramer, R. M. (1996). Members' responses to organizational identity threats: Encountering and countering the business week rankings. *Administrative Science Quarterly, 41,* 442–476. doi:10.2307/2393938

Ellemers, N., Spears, R., & Doosje, B. (2002). Self and social identity. *Annual Review of Psychology, 53,* 161–86. Available from http://www.socialsciences.leiden.edu

Ellis, C. (1991). Sociological introspection and emotional experience. *Symbolic Interaction, 14,* 23-50. doi:10.1525/si.1991.14.1.23

Ellis, C. (1999). Heartful autoethnography. *Qualitative Health Research, 9,* 669-683. doi:10.1177/104973299129122153

Ellis, C. (2000). Negotiating terminal illness: Communication, collusion, and coalition in caregiving. In J. Harvey & F.D. Miller (Eds.), *Loss and trauma: General and close relationship perspectives* (pp. 284-304). London: Brunner-Routledge.

Ellis, C. (2004). *The ethnographic I: A methodological novel about autoethnography.* Walnut Creek, CA: AltaMira Press.

Ellis, C. (2007). Telling secrets, revealing lives relational ethics in research with intimate others. *Qualitative Inquiry, 13,* 3-29. doi:10.1177/1077800406294947

Ellis, C. (2008). Autoethnography. In L. Given (Ed.), *The SAGE encyclopedia of qualitative research methods.* (pp. 49-52). Thousand Oaks, CA: SAGE Publications, Inc. doi:10.4135/9781412963909.n29

Ellis, C., & Bochner, A. P. (2000). Autoethnography, personal narrative, reflexivity: Researcher as subject. In N. K. Denzin, & Y. S. Lincoln (Eds.), *Handbook of Qualitative Research* (2nd ed., pp. 733-768). Thousand Oaks, CA: Sage.

Ellis, C. S., & Bochner, A. P. (2006). Analyzing analytic autoethnography an autopsy. *Journal of Contemporary Ethnography, 35*, 429–449. doi:10.1177/0891241606286979

Ellis, C., & Rawicki, J. (2013). Collaborative witnessing of survival during the Holocaust an exemplar of relational autoethnography. *Qualitative Inquiry, 19*, 366–380. doi:10.1177/1077800413479562

Ellis, C., Adams, T. E., & Bochner, A. P. (2011). Autoethnography: An overview. *Historical Social Research, 36*, 273-290. Retrieved from http://www.qualitative-research.net

Ellis, C., Bochner, A., Denzin, N., Lincoln, Y., Morse, J., Pelias, R., & Richardson, L. (2008). Talking and thinking about qualitative research. *Qualitative Inquiry, 14*, 254-284. doi: 10.1177/1077800407311959

Ellison, C. G., Finch, B. K., Ryan, D. N., & Salinas, J. J. (2009). Religious involvement and depressive symptoms among Mexican-origin adults in California. *Journal of Community Psychology, 37*, 171–193. doi:10.1002/jcop.20287

Elu, J., & Loubert, L. (2013). Earnings inequality and the intersectionality of gender and ethnicity in Sub-Saharan Africa: The case of Tanzanian Manufacturing. *American Economic Review, 103*, 289-292. doi:10.1257/aer.103.3.289

Engstrom, C. L. (2008). Autoethnography as an approach to intercultural training. *Rocky Mountain Communication Review, 5*, 17-31. Available from http://web.b.ebscohost.com.ezproxy.apollolibrary.com/

Esmail, S., Darry, K., Walter, A., & Knupp, H. (2009). Attitudes and perceptions towards disability and sexuality. *Disability & Rehabilitation, 32*, 1148-1155. doi:10.3109/09638280903419277

185

Essed, P. (2010). Towards a methodology to identify converging forms of everyday discrimination. *United Nations Division for the Advancement of Women, Commission on the Status of Women.* Retrieved from http://www.un.org/womenwatch

Etzion, D. (1984). Moderating effect of social support on the stress-burnout relationship. *Journal of Applied Psychology, 69,* 615-622. doi:10.1037//0021-9010.69.4.615

Falk, C. F., Dunn, E. W., & Norenzayan, A. (2010). Cultural variation in the importance of expected enjoyment for decision making. *Social Cognition, 28,* 609-629. doi:10.1521/soco.2010.28.5.609

Farber, B. (2000). Introduction: Understanding and treating burnout in a changing culture. *Journal of Clinical Psychology, 56,* 589-594. doi:10.1002/(SICI)1097-4679(200005)56:5<589::AID-JCLP1>3.0.CO;2-S

Fassett, D. L., & Warren, J. T. (2007). *Critical communication pedagogy.* Thousand Oaks, CA: Sage.

Finch, D. D. (2012). *The experiences of homeschool mothers* (Doctoral dissertation). Available from ProQuest Dissertations and Theses database. (UMI No. 3532770)

Fiske, A. (2002). Using individualism and collectivism to compare cultures—A critique of the validity. *Psychological Bulletin, 128,* 78-88. doi:10.1037//0033-2909.128.1.78

Flores, N. M., & Huo, Y. J. (2013). "We" are not all alike consequences of neglecting national origin identities among Asians and Latinos. *Social Psychological and Personality Science, 4,* 143–150. doi:10.1177/1948550612449025

Flynn, J. E. (2012). Critical pedagogy with the oppressed and the oppressors: Middle school students discuss racism and White privilege. *Middle Grades Research Journal, 7,* 95–110. Available from http://eric.ed.gov

Flynn, F. J., Chatman, J. A., & Spataro, S. E. (2001). Getting to know you: The influence of personality on impressions and performance of demographically different people in organizations. *Administrative Science Quarterly, 46,* 414–442. doi:10.2307/3094870

Foster, K., McAllister, M., & O'Brien, L. (2006). Extending the boundaries: Autoethnography as an emergent method in mental health nursing research. *International Journal of Mental Health Nursing, 15,* 44–53. doi:10.1111/j.1447-0349.2006.00402.x

Fox, R. (2014). Are those germs in your pocket, or am I just crazy to see you? An autoethnographic consideration of obsessive-compulsive disorder. *Qualitative Inquiry, 20,* 966–975. doi:10.1177/1077800413513732

Frable, E. S. (1993). Being and feeling unique: Statistical deviance. *Journal of Personality, 61,* 85-110. doi:10.1111/j.1467-6494.1993.tb00280.x

Frank, R., Redstone Akresh, I., & Bo, L. (2010). Latino immigrants and the U.S. racial order: How and where do they fit in? *American Sociological Review, 75,* 378-401. doi:10.1177/0003122410372216

Freeman, M. (2014). The hermeneutical aesthetics of thick description. *Qualitative Inquiry, 20,* 827–833. doi:10.1177/1077800414530267

Friberg, T. (2009). Burnout: From popular culture to psychiatric diagnosis in Sweden. *Culture, Medicine & Psychiatry, 33,* 538-558. doi:10.1007/s11013-009-9149-z

Friedkin, N. E. (2010). The attitude-behavior linkage in behavioral cascades. *Social Psychology Quarterly, 73,* 196-213. doi:10.1177/0190272510369661

Frost, D. M. (2011). Social stigma and its consequences for the socially stigmatized. *Social & Personality Psychology Compass, 5,* 824-839. doi:10.1111/j.1751-9004.2011.00394.x

Furham, A. (2012). Culture shock. *Journal of Psychology and Education, 7,* 9-22. Available from http://www.revistadepsicologiayeducacion.es

Furtner, M. R., Rauthmann, J. F., & Sachse, P. (2010). The socioemotionally intelligent self-leader: Examining relations between self-leadership and socioemotional intelligence. *Social Behavior & Personality: An International Journal, 38,* 1191-1196. doi:10.2224/sbp.2010.38.9.1191

Gale, K. (2014). Moods, tones, flavors living with intensities as inquiry. *Qualitative Inquiry, 20,* 998–1004. doi:10.1177/1077800413513725

Galupo, M., & Gonzalez, K. (2013). Friendship values and cross-category friendships: Understanding adult friendship patterns across gender, sexual orientation and race. *Sex Roles, 68,* 779-790. doi:10.1007/s11199-012-0211-x

Garcia, J. A. (1981). Yo soy Mexicano...: Self-identity and sociodemographic correlates. *Social Science Quarterly, 62,* 88–98. Available from http://www.blackwellpublishing.com

Gardner, L. D., & Lane, H. (2010). Exploring the personal tutor-student relationship: An autoethnographic approach. *Journal of Psychiatric and Mental Health Nursing, 17,* 342–347. doi:10.1111/j.1365-2850.2009.01527.x

Gardner, W. L., Gabriel, S., & Lee, A. Y. (1999). "I" value freedom, but "we" value relationships: Self-construal priming mirrors cultural differences in judgment. *Psychological Science, 10,* 321–326. Retrieved from http://www.jstor.org/stable/40063438

Garratt, D. (2014). Psychoanalytic-autoethnography troubling natural bodybuilding. *Qualitative Inquiry,* 1-11. doi:10.1177/1077800414542699

Gavilán, M. (2010). Persona multicultural, comunicación intercultural. La propuesta de Amin Maalouf [Multicultural person, intercultural communication. Amin Maalouf proposal]. *Comunicación y Sociedad, 14,* 199-216. Retrieved from http://www.publicaciones.cucsh.udg.mx/pperiod/comsoc/index.htm

Gearity, B. T., & Mertz, N. (2012). From "bitch" to "mentor": A doctoral student's story of self change and mentoring. *The Qualitative Report, 17,* 1-27. Retrieved from http://www.nova.edu/ssss/QR/QR17/gearity.pdf

Geertz, C. (1973). *The interpretation of cultures.* New York: Basic Books.

Geertz, C. (1988). *Works and lives: The anthropologist as author.* Stanford, CA: Stanford University Press.

Genkova, P. (2012). Cultural patterns and subjective culture as predictors of well-being: A cross-cultural study. *Psychology Research, 2,* 177-184. Retrieved from http://www.proquest.com/

Ghavami, N., Fingerhut, A., Peplau, L. A., Grant, S. K., & Wittig, M. A. (2011). Testing a model of minority identity achievement, identity affirmation, and psychological well-being among ethnic minority and sexual minority individuals. *Cultural Diversity & Ethnic Minority Psychology, 17,* 79-88. doi:10.1037/a0022532

Giampietro, G. (2008). *Doing ethnography*. Thousand Oaks, CA: Sage. doi:10.4135/9780857028976

Gilson, S. F., & DePoy, E. (2000). Multiculturalism and disability: A critical perspective. *Disability & Society, 15,* 207-218. doi:10.1080/09687590025630

Gilson, S. F., & DePoy, E. (2006). Explanatory legitimacy theory. In G. Albrecht (Ed.), *Encyclopedia of disability.* (pp. 700-703). Thousand Oaks, CA: SAGE Publications, Inc. doi:10.4135/9781412950510.n326

Given, L. M. (Ed.). (2008). *The SAGE encyclopedia of qualitative research methods.* Thousand Oaks, CA: Sage. doi:10.4135/9781412963909

Goldin, E. V. (2012). *Invisible to myself: Trigger words and the invisibly disabled identity* (Doctoral dissertation). Available from ProQuest Dissertations and Theses database. (UMI No. 1515826)

Gómez, A., Huici, C., Seyle, D., & Swann, J. B. (2009). Can self-verification strivings fully transcend the self-other barrier? Seeking verification of ingroup identities. *Journal of Personality & Social Psychology, 97,* 1021-1044. doi:10.1037/a0016358

Gomm, R., Hammersley, M., & Foster, P. (Eds.). (2009). *Case study method.* Thousand Oaks, CA: Sage. doi:10.4135/9780857024367

Grant, A. M., & Campbell, E. M. (2007). Doing good, doing harm, being well and burning out: The interactions of perceived prosocial and antisocial impact in service work. *Journal of Occupational & Organizational Psychology, 80,* 665-691. doi:10.1348/096317906X169553

Griffin, R. H. (2009). *The work of high school counselors' leadership for social justice: An analytic autoethnography* (Doctoral dissertation). Available from ProQuest Dissertations and Theses database. (UMI No. 3382098)

Gudykunst, W. B. (1983). Uncertainty reduction and predictability of behavior in low- and high-context cultures: An exploratory study. *Communication Quarterly, 31,* 49-55. Retrieved from http://www.ecasite.org

Hae Yeon, C., & Ferree, M. (2010). Practicing intersectionality in sociological research: A critical analysis of inclusions, interactions, and institutions in the study of inequalities. *Sociological Theory, 28,* 129-149. doi:10.1111/j.1467-9558.2010.01370.x

Hamdan, A. (2012). Autoethnography as a genre of qualitative research: A journey inside out. *International Journal of Qualitative Methods, 11,* 585-606. Retrieved from http://www.ualberta.ca

Hamilton, M., Smith, L., & Worthington, K. (2008). Fitting the methodology with the research: An exploration of narrative, self-study and auto-ethnography. *Studying Teacher Education, 4,* 17-24. doi:10.1080/17425960801976321

Hammershøj, L. (2009). The social pathologies of self-realization: A diagnosis of the consequences of the shift in individualization. *Educational Philosophy & Theory, 41,* 507-526. doi:10.1111/j.1469-5812.2007.00383.x

Hansen, N., & Philo, C. (2007). The normality of doing things differently: Bodies, spaces and disability geography. *Tijdschrift Voor Economische en Sociale Geografie (Journal of Economic & Social Geography), 98,* 493-506. doi:10.1111/j.1467-9663.2007.00417.x

Harley, D. A., Jolivette, K., McCormick, K., & Tice, K. (2002). Race, class, and gender: A constellation of positionalities with implications for counseling. *Journal of Multicultural Counseling and Development, 30,* 216-238. doi:10.1002/j.2161-1912.2002.tb00521.x

Harrell, S. P., & Bond, M. A. (2006). Listening to diversity stories: Principles for practice in community research and action. *American Journal of Community Psychology, 37,* 365-376. doi:10.1007/s10464-006-9042-7

Harrington, E. R. (2003). The social psychology of hatred. *Journal of Hate Studies, 3,* 49–82. Available from http://journals.gonzaga.edu

Harrison, M. E. (2011). *Discovering voices, discovering selves: Auto-ethnographic examinations of the relationships between Japanese queer sexualities and English as language and culture* (Doctoral dissertation). Available from ProQuest Dissertations and Theses database. (UMI No. 867276635)

Haseli, S., Vaezmousavi, S., & Seddighi, D. (2012). The effect of free self-talk on the performance of front-crawl. *Annals of Biological Research, 3,* 730-735. Retrieved from http://scholarsresearchlibrary.com/annals-of-biological-research/

Hayes, J. A., Chun-Kennedy, C., Edens, A., & Locke, B. D. (2011). Do double minority students face double jeopardy? Testing minority stress theory. *Journal of College Counseling, 14,* 117-126. doi:10.1002/j.2161-1882.2011.tb00267.x

Haynes, K. (2011). Tensions in (re)presenting the self in reflexive autoethnographical research. *Qualitative Research in Organizations and Management: An International Journal, 6,* 134-149. doi:10.1108/17465641111159125

Hendrix, K. G., Jackson, R. L., II, & Warren, J. R. (2003). Shifting academic landscapes: Exploring co-identities, identity negotiation, and critical progressive pedagogy. *Communication Education, 52,* 177–190. doi:10.1080/0363452032000156181

Hernandez, M. Y. (2009). Psychological theories of immigration. *Journal of Human Behavior in the Social Environment, 19,* 713-729. doi:10.1080/10911350902910898

Higgins, D. (2010). Sexuality, human rights and safety for people with disabilities: The challenge of intersecting identities. *Sexual & Relationship Therapy, 25,* 245-257. doi:10.1080/14681994.2010.489545

Ho, C. (2007). A framework of the foundation theories underlying the relationship between individuals within a diverse workforce. *Research & Practice in Human Resource Management, 15,* 1–13. Available from http://rphrm.curtin.edu.au

Ho, M. & Bauderb, H. (2011). 'We are chameleons': Identity capital in a multicultural workplace. *Social Identities, 18,* 281-297. doi:10.1080/13504630.2012.661997

Hoersting, R. C., & Jenkins, S. R. (2011). No place to call home: Cultural homelessness, self-esteem and cross-cultural identities. *International Journal of Intercultural Relations, 35,* 17-30. doi:10.1016/j.ijintrel.2010.11.005

Hogg, M. A. (2001). A social identity theory of leadership. *Personality & Social Psychology Review, 5,* 184-200. doi:10.1207/S15327957PSPR0503_1

Hogg, M. A. (2001a). Social categorization, depersonalization, and group behavior. In M. A. Hogg & R. S. Tindale (Eds.), *Blackwell handbook of social psychology: Group processes* (pp. 56-85). Oxford, England: Blackwell.

Hogg, M. A., & Terry, D. J. (2000). Social identity and self-categorization processes in organizational contexts. *Academy of Management Review, 25,* 121–140. doi:10.5465/AMR.2000.2791606

191

Hogg, M. A., & Reid, S. A. (2006). Social identity, self-categorization, and the communication of group norms. *Communication Theory, 16*, 7–30. doi:10.1111/j.1468-2885.2006.00003.x

Holcomb, T. K. (1997). Development of deaf bicultural identity. *American Annals of the Deaf, 14*, 289-293. Available from http://gupress.gallaudet.edu

Holman, S., J., Adams, T. E., & Ellis, C. (Eds.). (2013). *Handbook of autoethnography.* Walnut Creek, CA: Left Coast Press.

Holt, N. L. (2003). Representation, legitimation, and autoethnography: An autoethnographic writing story. *International Journal of Qualitative Methods, 2*, 1-22. Retrieved from http://www.ualberta.ca

Hong, Y., Morris, M. W., Chiu, C., & Benet-Martinez, V. (2000). Multicultural minds. A dynamic constructivist approach to culture and cognition. *American Psychologist, 55*, 709-720. doi:10.1037/0003-066X.55.7.709

Hong, Y., Wan, C., No, S., & Chiu, C. (2010). Multicultural identities. In S. Kitayama, & D. Cohen (Eds.). *Handbook of Cultural Psychology.* (pp. 323-345). New York: Guilford.

Hong, Y.-Y., Benet-Martínez, V., Chiu, C.-Y., & Morris, M. W. (2003). Boundaries of cultural influence construct activation as a mechanism for cultural differences in social perception. *Journal of Cross-Cultural Psychology, 34*, 453–464. doi:10.1177/0022022103034004005

Houghton, J. D., & Yoho, S. K. (2005). Toward a contingency model of leadership and psychological empowerment: When should self-leadership be encouraged? *Journal of Leadership & Organizational Studies, 11*, 65-83. Retrieved from http://www.baker.edu/

Hughes, S., Pennington, J. L., & Makris, S. (2012). Translating autoethnography across the AERA standards toward understanding autoethnographic scholarship as empirical research. *Educational Researcher, 41*, 209–219. doi:10.3102/0013189X12442983

Hughey, M. W., & Vidich, A. J. (1992). The new American pluralism: Racial and ethnic sodalities and their sociological implications. *International Journal of Politics, Culture & Society, 6*, 159-180. doi:10.1007/BF01395297

Hurd, E. (2012). A framework for understanding multicultural identities: An investigation of a middle level student's French-Canadian Honduran-American (Mestizo) identity. *Middle Grades Research Journal, 7,* 111-127. Available from http://eric.ed.gov/?id=EJ1006039

Hyers, L. L., & Hyers, C. (2008). Everyday discrimination experienced by conservative Christians at the secular university. *Analyses of Social Issues and Public Policy, 8,* 113-137. doi:10.1111/j.1530-2415.2008.00162.x

Jackman, G. R. (2009). *Who knew? An autoethnography of a first-year assistant principal* (Doctoral dissertation). Available from ProQuest Dissertations and Theses database. (UMI No. 3372864)

James, J. C., & Wu, C. (2006). Race, ethnicity, disability, and literature: Intersections and interventions. *MELUS, 31,* 3-13. doi:10.1093/melus/31.3.3

Jefferies, J. (2012). Mangling practices: Writing reflections. *Journal of Writing in Creative Practice, 5,* 73-84. doi:10.1386/jwcp.5.1.73_1

Jemmer, P. (2011). Self-talk: The spells of psycho-chaotic sorcery. *European Journal of Clinical Hypnosis, 9,* 51-58. Retrieved from http://www.ejch.com/

Jenerette, C., & Murdaugh, C. (2008). Testing the theory of self-care management for sickle cell disease. *Research in Nursing & Health, 31,* 355-369. doi:10.1002/nur.20261

Jones, R. S., Choe Kim, Y., & Cilente Skendall, K. (2012). (Re-) Framing authenticity: Considering multiple social identities using autoethnographic and intersectional approaches. *Journal of Higher Education, 83,* 698-723. Retrieved from http://www.ohiostatepress.org

Jost, J. T., & Kruglanski, A. W. (2002). The estrangement of social constructionism and experimental social psychology: History of the rift and prospects for reconciliation. *Personality & Social Psychology Review, 6,* 168–187. doi:10.1207/S15327957PSPR0603_1

Jupp, V. (Ed.). (2006). *The SAGE dictionary of social research methods.* Thousand Oaks, CA: Sage. doi:10.4135/9780857020116

Kahl, D. H. (2011). Autoethnography as pragmatic scholarship: Moving critical communication pedagogy from ideology to praxis. *International Journal of Communications, 5,* 1927–1946. Retrieved from http://ijoc.org

Kaltman, S., Hurtado de Mendoza, A., Gonzales, F. A., Serrano, A., & Guarnaccia, P. J. (2011). Contextualizing the trauma experience of women immigrants from Central America, South America, and Mexico. *Journal of Traumatic Stress, 24,* 635–642. doi:10.1002/jts.20698

Khosravi, S. (2007). The 'illegal' traveller: An auto-ethnography of borders. *Social Anthropology/Anthropologie Sociale, 15,* 321-334. doi:10.1111/j.0964-0282.2007.00019.x

Kiely, R. (2004). A chameleon with a complex: Searching for transformation in international service-learning. *Michigan Journal of Community Service Learning, 10,* 5-20. Retrieved from ERIC database. (EJ852915)

Kim, H., & Markus, H. R. (1999). Deviance or uniqueness, harmony or conformity? A cultural analysis. *Journal of Personality and Social Psychology, 77,* 785–800. doi:10.1037/0022-3514.77.4.785

Kim, M.-S., & Hubbard, A. S. E. (2007). Intercultural communication in the global village: How to understand "the other." *Journal of Intercultural Communication Research, 36,* 223–235. doi:10.1080/17475750701737165

Klinker, J., & Todd, R. H. (2007). Two autoethnographies: A search for understanding of gender and age. *Qualitative Report, 12,* 166-183. Retrieved from ERIC database. (EJ800174)

Knapp, J. R., & Dalziel, T. (2007). Agency theory and the effects of cognitive social categorization. In *Academy of Management Annual Meeting Proceedings* (pp. 1–6). Academy of Management. doi:10.5465/AMBPP.2007.26506659

Kmietowicz, Z. (2004). Doctors' careers are blighted by discrimination, says BMA. *BMJ (Clinical Research Ed.), 329,* 11. Retrieved from http://group.bmj.com/

Knell, M. (2006). *Burn-up of splash down.* Tyrone, GA: Authentic Publications.

Koch, T. (2006). Establishing rigour in qualitative research: The decision trail. *Journal of Advanced Nursing, 53,* 91-100. doi:10.1111/j.1365-2648.2006.03681.x

Kramer, R. M. (1998). Paranoid cognition in social systems: Thinking and acting in the shadow of doubt. *Personality & Social Psychology Review*, *2*, 251-275. doi:10.1207/s15327957pspr0204_3

Kreiner, G. E., Hollensbe, E. C., & Sheep, M. L. (2006). Where is the "me" among the "we"? Identity work and the search for optimal balance. *Academy of Management Journal*, *49*, 1031-1057. doi:10.5465/AMJ.2006.22798186

Kunz, M., Prkachin, K., & Lautenbacher, S. (2013). Smiling in pain: Explorations of its social motives. *Pain Research & Treatment* [Advance online publication]. doi:10.1155/2013/128093

Lam, C. S., Hector, T., Fong, C., & Corrigan, P. W. (2006). Chinese and American perspectives on stigma. *Rehabilitation Education, 20,* 269-279. doi:10.1891/088970106805065368

LaPierre, T. A., & Hill, S. A. (2013). Examining status discrepant marriages and marital quality at the intersections of gender, race, and class. *Advances in Gender Research, 17,* 113–136. doi:10.1108/S1529-2126(2013)0000017009

Lash, L. W., & Hodgetts, R. M. (1992). Mastering self-leadership: Empowering yourself for personal excellence. *Organizational Dynamics, 21,* 75-76. doi:10.1016/0090-2616(92)90067-W

Lau, P. Y., Yuen, M., & Chan, R. C. (2005). Do demographic characteristics make a difference to burnout among Hong Kong secondary school teachers? *Social Indicators Research, 71,* 491-516. doi:10.1007/s11205-004-8033-z

Lawson, T. F. (2008). "Whites only tree," hanging nooses, no crime? Limiting the prosecutorial veto for hate crimes in Louisiana and across America. *University of Maryland Law Journal of Race, Religion, Gender & Class, 8,* 123-197. Retrieved from http://www.law.umaryland.edu/journal/rrgc/index.asp

Leary, M. R., & Allen, A. B. (2011). Self-presentational persona: Simultaneous management of multiple impressions. *Journal of Personality & Social Psychology, 101,* 1033-1049. doi:10.1037/a0023884

Lee, H. (2008). Flexible acculturation. *Social Thought and Research, 29,* 49-73. Retrieved from http://kuscholarworks.ku.edu

Leung, A. K., & Chiu, C.-Y. (2010). Multicultural experience, idea receptiveness, and creativity. *Journal of Cross-Cultural Psychology, 41*, 723–741. doi:10.1177/0022022110361707

Levy, J. J., & Plucker, J. A. (2003). Assessing the psychological presentation of gifted and talented clients: A multicultural perspective. *Counselling Psychology Quarterly, 16*, 229–247. doi:10.1080/09515070310001610100

Lewis-Beck, M. S., Bryman, A., Futing, T. L. (Eds.). (2004). *The SAGE encyclopedia of social science research methods.* Thousand Oaks, CA: Sage. doi:10.4135/9781412950589

Libby, L., & Eibach, R. (2011). Self-enhancement or self-coherence? Why people shift visual perspective in mental images of the personal past and future. *Journal of Personality and Social Psychology, 5*, 714-726. doi:10.1177/0146167211400207

Linder, C. (2011). *Stories of anti-racist White feminist activists: "A conversation with myself"* (Doctoral dissertation). Available from ProQuest Dissertations and Theses database. (UMI No. 3464870)

Lindstrom, L., Harwick, R. M., Poppen, M., & Doren, B. (2012). Gender gaps: Career development for young women with disabilities. *Career Development and Transition for Exceptional Individuals, 35*, 108–117. doi:10.1177/0885728812437737

Liu, L., Friedman, R., Barry, B., Gelfand, M. J., & Zhang, Z. (2012). The dynamics of consensus building in intracultural and intercultural negotiations. *Administrative Science Quarterly, 57*, 269-304. doi:10.1177/0001839212453456

Liu, W., Pickett, T. R., & Ivey, A. E. (2007). White middle-class privilege: Social class bias and implications for training and practice. *Journal of Multicultural Counseling and Development, 35*, 194-206. doi:10.1002/j.2161-1912.2007.tb00060.x

LoBianco, A. F., & Sheppard-Jones, K. (2007). Perceptions of disability as related to medical and social factors. *Journal of Applied Social Psychology, 37*, 1-13. doi:10.1111/j.0021-9029.2007.00143.x

Loewen, G., & Pollard, W. (2010). The social justice perspective. *Journal of Postsecondary Education & Disability, 23*, 5-18. Retrieved from ERIC database. (EJ888640)

Lorenz, L. S. (2010). Visual metaphors of living with brain injury: Exploring and communicating lived experience with an invisible injury. *Visual Studies, 25,* 210-223. doi:10.1080/1472586X.2010.523273

Liu, J. H. (2011). Commentary on Furnham's culture shock, Berry's acculturation theory, and Marsella and Yamada's indigenous psychopathology: Being a call to action for pacific rim psychology. *Journal of Pacific Rim Psychology, 5,* 75–80. doi:10.1017/S183449090000060X

Lui, W. Y. (2009). *Rethinking cultural marginality in the postmodern age dialogical ambivalence of the multicultural self* (Master's thesis). Retrieved from http://urn.fi/URN:NBN:fi:jyu-200905131587

Luna, D., Ringberg, T., & Peracchio, L. A. (2008). One individual, two identities: Frame switching among biculturals. *Journal of Consumer Research, 35,* 279-293. doi:10.1086/586914

Lynam, M., & Cowley, S. (2007). Understanding marginalization as a social determinant of health. *Critical Public Health, 17,* 137-149. doi:10.1080/09581590601045907

Lyttle, A. D., Barker, G. G., & Cornwell, T. L. (2011). Adept through adaptation: Third culture individuals' interpersonal sensitivity. *International Journal of Intercultural Relations, 35,* 686-694. doi:10.1016/j.ijintrel.2011.02.015

Maddux, W. W., Adam, H., & Galinsky, A. D. (2010). When in Rome ... Learn why the Romans do what they do: How multicultural learning experiences facilitate creativity. *Personality and Social Psychology Bulletin, 36,* 731–741. doi:10.1177/0146167210367786

Magnusson, E. (2011). Women, men, and all the other categories: Psychologies for theorizing human diversity. *Nordic Psychology, 63,* 88-114. doi:10.1027/1901-2276/a000034

Mannarini, T., Rochira, A., & Talò, C. (2012). How identification processes and inter-community relationships affect sense of community. *Journal of Community Psychology, 40,* 951–967. doi:10.1002/jcop.21504

Mann-Feder, V., & Savicki, V. (2003). Burnout in Anglophone and Francophone child and youth workers in Canada: A cross-cultural comparison. *Child & Youth Care Forum, 32,* 337-354. doi:10.1023/B:CCAR.0000004506.61091.f3

Manz, C. C. (1986). Self-leadership: Toward an expanded theory of self-influence processes in organizations. *Academy of Management Review, 11,* 585-600. doi:10.5465/AMR.1986.4306232

Markus, R. H. (2013). *Clash! 8 cultural conflicts that make us who we are*. New York, NY: Penguin Group.

Marshall, S. E., & Read, J. G. (2003). Identity politics among Arab-American women. *Social Science Quarterly, 84,* 875–891. doi:10.1111/%28ISSN%291540-6237/issues

Martinez, A., & Merlino, A. (2014). I don't want to die before visiting Graceland a collaborative autoethnography. *Qualitative Inquiry, 20,* 990–997. doi:10.1177/1077800413513736

Masselot, A., & Bullock, J. (2013). Stuck at the cross-road: Intersectional aspirations in the EU anti-discrimination legal framework. *Australian and New Zealand Journal of European Studies (ANZJES), 2,* 3-16. Retrieved from http://www.eusanz.org/ANZJES/index.html

Matsumoto, D. (2007). Culture, context, and behavior. *Journal of Personality, 75,* 1285-1319. doi:10.1111/j.1467-6494.2007.00476.x

Maydell, E. (2010). Methodological and analytic dilemmas in autoethnographic research. *Journal of Research Practice, 6,* 1-13. Retrieved from http://jrp.icaap.org /index.php/jrp

McDonald, K. E., Keys, C. B., & Balcazar, F. E. (2007). Disability, race/ethnicity and gender: Themes of cultural oppression, acts of individual resistance. *American Journal of Community Psychology, 39,* 145-161. doi:10.1007/s10464-007-9094-3

McGibbon, E., & McPherson, C. (2011). Applying intersectionality & complexity theory to address the social determinants of women's health. *Women's Health & Urban Life, 10,* 59-86. Retrieved from http://www.utsc.utoronto.ca/~socsci/sever/journal /contents3.2.html

McIlveen, P. (2008). Autoethnography as a method for reflexive research and practice in vocational psychology. *Australian Journal of Career Development, 17,* 13-20. doi:10.1177/103841620801700204

McKenzie, C. (2011). *Exploring intersectionality, unravelling interlocking oppression: Feminist non-credit learning practices.* (Doctoral dissertation). Available from ProQuest Dissertations and Theses database. (UMI No. 920160905).

McMahon, B., West, S., Lewis, A., Armstrong, A., & Conway, J. (2004). Hate crimes and disability in America. *Rehabilitation Counseling Bulletin, 47,* 66-75. doi:10.1177/00343552030470020101

McMillan, J. H., & Schumacher, S. (2006). *Research in education: Evidence-based inquiry* (6th ed.). Boston, MA: Allyn & Bacon.

Meekosha, H. (2006). What the hell are you? An intercategorical analysis of race, ethnicity, gender and disability in the Australian body politic. *Scandinavian Journal of Disability Research, 8,* 161-176. doi:10.1080/15017410600831309

Melton, E. N., & Cunningham, G. B. (2014). Examining the workplace experiences of sport employees who are LGBT: A social categorization theory perspective. *Journal of Sport Management, 28,* 21–33. doi:10.1123/jsm.2011-0157

Mercadel-Butler, D. (2007). *Implementing peer coaching in a state funded pre-kindergarten program: An autoethnography* (Doctoral dissertation). Available from ProQuest Dissertations and Theses database. (UMI No. 3261592)

Merritt, R. D., & Harrison, T. W. (2006). Gender and ethnicity attributions to a gender- and ethnicity-unspecified individual: Is there a people = White male bias? *Sex Roles, 54,* 787–797. doi:10.1007/s11199-006-9046-7

Merryfeather, L. (2014). Passionate scholarship or academic safety an ethical issue. *Journal of Holistic Nursing,* 0898010114538320. doi:10.1177/0898010114538320

Mezzich, J. E., Ruiperez, M. A., Yoon, G., Liu, J., & Zapata-Vega, M. I. (2009). Measuring cultural identity: Validation of a modified Cortes, Rogler and Malgady bicultural scale in three ethnic groups in New York. *Culture, Medicine & Psychiatry, 33,* 451-472. doi:10.1007/s11013-009-9142-6

Mich, C. C., & Keillor, B. D. (2011). Ethnic identity: Understanding cultural differences within a culture. *Marketing Management Journal, 21,* 1-9. Retrieved from http://www.mmaglobal.org/jmm.htm

Milner, H. R. (2007). Race, culture, and researcher positionality: Working through the dangers seen, unseen, and unforeseen. *Educational Researcher, 36*, 388-400. doi:10.3102/0013189X07309471

Miller, A. S., & Hoffmann, J. P. (1999). The growing divisiveness: Culture wars or a war of words? *Social Forces, 78*, 721–745. doi:10.2307/3005573

Mills, A. J., Durepos, G., & Wiebe, E. (Eds.). (2010). *Encyclopedia of case study research.* Thousand Oaks, CA: Sage. doi:10.4135/9781412957397

Mizzi, R. (2010). Unraveling researcher subjectivity through multivocality in autoethnography. *Journal of Research Practice, 6,* 1-14. Retrieved from http://jrp.icaap.org/index.php/jrp

Moin, V., Duvdevany, I., & Mazor, D. (2009). Sexual identity, body image and life satisfaction among women with and without physical disability. *Sexuality & Disability, 27,* 83-95. doi:10.1007/s11195-009-9112-5

Moisander, J., & Valtonen, A. (Eds.). (2006). *Qualitative marketing research.* London, England: Sage. doi:10.4135/9781849209632

Molina, N. (2006). Medicalizing the Mexican: Immigration, race, and disability in the early-twentieth-century United States. *Radical History Review, 94,* 22-37. doi:10.1215/01636545-2006-94-22

Molinsky, A. (2007). Cross-cultural code-switching: The psychological challenges of adapting behavior in foreign cultural interactions. *Academy of Management Review, 32,* 622-640. doi:10.5465/AMR.2007.24351878

Moore, A. M., & Barker, G. G. (2012). Confused or multicultural: Third culture individuals' cultural identity. *International Journal of Intercultural Relations, 36,* 553-562. doi:10.1016/j.ijintrel.2011.11.002

Moriizumi, S. (2011). Exploring identity negotiations: An analysis of intercultural Japanese-U.S. American families living in the United States. *Journal of Family Communication, 11,* 85-104. doi:10.1080/15267431.2011.554359

Morris, R. (1993). Modernity's Prometheus. *Western Journal of Communication, 57,* 139-146. Retrieved from http://www.westcomm.org/

Mossman, T. (2012). "They're different from who I am": Making relevant identities in the middle through talk-in-interaction. *TESL Canada Journal, 29,* 103-123. Retrieved from http://eric.ed.gov/?id=EJ989905

Muehlenhard, C. L., & Peterson, Z. D. (2011). Distinguishing between sex and gender: History, current conceptualizations, and implications. *Sex Roles, 64,* 791-803. doi:10.1007/s11199-011-9932-5

Muncey, T. (2005). Doing autoethnography. *International Journal of Qualitative Methods 4,* 1-12. Retrieved from http://www.ualberta.ca/~iiqm/backissues/4_1/pdf/muncey.pdf

Mungo, S. J. (1981). Stress, burnout and culture shock: An experiential, pre-service approach. Retrieved from ERIC database. (ED211490)

Murphy, S. A. (2008). The role of emotions and transformational leadership on police culture: An autoethnographic account. *International Journal of Police Science & Management, 10,* 165–178. doi:10.1350/ijps.2008.10.2.72

Murphy-Keith, R. (2013). Living and leaving Lolita: An autoethnography of identification and transcendence. *Kaleidoscope: A Graduate Journal of Qualitative Communication Research, 12,* 87–105. Available from http://opensiuc.lib.siu.edu

Naples, N. A. (2009). Teaching intersectionality intersectionally. *International Feminist Journal of Politics, 11,* 566-577. doi:10.1080/14616740903237558

Nario-Redmond, M. R. (2010). Cultural stereotypes of disabled and non-disabled men and women: Consensus for global category representations and diagnostic domains. *British Journal of Social Psychology, 49,* 471-488. doi:10.1348/014466609X468411

Neck, C. P., Ashcraft, R. F., & VanSandt, C. V. (1998). Employee self-leadership: Enhancing the effectiveness of nonprofits. *International Journal of Organization Theory & Behavior, 1,* 521-551. Retrieved from http://www.pracademics.com /ijotb.html

Neck, C. P., & Houghton, J. D. (2006). Two decades of self-leadership theory and research: Past developments, present trends, and future possibilities. *Journal of Managerial Psychology, 21,* 270-295. doi:10.1108/02683940610663097

Neck, C. P., & Manz, C. C. (1992). Thought self-leadership: The influence of self-talk and mental imagery on performance. *Journal of Organizational Behavior, 13,* 681-699. doi:10.1002/job.4030130705

Nelson, J. K., Zaccaro, S. J., & Herman, J. L. (2010). Strategic information provision and experiential variety as tools for developing adaptive leadership skills. *Consulting Psychology Journal: Practice and Research, 62,* 131-142. doi:10.1037/a0019989

Nevin, A., Smith, R., & McNeil, M. (2008). Shifting attitudes of related service providers: A disability studies & critical pedagogy approach. *International Journal of Whole Schooling, 4,* 1-12. Available from http://www.wholeschooling.net

Nezlek, J. B., Schütz, A., & Sellin, I. (2007). Self-presentational success in daily social interaction. *Self & Identity, 6,* 361-379. doi:10.1080/15298860600979997

Ngunjiri, F., Hernandez, K. C., & Heewon, C. (2010). Living autoethnography: Connecting life and research. *Journal of Research Practice, 6,* 1-17. Retrieved from http://jrp.icaap.org/index.php/jrp

Nosek, M. A., & Hughes, R. B. (2003). Psychosocial issues of women with physical disabilities: The continuing gender debate. *Rehabilitation Counseling Bulletin, 46,* 224-233. doi:10.1177/003435520304600403

Ochs, M., Niewiadomski, R., Brunet, P., & Pelachaud, C. (2012). Smiling virtual agent in social context. *Cognitive Processing, 13 (Suppl. 2),* S519-S532. doi:10.1007/s10339-011-0424-x

Ojeda, V. D., & Bergstresser, S. M. (2008). Gender, race-ethnicity, and psychosocial barriers to mental health care: An examination of perceptions and attitudes among adults reporting unmet need. *Journal of Health and Social Behavior, 49,* 317-334. doi:10.1177/002214650804900306

Oliver, M. (1986). Social policy and disability: Some theoretical issues. *Disability, Handicap & Society, 1,* 5-17. doi:10.1080/02674648666780021

Oliver, M. (1998). Theories in health care and research: Theories of disability in health practice and research. *British Medical Journal, 317,* 1446-1449. Available from http://www.ncbi.nlm.nih.gov

Oliver, M. (2010). Editorial perspective: Writing qualitative manuscripts. *Journal of Professional Counseling: Practice, Theory & Research, 38,* 1-4. Retrieved from http://www.txca.org

Orbe, M. P., & Drummond, D. K. (2009). Negotiations of the complicitous nature of US racial/ethnic categorization: Exploring rhetorical strategies. *Western Journal of Communication, 73,* 437-455. doi:10.1080/10570310903279091

Ortoleva, S., & Knight, A. (2012). Who's missing? Women with disabilities in U.N. Security Council Resolution 1325 National Action Plans. *ILSA Journal of International & Comparative Law, 18,* 395-412. Retrieved from http://www.nsulaw.nova.edu/orgs/ILSAJournal/index.cfm

Ovadia, S. (2001). Race, class, and gender differences in high school seniors' values: Applying intersection theory in empirical analysis. *Social Science Quarterly (Wiley-Blackwell), 82,* 340-356. Available from http://www.wiley.com

Oxford, W. H. (1977). Monoculturalism versus multiculturalism. *Speech Education, 5,* 1-14. Retrieved from http://facstaff.uww.edu/wca/journals1.html

Ozyurt, S. (2013). Negotiating multiple identities, constructing Western-Muslim selves in the Netherlands and the United States. *Political Psychology, 34,* 239–263. doi:10.1111/j.1467-9221.2012.00924.x

Padilla, L. M. (2001). 'But you're not a dirty Mexican': Internalized oppression, Latinos & Law. *Texas Hispanic Journal of Law & Policy, 7,* 58-113. Retrieved from http://www.utexas.edu/law/journals/thjlp/

Parent, M. C., & DeBlaere, C., & Moradi, B. (2013). Approaches to research on intersectionality: Perspectives on gender, LGBT, and racial/ethnic identities. *Sex Roles, 68,* 639–645. doi:10.1007/s11199-013-0283-2

Park, J. H., Faulkner, J., & Schaller, M. (2003). Evolved disease-avoidance processes and contemporary anti-social behavior: Prejudicial attitudes and avoidance of people with physical disabilities. *Journal of Nonverbal Behavior, 27,* 65-87. doi:10.1023/A:1023910408854

Pearson, H. (2010). Complicating intersectionality through the identities of a hard of hearing Korean adoptee: An autoethnography. *Equity & Excellence in Education, 43,* 341-356. doi:10.1080/10665684.2010.496642

Pearson, E. H. (2012). *A methodological approach to examining racial and ethnic minorities with disabilities: Intersecting and interlocking race/ethnicity, disability, and gender*

(Doctoral dissertation). Available from ProQuest Dissertations and Theses database. (UMI No. 1519195)

Peipina, O. (2009). The role of ethnic identity in the modern multi-ethnic society. *Ethnicity, 2009*(2), 74-92. Retrieved from http://www.du.lv/en

Pelias, R. J. (2000). The critical life. *Communication Education, 49,* 220-228. doi:10.1080/03634520009379210

Pensoneau-Conway, S. L., & Toyosaki, S. (2011). Automethodology: Tracing a home for praxis-oriented ethnography. *International Journal of Qualitative Methods, 10,* 378-399. Available from http://ejournals.library.ualberta.ca

Pereira, R. H. (2012). Rigour in phenomenological research: Reflections of a novice nurse researcher. *Nurse Researcher, 19,* 16-19. Retrieved from http://connection.ebscohost.com/

Pérez Huber, L. (2010). Using Latina/o Critical Race Theory (LatCrit) and Racist Nativism to explore intersectionality in the educational experiences of undocumented Chicana college students. *Educational Foundations, 24,* 77-96. Retrieved from http://eric.ed.gov/?id=EJ885982

Perlmutter, P. (2006). Risk and reluctance in criticizing minorities. *Society, 43,* 39-44. doi:10.1007/BF02687594

Peters, S. (2006). Disability culture. In G. Albrecht (Ed.), *Encyclopedia of disability.* (pp. 413-477). Thousand Oaks, CA: SAGE Publications, Inc. doi:10.4135/9781412950510.n224

Phinney, J. S., & Ong, A. D. (2007). Conceptualization and measurement of ethnic identity: Current status and future directions. *Journal of Counseling Psychology, 54,* 271-281. doi:10.1037/0022-067.54.3.271

Pichon, H. W. (2013). Telling their stories: The use of autoethnography as an instructional tool in an introductory research course. *The Qualitative Report, 18,* 1-8. Retrieved from http://www.nova.edu

Pines, A. M. (2004). Adult attachment styles and their relationship to burnout: A preliminary, cross-cultural investigation. *Work & Stress, 18,* 66-80. doi:10.1080/02678370310001645025

Pines, A., Neal, M. B., Hammer, L. B., & Icekson, T. (2011). Job burnout and couple burnout in dual-earner couples in the sandwiched generation. *Social Psychology Quarterly, 74,* 361-386. doi:10.1177/0190272511422452

Pitts, V. (2005). Feminism, technology and body projects. *Women's Studies, 34,* 229-247. doi:10.1080/00497870590964129

Platero, R. (2008). Outstanding challenges in a post-equality era: The same-sex marriage and gender identity laws in Spain. *International Journal of Iberian Studies, 21,* 41-49. doi:10.1386/ijis.21.1.41/3

Pohlert, E. (2008). *An autoethnography of multiethnicity and identity: Negotiating and shifting perspectives in multiethnic contexts* (Doctoral dissertation). Available from ProQuest Dissertations and Theses database. (UMI No. 3298897)

Pompper, D. (2010). Researcher-researched difference: Adapting an autoethnographic approach for addressing the racial matching issue. *Journal of Research Practice, 6,* 1-16. Retrieved from http://jrp.icaap.org/index.php/jrp

Pope, M., Barret, B., Szymanski, D. M., Chung, Y. B., Singaravelu, H., Mclean, R., & Sanabria, S. (2004). Culturally appropriate career counseling with gay and lesbian clients. *Career Development Quarterly, 53,* 158–177. Available from http://eric.ed.gov

Poulos, C. N. (2014). My father's ghost a story of encounter and transcendence. *Qualitative Inquiry, 20,* 1005–1014. doi:10.1177/1077800414530317

Prince, E. K. (2006). *The heart of leadership: An autoethnographic study of issues that impact education leadership* (Doctoral dissertation). Available from ProQuest Dissertations and Theses database. (UMI No. 3214370)

Purdie-Vaughns, V., & Eibach, R. (2008). Intersectional invisibility: The distinctive advantages and disadvantages of multiple subordinate-group identities. *Sex Roles, 59,* 377-391. doi:10.1007/s11199-008-9424-4

Qin, X. (2011). Multiculturalism in the current American society. *US-China Foreign Language, 9,* 666-672. Retrieved from http://connection.ebscohost.com

QSR International. (2013). NVivo10: Getting started. Retrieved from http://www.qsrinternational.com

Quinn, M. L. (2009). *Autoethnography: My journey from educator to educator-activist* (Doctoral dissertation). Available from ProQuest Dissertations and Theses database. (UMI No. 3320017)

Radley, A., & Taylor, D. (2003). Remembering one's stay in hospital: A study in photography, recovery and forgetting. *Health, 7,* 129-159. doi:10.1177/1363459303007002872

Ramey, M. (2007). Americans With Disabilities Act: A history of rights. *Journal of Philosophy & History of Education, 57,* 128-135. Retrieved from http://www.ebscohost.com/

Ransford, H., & Miller, J. (1983). Race, sex and feminist outlooks. *American Sociological Review, 48,* 46-59. Available from http://www.asanet.org

Reed-Danahay, D. (2009). Anthropologists, education, and autoethnography. *Reviews In Anthropology, 38,* 28-47. doi:10.1080/00938150802672931

Rembis, M. A. (2010). Yes we can change: Disability studies—enabling equality. *Journal of Postsecondary Education & Disability, 23,* 19-27. doi:10.1007/s11195-009-9133-0

Remenyi, D., Grant, K. A., & Pather, S. (2005). The chameleon: A metaphor for the chief information officer. *Journal of General Management, 30,* 1-11. Retrieved from http://www.braybrooke.co.uk

Rees, S., & Pease, B. (2007). Domestic violence in refugee families in Australia: Rethinking settlement policy and practice. *Journal of Immigrant & Refugee Studies, 5,* 1-19. doi:10.1300/J500v05n02_01

Rhodes, M. (2013). How two intuitive theories shape the development of social categorization. *Child Development Perspectives, 7,* 12–16. doi:10.1111/cdep.12007

Ribbens, J., & Edwards, R. (1998). Hearing my feeling voice? An autobiographical discussion of motherhood. In J. Ribbens, & R. Edwards (Eds.), *Feminist dilemmas in qualitative research* (pp. 25-39). London, England: Sage. doi:10.4135/9781849209137.n2

Rigoni, I. (2012). Intersectionality and mediated cultural production in a globalized post-colonial world. *Ethnic & Racial Studies, 35,* 834-849. doi:10.1080/01419870.2011.628035

Riordan, N. O. (2014). Autoethnography: Proposing a new research method for information systems research." *Proceedings of the European Conference on Information Systems (ECIS) 2014*. Retrieved from http://aisel.aisnet.org/ecis2014/proceedings/track03/6

Robertson, T. (2006). Dissonance effects as conformity to consistency norms: The effect of anonymity and identity salience. *British Journal of Social Psychology, 45,* 683-699. doi:10.1348/014466605X82855

Rodríguez-García, D. (2010). Beyond assimilation and multiculturalism: A critical review of the debate on managing diversity. *Journal of International Migration & Integration, 11,* 251-271. doi:10.1007/s12134-010-0140-x

Rohmer, O., & Louvet, E. (2009). Describing persons with disability: Salience of disability, gender, and ethnicity. *Rehabilitation Psychology, 54,* 76-82. doi:10.1037/a0014445

Rondero, V. H., & Mendoza, C. T. (2011). Shame resilience: A strategy for empowering women in treatment for substance abuse. *Journal of Social Work Practice in the Addictions, 11,* 375-393. doi:10.1080/1533256X.2011.622193

Roush, S. E., & Sharby, N. (2011). Disability reconsidered: The paradox of physical therapy. *Physical Therapy, 91,* 1715-1727. doi:10.2522/ptj.20100389

Rudmin, F. W. (2003). Critical history of the acculturation psychology of assimilation, separation, integration, and marginalization. *Review of General Psychology, 7,* 3-37. doi:10.1037/1089-2680.7.1.3

Rule, P., & Modipa, T. (2012). "We must believe in ourselves": Attitudes and experiences of adult learners with disabilities in KwaZulu-Natal, South Africa. *Adult Education Quarterly, 62,* 138-158. doi:10.1177/0741713611400303

Ruwanpura, K. N. (2008). Multiple identities, multiple-discrimination: A critical review. *Feminist Economics, 14,* 77-105. doi:10.1080/13545700802035659

Ryan, G. W., & Bernard, H. R. (2003). Techniques to identify themes. *Field Methods, 15,* 85-109. doi:10.1177/1525822X02239569

Ryan-Nicholls, K., & Will, C. (2009). Rigour in qualitative research: Mechanisms for control. *Nurse Researcher, 16,* 70-85. Retrieved from http://www.nursing-standard.co.uk/

Ryder, A. G., Alden, L. E., & Paulhus, D. L. (2000). Is acculturation unidimensional or bidimensional? A head-to-head comparison in the prediction of personality, self-identity, and adjustment. *Journal of Personality and Social Psychology,79*, 49-65. doi:10.1037/0022-3514.79.1.49

Saayman, T., & Crafford, A. (2011). Negotiating work identity. *SAJIP: South African Journal of Industrial Psychology, 37,* 207-218. doi:10.4102/sajip.v37i1.963

Sacharin, V., Lee, F., & Gonzalez, R. (2009). Identities in harmony: Gender-work identity integration moderates frame switching in cognitive processing. *Psychology of Women Quarterly, 33,* 275–284. Available from http://www.sagepub.com

Salazar, C. F., & Abrams, L. P. (2005). Conceptualizing identity development in members of marginalized groups. *Journal of Professional Counseling: Practice, Theory & Research, 33,* 47–59. Available from http://www.txca.org

Saldaña, J. (2013). *The coding manual for qualitative researchers* (2nd ed.). Thousand Oaks, CA: Sage.

Sambrook, S. A., Jones, N., & Doloriert, C. (2014). Employee engagement and autoethnography: being and studying self. *Journal of Workplace Learning, 26,* 172 – 187. doi:10.1108/JWL-09-2013-0072

Sariyant, T. P. (2002). *Knowing and understanding through auto/ethnography: Narrative on transformative learning experience* (Doctoral dissertation). Available from ProQuest Dissertations and Theses database. (UMI No. 3039391)

Sarkisian, N., & Gerena, M. (2005). Extended family integration among Latinos/as and Euro Americans: Cultural and structural determinants of ethnic differences. *Conference Papers—American Sociological Association,* pp. 1-33. Retrieved from http://www.asanet.org/

Sarkisian, N., Gerena, M., & Gerstel, N. (2007). Extended family integration among Euro and Mexican-Americans: Ethnicity, gender, and class. *Journal of Marriage and Family, 69,* 40–54. doi:10.1111/j.1741-3737.2006.00342.x

Schneider, C. E. (2011). *Running for normalcy, identity development, and the disability blues: An auto-ethnography that explores one man's quest to understand his identity*

(Doctoral dissertation). Available from ProQuest Dissertations and Theses database. (UMI No. 849651428)

Schilbach, L., Eickhoff, S. B., Mojzisch, A., & Vogeley, K. (2008). What's in a smile? Neural correlates of facial embodiment during social interaction. *Social Neuroscience, 3*, 37-50. doi:10.1080/17470910701563228

Schwartz, S. J., & Zamboanga, B. L. (2008). Testing Berry's model of acculturation: A confirmatory latent class approach. *Cultural Diversity & Ethnic Minority Psychology, 14*, 275-285. doi:10.1037/a0012818

Scott, J. A. (2012). "Cripped" heroes: An analysis of physically disabled professionals' personal narratives of performance of identity. *Southern Communication Journal, 77*, 307-328. doi:10.1080/1041794X.2012.673852

Scullion, P. (2010). Models of disability: Their influence in nursing and potential role in challenging discrimination. *Journal of Advanced Nursing, 66*, 697-707. doi:10.1111/j.1365-2648.2009.05211.x

Sedikides, C., & Brewer, M. B. (2001). Individual self, relational self, and collective self: Partner, opponents, or strangers? In C. Sedikides, & M. B. Brewer (Eds.), Individual self, relational self, collective self. (pp. 1-4). Ann Arbor, MI: Psychology Press.

Shank, G. D. (2006). *Qualitative research: A personal skills approach* (2nd ed.) Upper Saddle River, NJ: Pearson Merrill Prentice Hall.

Shankar, A., Elliott, R., & Fitchett, J. A. (2009). Identity, consumption and narratives of socialization. *Marketing Theory, 9*, 75–94. doi:10.1177/1470593108100062

Shaw, L. R. Chan, F., & McMahon, B. T. (2012). Intersectionality and disability harassment: The interactive effects of disability, race, age, and gender. *Rehabilitation Counseling Bulletin, 55*, 82–91. doi:10.1177/0034355211431167

Shen, W., & Dumani, S. (2013). The complexity of marginalized identities: The social construction of identities, multiple identities, and the experience of exclusion. *Industrial & Organizational Psychology, 6*, 84–87. doi:10.1111/iops.12013

Shenton, A. K. (2004). Strategies for ensuring trustworthiness in qualitative research projects. *Education for Information, 22*, 63-75. doi:10.1016/S0740-8188(04)00025-8

Sherr, M., & Montesino, M. (2009). Hate crime based on ethnicity and religion: A description of the phenomenon in the United States since 2000. *International Journal of Diversity in Organisations, Communities & Nations, 9,* 23-37. Retrieved from http://ondiversity.com/publications/journal

Sherry, M. (2006). Identity. In G. Albrecht (Ed.), *Encyclopedia of disability.* (pp. 907-915). Thousand Oaks, CA: SAGE Publications, Inc. doi:10.4135/9781412950510.n430

Shen, W., & Dumani, S. (2013). The complexity of marginalized identities: The social construction of identities, multiple identities, and the experience of exclusion. *Industrial & Organizational Psychology, 6,* 84–87. doi:10.1111/iops.12013

Shibata, S. (2012). Macro-and micro-language learning counseling: An autoethnographic account. *Studies in Self-Access Learning Journal, 3,* 108–121. Retrieved from http://sisaljournal.org

Shinhwan, P. (2006). Pastoral counselling of Korean Clergy with burnout : Culture and narcissism. *Asia Journal of Theology, 20,* 241-255. Retrieved from http://www.library.wisc.edu/guidelines/SEAsia/refbib/pssea.html

Simpson, G. (2010). From inclusion to exclusion: Some unintended consequences of valuing people. *British Journal of Learning Disabilities, 38,* 180-186. doi:10.1111/j.1468-3156.2009.00572.x

Sin, S. (2010). Considerations of quality in phenomenographic research. *International Journal of Qualitative Methods, 9,* 305-319. Retrieved from http://www.ualberta.ca/~iiqm/

Sinclair, S., Hardin, C. D., & Lowery, B. S. (2006). Self-stereotyping in the context of multiple social identities. *Journal of Personality and Social Psychology, 90,* 529-542. doi:10.1037/0022-3514.90.4.529

Smart, J. F. (2009). The power of models of disability. *Journal of Rehabilitation, 75,* 3-11. Retrieved from http://www.nationalrehab.org/website/pubs/index.html

Smith, C. (2005). Epistemological intimacy: A move to autoethnography. *International Journal of Qualitative Methods, 4,* 1-7. doi:10.1177/1094428105280126

Smith, F. W., & Schyns, P. G. (2009). Smile through your fear and sadness: Transmitting and identifying facial expression signals over a range of viewing distances. *Psychological Science, 20*, 1202-1208. doi:10.1111/j.1467-9280.2009.02427.x

Smith, P., & Routel, C. (2010). Transition failure: The cultural bias of self-determination and the journey to adulthood for people with disabilities. *Disability Studies Quarterly, 30*, 1. Retrieved from http://www.dsq-sds.org/

Smith-Sullivan, K. (2008). *The autoethnographic call: Current considerations and possible futures* (Doctoral dissertation). Available from ProQuest Dissertations and Theses database. (UMI No. 304462879)

Söder, M. (2009). Tensions, perspectives and themes in disability studies. *Scandinavian Journal of Disability Research, 11*, 67-81. doi:10.1080/15017410902830496

Song, E. (2009). Coping with intercultural transactions in multicultural societies. *Social Behavior & Personality: An International Journal, 37*, 273-288. doi:10.2224/sbp.2009.37.2.273

Soto, J. A., Armenia, B. E., Perez, C. R., Zamboanga, B. L., Umana-Taylor, A. J., Lee, R. M., . . . Ham, L. S. (2012). Strength in numbers? Cognitive reappraisal tendencies and psychological functioning among Latinos in the context of oppression. *Cultural Diversity & Ethnic Minority Psychology, 18*, 584-594. doi:10.1037/a0029781

Speicher, B. (2010). Multicultural messages in public discourse. *International Journal of Diversity in Organisations, Communities & Nations, 10*, 15-28. Retrieved from http://ondiversity.com/publications/journal

Spry, T. (1995). In the absence of word and body: Hegemonic implications of "victim" and "survivor" in women's narratives of sexual violence. *Women and Language 13*, 1-27. Available from http://search.proquest.com

Spry, T. (2001). Performing autoethnography: An embodied methodological praxis. *Qualitative Inquiry, 7*, 706–732. doi:10.1177/107780040100700605

Stamm, B., Stamm, H. E., Hudnall, A. C., & Higson-Smith, G. (2004). Considering a theory of cultural trauma and loss. *Journal of Loss & Trauma, 9*, 89-111. doi:10.1080/15325020490255412

Staunces, D. (2003). Where have all the subjects gone? Bringing together the concepts of intersectionality and subjectification. *NORA: Nordic Journal of Women's Studies, 11,* 101-110. doi:10.1080/08038740310002950

Stinson, A. B. (2010). *An autoethnography: A mathematics teacher's journey of identity construction and change* (Doctoral dissertation). Available from ProQuest Dissertations and Theses database. (UMI No. 3401616)

Stone, S. D. (2005). Reactions to invisible disability: The experiences of young women survivors of hemorrhagic stroke. *Disability & Rehabilitation, 27,* 293-304. doi:10.1080/09638280400008990

Stow, B. D. (2005). *Examining (my)self: An autoethnographic exploration of cultural identity negotiation* (Master's thesis). Retrieved from http://hdl.handle.net/2346/1040

Strolovitch, D. Z. (2006). Do interest groups represent the disadvantaged? Advocacy at the intersections of race, class, and gender. *Journal of Politics, 68,* 894-910. doi:10.1111/j.1468-2508.2006.00488.x

Struthers, J. (2012). *Analytic autoethnography: A tool to inform the lecturer's use of self when teaching mental health nursing?* (Doctoral dissertation). Available from http://eprints.lancs.ac.uk/62512/

Sultana, A. M. (2011). Measuring gender role identity and awareness among women towards their right in family. *Australian Journal of Basic & Applied Sciences, 5,* 1558-1562. Retrieved from http://connection.ebscohost.com/

Sussman, N. M. (2000). The dynamic nature of cultural identity throughout cultural transitions: Why home is not so sweet. *Personality and Social Psychology Review, 4,* 355-373. doi:10.1207/S15327957PSPR0404_5

Tabak, A., Çelik, M., & Türköz, T. (2011). Self- leadership in public sector. *Interdisciplinary Journal of Contemporary Research in Business, 3,* 114-133. Retrieved from http://connection.ebscohost.com/

Tadmor, C. T., Galinsky, A. D., & Maddux, W. W. (2012). Getting the most out of living abroad: Biculturalism and integrative complexity as key drivers of creative and professional success. *Journal of Personality & Social Psychology, 103,* 520-542. doi:10.1037/a0029360

Tajfel, H. (1982). Social psychology of intergroup relations. *Annual Review of Psychology, 33,* 1-39. doi:10.1146/annurev.ps.33.020182.000245

Tajfel, H., Richardson, A., & Everstine, L. (1964). Individual consistencies in categorizing: A study of judgmental behavior. *Journal of Personality, 32,* 90-108. doi:10.1111/1467-6494.ep8933218

Tanis, M., & Postmes, T. (2005). A social identity approach to trust: Interpersonal perception, group membership and trusting behaviour. *European Journal of Social Psychology, 35,* 413-424. doi:10.1002/ejsp.256

Taub, D. E., McLorg, P. A., & Fanflik, P. L. (2004). Stigma management strategies among women with physical disabilities: Contrasting approaches of downplaying or claiming a disability status. *Deviant Behavior, 25,* 169-190. doi:10.1080/01639620490269012

Tedlock, B. (2005). The observation of participation and the emergence of public ethnography. In N. K. Denzin and Y. S. Lincoln (Eds.), *Handbook of qualitative research* (3rd ed., pp. 467–482). Thousand Oaks, CA: Sage.

Theodorakis, Y., Hatzigeorgiadis, A., & Chroni, S. (2008). Self-talk: It works, but how? Development and preliminary validation of the functions of self-talk questionnaire. *Measurement in Physical Education & Exercise Science, 12,* 10-30. doi:10.1080/10913670701715158

Thomas, E., & Magilvy, J. (2011). Qualitative rigor or research validity in qualitative research. *Journal for Specialists in Pediatric Nursing, 16,* 151-155. doi:10.1111/j.1744-6155.2011.00283.x

Thunman, E. (2012). Burnout as a social pathology of self-realization. *Distinktion: Scandinavian Journal of Social Theory, 13,* 43-60. doi:10.1080/1600910X.2012.648744

Thyer, B. A. (Ed.). (2001). *The Handbook of Social Work Research Methods.* Thousand Oaks, CA: Sage. doi:10.4135/9781412986182

Tindongan, C. W. (2012). *"What are you?" Exploring the lived identity experiences of Muslim immigrant students in U.S. public school* (Doctoral dissertation). Available from ProQuest Dissertations and Theses database. (UMI No. 1034458767)

213

Tolich, M. (2010). A critique of current practice: Ten foundational guidelines for autoethnographers. *Qualitative Health Research, 20,* 1599–1610. doi:10.1177/1049732310376076

Torres, L., & Rollock, D. (2009). Psychological impact of negotiating two cultures: Latino coping and self-esteem. *Journal of Multicultural Counseling and Development, 37,* 219-228. doi:10.1002/j.2161-1912.2009.tb00104.x

Torres, V., Martinez, S., Wallace, L. D., Medrano, C. I., Robledo, A. L., & Hernandez, E. (2012). The connections between Latino ethnic identity and adult experiences. *Adult Education Quarterly, 62,* 3-18. doi:10.1177/0741713610392765

Trahan, A. (2011). Qualitative research and intersectionality. *Critical Criminology, 19,* 1-14. doi:10.1007/s10612-010-9101-0

Trahar, S. (2009). Beyond the story itself: Narrative inquiry and autoethnography in intercultural research in higher education. *Forum Qualitative Sozialforschung / Forum: Qualitative Social Research, 10* Retrieved from http://www.qualitative-research.net

Turnbull, H. R., & Stowe, M. J. (2001). Five models for thinking about disability: Implications for policy responses. *Journal of Disability Policy Studies, 12,* 198-205. doi:10.1177/104420730101200305

Tuura, B. M. (2012). *Tensions within teaching: An autoethnography of an American teacher* (Doctoral dissertation). Available from ProQuest Dissertations and Theses database. (UMI No. 3554603)

Tyrrell, Z. (2010). A cognitive behavioural model for maintaining processes in burnout. *Cognitive Behaviour Therapist, 3,* 18-26. doi:10.1017/S1754470X10000024

Ungvari, G., Mullen, P., & Sandor, G. (2000). Reactive psychoses revisited. *Australian & New Zealand Journal of Psychiatry, 34,* 458-467. doi:10.1046/j.1440-1614.2000.00752.x

Unsworth, K. L., & Mason, C. M. (2012). Help yourself: The mechanisms through which a self-leadership intervention influences strain. *American Psychological Association, 17,* 235-245. doi:10.1037/a0026857

Van Herk, K. A., Smith, D., & Andrew, C. (2011). Examining our privileges and oppressions: Incorporating an intersectionality paradigm into nursing. *Nursing Inquiry, 18,* 29-39. doi:10.1111/j.1440-1800.2011.00539.x

Van House, N. A. (2011). Personal photography, digital technologies and the uses of the visual. *Visual Studies, 26,* 125-134. doi:10.1080/1472586X.2011.571888

Verkuyten, M. (2006). Multicultural recognition and ethnic minority rights: A social identity perspective. *European Review of Social Psychology, 17,* 148-184. doi:10.1080/10463280600937418

Verkuyten, M., & de Wolf, A. (2002). Ethnic minority identity and group context: Self-descriptions, acculturation attitudes and group evaluations in an intra- and intergroup situation. *European Journal of Social Psychology, 32,* 781-800. doi:10.1002/ejsp.121

Verkuyten, M., & deWolf, A. (2002a). Being, feeling and doing: Discourses and ethnic self-definitions among minority group members. *Culture & Psychology, 8*(4), 371–399. doi:10.1177/1354067X0284001

Vicent, R., Sanz, B., & Mocha, M. (2009). Efecto camaleón. El arte de gestionar la diversidad [Chameleon effect: The art of negotiating diversity]. *Psychosocial Intervention/Intervencion Psicosocial, 18,* 47-55. Retrieved from http://www.copmadrid.org/

Viggiani, P. A., Charlesworth, L., Hutchison, E. D., & Faria, D. (2005). Utilization of contemporary literature in human behavior and social justice coursework. *Social Work Education, 24,* 57-96. doi:10.1080/0261547052000324991

Vivero, V., & Jenkins, S. (1999). Existential hazards of the multicultural individual: Defining and understanding 'cultural homelessness. *Cultural Diversity and Ethnic Minority Psychology, 5,* 6-26. doi:10.1037/1099-9809.5.1.6

Voigts, J. (2009). *International sojourns and acquired disabilities as intercultural experiences: A journey of personal transformation* (Doctoral dissertation). Available from ProQuest Dissertations and Theses database. (UMI No. 304140989)

Wall, S. (2006). An autoethnography on learning about autoethnography. *International Journal of Qualitative Methods, 5,* 1-12. Retrieved from http://www.ualberta.ca

Wall, S. (2008). Easier said than done: Writing an autoethnography. *International Journal of Qualitative Methods, 7,* 38-53. Retrieved from http://www.ualberta.ca

Walters, K., & Auton-Cuff, F. (2009). A story to tell: The identity development of women growing up as third culture kids. *Mental Health, Religion & Culture, 12,* 755-772. doi:10.1080/13674670903029153

Wang, C. C. (1999). Photovoice: A participatory action research strategy applied to women's health. *Journal of Women's Health, 8,* 185-192. doi:10.1089/jwh.1999.8.185

Ward, C., & Rana-Deuba, A. (1999). Acculturation and adaptation revisited. *Journal of Cross-Cultural Psychology, 30,* 422–442. doi:10.1177/0022022199030004003

Ward, C. (2008). Thinking outside the Berry boxes: New perspectives on identity, acculturation and intercultural relations. *International Journal of Intercultural Relations, 32,* 105-114. doi:10.1016/j.ijintrel.2007.11.002

Ward, C., Bochner, S., & Furnham, A. (2001). *The psychology of culture shock* (2nd Ed.). Philadelphia, PA: Routledge.

Ward, C., Stuart, J., & Kus, L. (2011). The construction and validation of a measure of ethno-cultural identity conflict. *Journal of Personality Assessment, 93,* 462–473. doi:10.1080/00223891.2011.558872

Warner, D., & Brown, T. (2010). The intersectionality of race/ethnicity and gender in age-trajectories of disability. *Conference Papers—American Sociological Association,* pp. 1852. doi:10.1016/j.socscimed.2011.02.034

Warner, L., & Shields, S. (2013). The intersections of sexuality, gender, and race: Identity research at the crossroads. *Sex Roles, 68,* 803–810. doi:10.1007/s11199-013-0281-4

Warren, J. T. (2001). Absence for whom? An autoethnography of white subjectivity. *Cultural Studies/Critical Methodologies, 1,* 36-49. doi:10.1177/153270860100100104

Warren, J. (2009). Autoethnography. In S. Littlejohn, & K. Foss (Eds.), *Encyclopedia of Communication Theory.* (pp. 69-70). Thousand Oaks, CA: SAGE Publications, Inc. doi:10.4135/9781412959384.n25

Weathers, M. R. (2012). *Using photovoice to communicate abuse: A co-cultural theoretical analysis of communication factors related to digital dating abuse.* Available from ProQuest Dissertations and Theses database. (UMI No. 1015033765)

Willem, H. (2009). Family matters: Community, ethnicity, and multiculturalism. *Church History and Religious Culture, 89,* 53-63. doi:10.1163/187124109X407998

Williams, C. B. (2005). Counseling African American women: Multiple identities--Multiple constraints. *Journal of Counseling & Development, 83,* 278–283. doi:10.1002/j.1556-6678.2005.tb00343.x

Willis, J. W. (2007). *Foundations of qualitative research: Interpretive and critical approaches.* Thousand Oaks, CA: Sage.

Wong, B. (2010). Accommodating disadvantaged cultural minorities. *At the Interface/Probing the Boundaries, 73,* 109-135. Retrieved from http://www.rodopi.nl

Wortley, S. (2003). Hidden intersections: Research on race, crime, and criminal justice in Canada. *Canadian Ethnic Studies, 35,* 99-117. Retrieved from http://www.umanitoba.ca/publications/ces/

Yassour-Borochowitz, D. (2012). "Only if she is sexy": An autoethnography of female researcher-male participants relations. Equality, Diversity and Inclusion: An International Journal, 31, 402-417. doi:10.1108/02610151211235433

Yilmaz, I. (2001). Law as chameleon: The question of incorporation of Muslim personal law into the English law. *Journal of Muslim Minority Affairs, 21,* 297-308. doi:10.1080/1360200120092879

Yoon, E. (2011). Measuring ethnic identity in the Ethnic Identity Scale and the Multigroup Ethnic Identity Measure-Revised. *Cultural Diversity and Ethnic Minority Psychology, 17,* 144-155. doi:10.1037/a0023361

Young, I. M. (1990). *"Five Faces of Oppression."* From *Justice and the Politics of Difference.* Princeton, NJ: Princeton University Press.

Zaharna, R. S. (1989). Self-shock: The double-binding challenge of identity. *International Journal of Intercultural Relations, 13,* 501-525. doi:10.1016/0147-1767(89)90026-6. Available from www.sciencedirect.com

Zaykowski, H. (2010). Racial disparities in hate crime reporting. *Violence and Victims, 25,* 378-394. doi:10.1891/0886-6708.25.3.378

Zotero. (n.d.). Grab your research with a single click. Retrieved from https://www.zotero.org/

Appendix A

Life Story Interview Labovian Approach

Andrews et al. (2008) discussed the Labovian approach including an abstract (A), an orientation (O), a complicating action (CA), a result (R), an evaluation (E), and a coda (C) will guide the data collection for this qualitative analytic autoethnography.

Abstract. What is my story about? How does my story begin? What happened in Mexico that motivated me to immigrate? What happened in the United States after I immigrated? What happened during social interactions?

Orientation. Why are my experiences interacting with different cultures important enough to be shared? Who influenced me to behave as a cultural chameleon? Where do I behave as a cultural chameleon? When do I believe I need to mix behaviors? Why do I think is important to make my privacy public? Who are benefiting from my disclosure?

Complicating action. What do I think are the benefits of mixing behaviors? What barriers did I overcome by mixing behaviors? How did I manage discrimination, stigmatization, or rejection by mixing behaviors? How and why mixing behaviors play as a shield or bubble to protect achieving my dreams and goals.

Evaluation. How would my life be today if I had not mixed behaviors? How did I manage my inner emotions when I noticed I needed to mix behaviors? How did I know I needed to mix behaviors? How did I learn that mixing behaviors could be a strategy to overcome social barriers? How and why did I keep my behavior of mixing identities as a sealed personal secret? How people acted or re-acted when noticed I mixed behaviors? How did I respond to people when they noticed I mixed behaviors?

Result. Why do I continue mixing behaviors during social situations? How is mixing behaviors easier now than before? What did I gain by mixing behaviors? What did I lose by mixing behaviors? What happened during mixing behaviors that I believe my feelings and emotions are vulnerable today? How do I know that my feelings and emotions are stronger and not weaker? How perceiving the need of mixing behaviors during social interactions has affected my trust on other people? What did I achieve by mixing behaviors?

Coda. Where do I perceive myself now compared to before mixing behaviors? What could have happened if I did not mix behaviors? Why do I want to continue mixing behaviors during social interactions? What does mixing behaviors represent for me now compared when I did not know about mixing behaviors as a strategy to continue my path in life?

Appendix B

Labovian Life Story Interview

DataSet_1

Abstract

What is my story about?

I am a woman with physical disabilities, a polio survivor, who uses a wheelchair for her self-sufficiency. I am humble sharing my cultural experiences. I am not superior or a victim or I want to neither censure nor blame anyone, this is my story. It will not be difficult to image my successes and failures through life based on my visible disability. It will be hard to understand my journey interconnecting my cultures --as an immigrant with disabilities-- with the American disability culture. But it will be harder if not impossible to comprehend how I dealt with conflicts and stresses emerging when multiple cultures crossed influencing me and my life's trajectory as an adult with multiple cultures. My story is about the multiple cultures I represent, their intersectionality, and how I behave during social interactions.

How does my story begin?

I was born average, as an able-body baby. At two years of age, my life and the life of all around me changed suddenly. I was diagnosed with poliomyelitis, which paralyzed my body from the neck down. Poliomyelitis is a virus caused by polioviruses originating paralysis, known as paralytic poliomyelitis or polio for short.

According to some relatives who witnessed my setback, after I received the polio vaccination, the paralyzing virus infected me. After the contagion, medical experts argued that many children did not show any symptoms or illness, but the child could have had high temperature making his or her body weak. The body's weakness allowed the virus to evolve and move rapidly leaving muscle atrophy, without sensory, affecting larger motor neurons of spinal cord and medulla. In my case, according to my relatives, I was playing at a park, I tumbled and lost physical mobility, but they remembered that, few days earlier, I had some symptoms similar to having a cold with fever. Agreeing to their recalling, I want to believe

220

that the fever of my "cold" took the virus around my entire body leaving me totally paralyzed.

There are other speculations about how I acquired my disability. One story indicated that I was a victim of witchcraft done by some relatives who not accepted my existence as blood related; according to this story, I was a baseborn child. Other story involves a provoked accident where a group of children, relatives, upset at my existence jumped, all at the same time, on top of my small body causing spine damage.

There are different stories, but the only one I accept, as a fact, based on scientific and medical studies, is that I was infected with polio at age of two. After four years of surgeries, physical therapy, and training, half of my body reestablished, but my legs did not respond, leaving me dependent on braces, crutches, and finally on a wheelchair. I acquired a disability –according to who witnessed it.

Although I have had the disability almost all my life, I did not see myself as "disabled" or having a disability, as bicultural, or as multicultural. I had a regular childhood with other children with and without disabilities, with struggles and accomplishments, and excitements and troubles, as any child might experience. I never thought or occurred to me that I wanted to be "normal" or to be like everybody else around me. I saw myself as a person, with a difference, but such difference was not a major aspect of who I was, I was me –Cecilia.

During my childhood and adolescence, I had issues such as pleasing people, searching for love, to be liked, to be loved, to be accepted, and to fit-in. During a few years of my teen age, I drank, consumed drugs, smoked, and faced three suicidal attempts. I did not relate those behaviors to my disability, I thought my conduct was the result of abandonment, the violence I witnessed, or the rejection I faced for being a baseborn child. Many people call this behavior as denial, but based on my own perception, it was just life, I never thought it was because of my disability.

221

I can say that I never looked for normality because I did not see my disability as an aspect of abnormality. Yes. I went to three schools specially designed for children with disabilities, but I never questioned the reasons of attending those schools. I finished pre-college and I graduated as a computer programmer with "normal" people. I interacted with both people with and without disabilities –I was like everybody else, I thought.

In my childhood, I learned different skills at school and after school. I learned oil painting, pencil drawing, play guitar, different crafts as crocheting, knitting, ceramics, and many other skills designed to survive for people with disabilities. I think the schools I attended were designed to prepare students with disabilities to do different types of crafts and other skills not only as a hobby but also as a way for survival.

During my adolescence, I achieved a category of one of the best wheelchair basketball players in Mexico. Yes. The team players were people with disabilities only. I could not walk and I wanted to play then that was my place. Later on, I became part of the national Mexican team representing my country in a couple of Pan Americans (i.e., Halifax, Canada and Mayaguez, Puerto Rico), and I was selected to participate in two Paralympics, but I missed those opportunities. I had an accident while training for the Paralympics games and I was failing the class of chemistry –I had a life like everybody else.

I also participated in nationals, statewide, and local competitions and won several medals for different sports as tennis table, javelin throw, discus throw, and other sports, not just basketball.

I loved sports like any other sports person would do. I had hundreds of gold, silver, and bronze medals or first, second, and third place, although I piled them up in a box in Mexico, I really did not care keeping them as part of my memories, except for two -the bronze medals I received in Canada and Puerto Rico with my basketball team.

My family did not attend any of my local or national games, except for one sibling. I was a troubled teen, and my relatives preferred not to face the embarrassment they could have encountered if they were part of my support team. The medals I had won were for me only; they did not have any sentimental or emotional value. I had them in a box and later I gave them away or trashed them.

Later on, still in my teen age, I experienced discrimination, biases, and prejudices based on my wheelchair or the disability, but I kept moving on or forward. I remember my best friend's cousin, teen ager also, kept calling me on the phone, and we ended chatting for hours. I can say that it was a phone-date, until he asked meeting me in person. When we met, he was disillusioned, he could not believe that I had a disability and I had to use a wheelchair; he terminated "the dating relationship" accusing me of hiding the truth from him.

In our phone conversations, I did not mention my disability because, first, I thought my best friend had told him about it, and second, it never occurred to me that my disability could be an issue in such a romantic and loving relationship. It was not like "don't ask, don't tell" or "hiding the truth" it was just not necessary – I thought. He never talked to me again, he avoided even crossing to my pathway, and my best friend did the same, he ended a wonderful friendship of several years.

Before he broke our friendship, I asked him for the reasons he did not disclose my disability to his cousin, and he responded that he did not think it was necessary. His cousin was happy, I was happy, triggering happiness for him too. Later, I found out the reason he ended our friendship. His family pressured him to break our friendship because they did not know I had a disability either. Such experience could be defined as a very disturbing experience by many people, but for me was like, "Oh well!" Yes. I felt bad and cried because I missed him, I do not remember crying because he did not accept me the way I was.

During the four years attending pre-college, I was the only person using a wheelchair. I was popular, funny, and loved. I also like to cut classes, which got me in trouble many times.

223

Everybody in the school liked me, respected me, and supported me. The school administration made the school accessible for me. The school was an old building, and historic building, and it was not accessible for people using a wheelchair. The administration staff built some ramps for me, and my classes that supposed to be in the second floor were rescheduled to be in the first floor. If I had a special class in the second level and the teacher could not change the class to the lower floor, my classmates would take me (a group of strong men) up and down the stairs.

I had a team making my school days enjoyable and possible because if I would not have them, my education story would be much more different. I graduated thanks to my love for education and thanks to my classmates who thought me the meaning of teamwork, the necessity of self-leadership, and that being different did not have to be a barrier for friendship, a drama, or a tragic experience. After we graduated, we planned attending the UNAM (Universidad Autónoma de México) together, but after my father denied any type of support for me to attend UNAM, we took different paths. My team of classmates continued their education as doctors and attorneys, and I attended a short career as computer programmer.

Few years later, I needed to make some income to survive and to support my family, but the discrimination, multiple and varied, pushed me to find odd jobs for women. I became the first woman with and without disabilities to work as shoe shining in Mexico –the entire country not just in the City. Becoming the first shoe shiner, I believed, I opened doors for various women with or without disabilities to become economic independent, but it came with its own story of difference of treatment.

My mother, one older sibling, and I supplicated and bought out the leader to allow me joining the shoe shiners group, but I had an intense restriction. I was not allowed in the meetings, reunions, or anything that required being present, including stepping into the office to pay my fees. The union's leader sent a "special" group to collect the fees I needed to pay for my spot.

He stated that it was embarrassing for him, and for the group of shoe shiners, to have a "wheelchaired invalid" one in the group.

Although, his group did not accept women, my gender was not the issue; the issue was the wheelchair embarrassed him or them. According to him, if people saw me as part of the shoe shiners, the group could lose reputation, business, and allies. I was a bad icon for the group. After becoming a shoe shiner many people, including my former pre-college classmates, did not want to shake my "filthy" hand or to be seen with me or turned around to avoid me. I did not care because those former classmates were not part of my team. I never saw my team again. I am not sure how I would do or not do if my team rejected me too for being a shoe shiner.

Few months later, during the day, I did shoe shining and at night, I panhandled pleading for money with a group of friends with different disabilities. When I asked for money, I did not tell people that I needed the money to support my family or that I could not get a job as computer programmer. People saw the wheelchair and assumed whatever they wanted to assume. I had the education, the wiliness, the desire, and the wheelchair too. I did not need to explain anything because people saw the wheelchair and assumed whatever they believed. The discrimination against people with disabilities in Mexico stopped my opportunities for employment.

While begging for money, I saw the opportunity to enroll at UNAM to continue my education. I thought I could go to school after or before shoe shinning, in the evenings or mornings, and I could pay for my school supplies with the money collected by panhandling. I went to UNAM to visit campus and to find options in case I needed some help getting into the buildings or to attend my classes. I found some difficulties with transportation, accessibility, and time, but I decided that I was going back to school to become a Medical Examiner, but I never thought about the accessibility problems when doing the actual work. The university was not accessible or adaptable to my physical needs. I postponed my plans to return to school because I needed to think about a different career that would allow me to have less problems learning and performing with my wheelchair.

What happened in Mexico that motivated me to immigrate?

My troubled attitude and my need to solicit money on the streets, forced my mother to toss me out of Mexico. I needed to "visit" my father and share my bad behaviors and the consequences with him. I remember I promised to myself not only that I would try to make a meaning of my new experiences, but also I told to my internal 'I' that I would go back home if things did not work for me. In a wheelchair, I survived 25 years in the third largest city of the world; I could make another 25 with no problems, and I would go return to school.

In 1989, one of my brothers and I emigrated from Mexico the United States. It was easier than we were told it would be. There were three options for us, first, getting permission either to enter to the new country or second, to enter illegally by crossing the river –el Rio Grande. The third option was to cross the border legally with a relative. We needed a passport and a visa to cross the border. After a long talk, we agreed that crossing illegally was not an option because my wheelchair was very heavy and would sink crossing the Rio Grande and too old to take days of pushing. If the wheelchair did not make it, meant, I would not make it either. My brother and I did not want to leave our country and we made all possible excuses. If our only option were to cross illegally, crossing the Rio Grande, we would do it, if we wanted to emigrate. The wheelchair issue was more an excuse and way of feeling safe than a safety issue.

We decided to travel with our relative and we aimed for authorization by going to the American embassy. We were afraid going there because many told us that in order to enter to the United States we had to have money, assets, education, and a secured place to live –we had none. Some people said that because of my wheelchair, it would be harder to obtain a tourist or student visa because the United States' society thought disabled immigrants were a burden to their country. We decided to try anyway because crossing the border illegally was not an option –for us. We were hoping the American embassy would deny any type of entrance for us.

One Monday, early in the morning, we arrived to the American embassy to meet with the relative we were traveling, and surprised we saw hundreds of people in line and many more arriving. Some people even had tents and blankets, as they spent the night there saving their spot in line. We were, probably, the number 350 in line or worse. But right after we found our right spot in line, we saw a woman waving to us from a place inside the embassy. She gestured to approach her.

We asked someone else to watch our spot then we went to see what she needed from us. Concerned, we wondered if did something wrong. She asked us the reason we were there, we explained our motives, and few minutes later, we had a tourist visa with no expiration date. We could enter to America and stay as long as we wanted or until our passport expired. We went back in line to thank the person watching our space and we left the American embassy with a passport and a visa in less than 10 minutes. Our relative could not believe we got our visa without her presence and signature. In February of 1989, we took a taxi to the bus station to start our journey to the United States of America. It was easy enough for me to think, "Things happen for a reason."

What happened in the United States after I immigrated?
My life has offered constant positive and negative encounters before and after I immigrated to the land of opportunities. Although, in pre-college I learned about identities, cultures, multiculturalism, and the meaning of "I," I was not aware that, in some point of my life, I could experience struggles and pressures emerging from several and different expectations based on multicultural relationships. I was not aware that when a person immigrates onto a new cultural experience, uncertainty emerges if the person cannot or does not want to cope or adapt to the new culture. I did not have any idea about ambiguity or the need of coping skills. I only knew that, when the bus crossed the border between United States and Mexico, I felt homesick, and then my story of cultural intersections suddenly emerged.

When I arrived to the United States my first experience was that, I was not welcomed. The apartment I supposed to stay had several stairs. The bedroom and bathroom were in the second floor, and the kitchen and living room in the lower floor. The apartment was so small that it was difficult for me to enter and harder to move around with my wheelchair. I felt sad and homesick; I wanted to run back to Mexico, to my home. I felt some tears trying to escape from my eyes, but I did not allow myself to cry. Less than two weeks passed when my "hostess" moved to an apartment in a second floor with no elevator, and where my chair did not fit. The change between apartments was from bad to worse. I experienced blatant rejection.

During my first weeks after I arrived to the Unites States, I noticed some behaviors that seemed strange to me but I thought it was my unfamiliarity to town. I did not know many people, and the few relatives I had here were not close to me since my birth. I was a baseborn child, the result of a horrible immorality, to make it worse, I had a visible disability, and they preferred to keep me away, far away from them. I wanted to believe that those rejecting behaviors were my imagination or my personal perception because I was homesick. I missed my home, and I was somewhat defensive. I questioned those strange behaviors and I began blaming them to my imagination. I was being a drama –I thought.

What happened during social interactions?
When I started socializing was because I accompanied to my brother to his activities. He liked attending the Catholic Church in Mexico City, and then when we arrived here, we started attending the Catholic mass; actually, I accompanied him just to avoid being alone at "home" and to meet some people in town. I was not a church person.

Although the mass was in Spanish, for the Latino and Hispanic community, something seemed odd because people behaved toward me as if I came from another planet. As if, they never saw a woman in a wheelchair. Some people were singing the mass while staring at my wheelchair, too many people staring. It was more than uncomfortable. I remember my sibling

228

telling me in Spanish, "No les hagas caso manita" ("Do not put attention, sis"), because the gazing distressed me.

For some people I was the invalid Chilanga, for others I was the "poor thing" some preferred to stay away from me as if I had a contagious illness, and others totally ignored me. Although I was friendly, said hi to people, and smiled, when my brother was not with me, I was alone, isolated, and few people crossed some words with me. I did not want to go there anymore. I felt like trapped in a cage, like in a circus, where people can look at the caged freak saying hi to them. I had better things to do or better places for me to encounter rejection. I stopped going.

Roughly, two years after I immigrated to America and I wanted to learn sign language at the same time I was learning English, I encountered my position as a multicultural person when I met with a disability service provider. The consultation lasted more than 45 minutes, but this is what I synthetized from the meeting, "…a woman in a wheelchair who emigrated from Mexico cannot learn sign language because of her physical limitations and strong accent. More opportunities will develop when she attends English as second language (ESL). The local Latino or Hispanics services will provide her with relevant information…" There, I learned something that struck my truth. The awareness not only gave me goosebumps but also located me in an unknown personal authenticity. I became aware that being multicultural was an issue.

I needed to learn English. I needed to communicate with people other than Spanish speakers. I signed up to take classes in the morning, afternoon, and evenings, and when I did not have classes a mentor was assigned to me. It took me about two or three months to communicate in English, limited, but I did not need an interpreter. A local newspaper and an organization providing services for people with disabilities noticed my determination to learn and invited me to be part of a disability awareness program. A newspaper and a governmental organization preparing a documentary interviewed me and videotaped my regular day activities with other people with disabilities.

229

About the same time, I was helping a woman to set up appointments for her to sell her product. I worked from home making phone calls inviting people to listen to her presentation and her product. She was beautiful, smart, well educated, and determined to get what she wanted. She told me that her dad was African American and her mother Hispanic. She was the first Hispanic-African American person I had met in the U.S.

One morning she arrived to my apartment, had a newspaper in her hand, and tossed it on my table. She said, "Did you see this shit?" I opened the newspaper and I saw my picture. I felt so proud, happy, exciting that I was making history in this country. I asked her, "What shit? Do not you think this is good?" She responded, "No. This is bull shit! They picture you as an idiot, ignorant idiot, coming from Mexico. They said you were just dumb there, but coming here, you have become a brilliant star! Smart, intelligent, an example, an inspiration... full of shit!"

I told her that I did not read that and I asked her to explain what the article really said about me. Her answer was somewhat despicable telling me that I would not understand it even if it were in my language indicating that it was my ego. She suggested calling the newspaper and complaining about the article, which I did, but later called them apologizing and explaining that my limited English helped me to misunderstand their article about me.

When I shared her behavior and comments about the newspaper article with some of my classmates, their comments puzzled me even more. I remember one of them saying, "Creo que estas confundida. Estas pensando en lo que tú "amiga" o "jefa" te dijo. Creo que está equivocada, a lo mejor celosa... envidia. Lo único que quiero decirte es que debes de tener en cuenta de que aquí tu peor enemigo son los Mexicanos, los Chicanos, y claro los mixtos (I think you are confused. You are thinking about what your "friend" or "boss" told you. I think she is wrong, perhaps, jealous... envious. The only thing I want to tell you is that you must be aware that your worst enemy here are Mexicans, Chicanas, and of course, mixed)." Her comment seemed out of place because she was from Mexico as well, and I could not grasp what she meant by her comment.

Another classmate interrupted her saying, "¡Los mixtos son malos! ¡Están enojados con cualquiera que se les ponga al frente! ¡Aguas!" (Mixed are bad! They are angry with anyone who steps in front of them! Watch out!)" My other classmate continued saying, "Eres nueva aquí, en América y estas luchando fuerte. No escuches. ¡Los Mexicanos le echan tierra a los mismos Mexicanos! ¡Solo acuérdate! (You are new here, in America, and you are working hard. Do not listen. Mexicans pour dirt over Mexicans! Remember that!)" I listened to their words, but I doubted what they were saying because, in my perception, it was impossible that a woman so smart, educated, and pretty, would want to hurt me.

After such experience with the newspaper article, when the documentary was released and aired I did not show it to anyone. If people saw it on the news or somewhere else was OK but I did not show it nor discussed it, I felt disempowered and afraid of the possible comments or responses. My family watched it through the local news, but I did not discuss about it –I did hide it.

After analyzing my classmates' comments, "… be aware… your worst enemies… are other Mexicans, Chicanas… mixed are angry… watch out… Mexicans pour dirt over Mexicans…" something saddened deep inside of me. I understood that strange people's behavior I could not understand. The people's behavior I had have faced for many months, but I thought it was me feeling melancholic, lonely, sad, and needed to go back home –my country. It was not me; something unfamiliar was happening around me, in my new environment. I perceived that I was meeting angry people. I was entering into an angry culture, an unfamiliar territory for me.

During my social interactions I have heard people telling me that I am not smart or intelligent, or an example, or an inspiration, or that my activities were not doing any favor to my fellow Americans. I have had numerous experiences including people refusing to shake

231

my hand and calling me "loser" "fucking Mexican." Some people (Hispanics or Latinos) intimidated me saying that I needed to hide to avoid the "migra" (immigration officers) or I would be deported. Some suggested not speaking Spanish in front of strangers or not speaking Spanish at all. Some advised me to tell people that I was Native American who lived in an Indian reservation all my life.

I remember concluding a training to become employed (actually it was my first official job within the US) and the person working with me said that the best place she could place me was within a factory because, according to her, I had no skills, did not speak English enough to work in an office, and I had limited qualifications. She said that my best option was to talk to "business or organizations run by my own people" asking them to hire me. I was not sure who were my own. I did not speak a perfect English, but enough to have a professional conversation, I was a computer savvy knowing more than just turning the computer off or on, and I was a quick learner with teaching skills, but that did not count for her. I needed to ask to my own people to hire me.

I shared my experience with a White man with physical disabilities who used a wheelchair as well and he told me to file a formal complaint. His argument was that I was not helping the disability movement taking shit (as he mentioned) from service providers. According to him, I needed to do something about it, and my best option was to file a lawsuit.

I tried to explain to him that filing lawsuits would not be an option for me, mainly because I would spend my entire life filing to correct too many behaviors. I also explained that I like to educate people instead of complaining. He was very upset indicating that if I did not do anything about it, they (perpetrators) would do the same to them –Americans with disabilities.

I told him that I agreed with the theory that this country was the land of lawsuits but not for me because I had too many social classifications and I would not have success with any claims. When I explained my social categorizations as being Mexican, Latina or Hispanic, in a wheelchair, woman, immigrant, and brown, he mentioned my accent, which I had forgotten, but he was right, my accent falls into a different minority.

He knew about my concerns and that I did not have a chance to win a case, but he did not understand the intersection of those social categorizations. He continued arguing with me and bringing other interesting topics to the conversation. One topic was when I had the opportunity to participate in a phone conference with the President of the United States, at that time Mr. Bill Clinton.

My friend highlighted that Americans with disabilities gave me the opportunity of my life talking to the President and I had failed. Yes. I had a phone conference with Mr. Clinton, but my perception is that the people, who invited me or put me in such challenging situation, as talking to a President of a nation, set me up for failure. I did not have much interaction or knowledge about disabilities within the US, and I did not have a mentor or guidance to tell me what "they" were expecting from me. I feel like they tried to prove me stupid or worse.

I feel, now and then, as if someone (or too many) wanted to mold me as they pleased. I was like the immigrant doll that needed to be "fixed" or "rescued" to acculturate and by molding her as clay was their only idea. He complaint, more than once, about my strong accent highlighting my "fucked ups" (as he said) during the phone conference.

In the argument, I perceived the intersection of my cultures because I was not sure where the next attack would be based on. He had options to choose from to continue and to base his complaints, if it was not my immigration status or my accent; it was my gender and my ethnicity; my social status and my disability, or whatever he wanted to bring to the table.

In another time a similar situation was ready to happen with another White man in a wheelchair, I kept quiet, and smiled at him trying to bring the best of me. I mixed behaviors to avoid explaining my situation, the cultural intersection, and my feelings about it. I remember it worked because he changed the conversation. After those experiences, I adopted

233

to mix behaviors when I could not or did not want to argue about my own life with someone else.

Other interactions have included telling me, politely, that I embarrassed them, that I am a token, that some jobs were "specially" developed for me because of my tokenism, and I have been called a "wannabe." Other comments included that because of my disability God sent people to help me, that I am a burden, or that I always need physical help and emotional support. For some people I am a broken doll, for others I am suffering, and for others I am the poor girl. I have been told that I have a chip on my shoulder because of my activism and advocacy for people with disabilities.

Some people even tried to push my locked wheelchair to get me out of a place where they thought I did not belong there. Others have been disgusted meeting me in person and others have told me "There is always something" with me. Without overlooking the comments I have heard telling me to be aware that I could cause revulsion to some average people. That I could never be somebody in life because I was already nothing, nobody, or that God had punished me with my disability. That I am burnout, that I need mental health support to acculturate, or that I need to go back where I belong, just to mention some because I can go and on, being multicultural brings to my life many and constant challenges.

Orientation

Why are my experiences interacting with different cultures important enough to be shared?
I think my experiences during cultural interactions are important to share because I do not recommend, to anybody, to mix behaviors to blend into a culture to fit-in or to adjust. It is difficult to realize the struggles of physical and emotional adjustments that I, as a multicultural person, experience. The challenges I encounter as a person with multiple social classifications are innumerable, happen daily, and constantly.

Some of the challenges I faced encouraged me to mix behaviors and, sometimes, to segregate avoiding those complicated interactions and to keep them away from my life's trajectory. The

234

interactions pretending to be docile, quiet, submissive, dramatic, pleasant, adapted, integrated, acculturated, marginalized, and suffering trying to please society's expectations are hard to carry with me, they are disturbing, and make my life's pathway harder than it should be. I only wanted to be me; I only wanted to integrate to my new culture as an active member of the community.

After listening to a Latina girl, 11 or 12 years old who told me, "Cecy, when my friends and I are playing on our street and we see the police driving around we say, 'act White'", the girl laughed. I asked, "You're kidding me, right?" She responded, "Nope! We are Mexicans!" My first thought was that the girl and her friends were mixing behaviors unintentionally. I inquired, "How do Whites act? Or what do they do that the police will not bother them?" Her brother, about 13 years old, joined the conversation and both shared their experiences as Latinos or Mexicans. They also shared how they have to behave to fit-in or to protect themselves from stereotypes, profiles, or discrimination, although they are Americans by birth.

I was not surprised or shocked listening to their stories, but it hurt. My experiences were or are the same or worse adding my other social classifications. I acted quiet, happy, dramatic, disabled, satisfied, normal, evading speaking Spanish, or making sure people from Mexico do not know I am native from Mexico City or Chilanga, all to please others and to avoid drama. Been there. Done that. The difference among those children and I is that I am an adult; I was an adult when I learned that I needed to mix behaviors to avoid rejection, retaliation, and whatever comes with being different. They are just children developing. They should not have to mix behaviors.

I was sad, deeply sad that children had to mix behaviors to protect themselves from the stereotypes or from the stout profiles targeting certain racial and ethnic minority groups. Mixing behaviors, for me, is more than behaving according to the selected culture, mixing behaviors is hiding the self, the real self, because the self feels threatened by the external situations. Children should feel safe and should not have to face the need to "act White" or to mix behaviors to protect themselves or just to feel safe.

I think my experiences interacting with different cultures are important enough to be shared because mixing behaviors is happening more than known or expected. Mixing behaviors is happening within children, among children, Americans or not, immigrants or not, adults, and perhaps within elderly people as well. I think many people are adopting mixing behaviors as a reality, as a way of living, and as a protective shield, but there is the risk of losing identity trying to fit-in or to adjust –to belong somewhere.

Who influenced me to behave as a cultural chameleon?
I influenced myself to behave as a cultural chameleon to protect my inner self against the angry monster that society carries in its shoulders. I believe on me. I have faith on me. I avoid drama to keep peace in me. I spent and wasted so much time and energy attempting to please the expectations of varied external influences --people. I realized that, at some point in my life, something had destroyed my compound uniqueness, my authentication when my multicultural individuality crossed and conflicted with each other based on perceptions, assumptions, expectations, and desires including my own.

I felt I had to do something to maintain my existence in peace or I would be one more statistic. I influenced myself to behave as a cultural chameleon to protect my inner self, to reach my goals, and to dismiss the possible impact that being different could cause on me. I influenced myself because I am, I have goals, dreams, desires, and being just me does not fit with each one of my social classifications or altogether.

I love dancing, singing, playing, being happy and loud. According to some personality style tests, I am a go-getter and an extroverted, but I can be an introvert as well. Yes. I agree with those tests because I am happy and I am a people person, but I know when to switch between extrovert and introvert or vice versa, depending on the situation. I still sing, dance, joke, and play at home where my dogs do not care if the singer is not JLo or if I cannot move my wheelchair to the music's rhythm. My dogs do not expect me acting to please them as people do.

During my first cultural experiences in which I did not understand the rejection based on my social classifications and the intersection of those classifications, I did not know what to do. I was not sure how to respond and, at the same time, how to avoid retaliation or any other behavior forcing me to protect myself. I realized that if I kept quiet, smiled, or excused myself worked for some situations, but not for others. I could not just become the follower of such angriness road filled with rejection, stereotypes, discrimination, and so forth and still maintain my inner self happy and motivated. There was not a road for me to join and follow. My only option was to build my own pathway to follow and that is what I did by mixing behaviors.

My dreams since I was a child were to have my own place and a dog, to drive, to be a doctor or an attorney, and I wanted to be me. In my young adulthood, living in the US, I wanted to reach the American dream and enjoy the land of the opportunities. I wanted to appreciate what Americans with disabilities have done for people with disabilities and, at the same time, helping them to continue their progress and integrate with them to continue such progress.

I wanted to help the Latino and Hispanic community to tell and show that "si se puede." I wanted to learn as much as I could and living in the land of the opportunities, and those opportunities were available for me too. I was not willing to challenge people, perceptions, or behaviors by fighting, arguing, or confronting anybody in order for me to live my life and to reach my dreams. My option was to mix behaviors to allow myself reaching the most impossible dreams I had. I influenced myself to mix behaviors with a goal in mind, and faith in my heart.

Where do I behave as a cultural chameleon?
I behave as a cultural chameleon everywhere I perceive it as necessary. This could be in conferences, in jobs, in social media, with my family or friends, during appointments with

doctors or medical providers, job interviews, and volunteering. I behave as a cultural chameleon in any social interaction where I perceive people's need of power, people's need to disempowering someone, where I am perceived as vulnerable, and when my challenges are stronger than manageable.

I behave as a cultural chameleon everywhere I see or perceive that my inner self may be disturbed, mistreated, or questioned, where I perceive that my dreams, goals, and plans could be diverged or threatened, where I feel unsafe or unwelcomed, where I perceived a discriminatory, stereotyping, and prejudicing environment. I behave as cultural chameleon when I need to protect my inner self.

When do I believe I need to mix behaviors?
I mix behaviors where I cannot be I, when I perceive high expectations from people, or when the "rules of normality" are strong. I mix behaviors when I perceived the lack of sensitivities to disabilities, or when I feel someone is hungry of power, or when I see that people see me as vulnerable.

These types of situations are common in my daily activities and sometimes, depending on my wiliness to educate, I respond indirectly educating the person or simply ignoring the behavior and continue doing what I need to do. My approach to educate or to ignore could be taken well, wrong, or bad. I have experienced people admiring my self-sufficiency or questioning it. It is up to them to believe what they prefer to believe because I am not willing to explain my life to every person who questions it. What people can think is their problem, not mine. My problem is to do what I need to do without letting negative vibes to disturb me nor my goals. But I had to learn how to do it and how to avoid internalizing its possible effects.

Why do I think is important to make my privacy public?
My thoughtful reflections related to my dissertation's topic helped me to appreciate that my story might relate to other people experiencing multicultural clashes, or to people aiming to deal with one culture at a time, or to people who adopted the strategy of mixing behaviors for

social survival. Mixing behaviors, I believe, is happening strongly and more often and, unfortunately, is affecting multicultural people in a myriad of ways. I think the behavior of mixing behaviors is being adopted as a way of living not as a tool for inner harmony.

When I listened to the children discussing "act White" to protect themselves or to avoid being targeted as an ethnic minority group, confirmed to me that mixing behaviors is happening more than usual. I am not the only one who feels like "fish out of water" or "ni de aquí ni de allá" (neither from here nor there). I am intrigued by the topics of burnout, rejection, losing identity, other topics, and their possible connection with feeling like fish out of water and disclosing my privacy may reveal that this is happening to someone and the topics may relate to other people as well.

I remember I read a journal where the author discussed people losing their third culture could end in violence. What interested me more was to reflect on the excessively violence experienced within the United States and its association of losing the third identity, and the need of mixing behaviors to fit-in or to adjust to a culture. Rejection takes more than coping skills, assertiveness, self-esteem, education, and so forth. Disclosing feelings of rejection takes exposing one's self to vulnerability and retaliation.

I remember one time I was tagged as violent because I spoke up about an aggressive cultural interaction that was affecting me at work and I needed to defend myself. I knew I was going to face retaliation but I took the chance. I had to stop the aggression against me for my own sake. I ended being tagged as violent because I was not willing to accept to continue being harassed, discriminated, and suppressed. Another occasion, or more than once, I spoke up about the difference of treatment I was facing and I was demanded to confront the person discriminating me or I would lose my job. After these experiences and many others, I decided not to speak up to avoid putting myself facing retaliation or making myself exposed to others. I had enough with my cultural interactions; I did not want to add more to my already filled plate.

Who are benefiting from my disclosure?

I want to believe that many people could benefit from my disclosure. Just thinking on the educational potential value that my story could represent, encouraged me to disclose how I manage the intersectionality of cultures. I believe not only multicultural people could benefit from my disclosure but also people around them. I have searched for information related to fitting into different cultures but I could not find any information on how to respond to one culture at a time or when to be or not to be multicultural.

I believe one possible benefit, based on my cultural personal experiences, is to inform scholars, interested professionals, and any other people interested that this is phenomenon is happening more than expected. Another possible benefit is to share that leading oneself through the path desired, is possible by ignoring or stopping negative vibes before the negativity enters and disturbs our inner self. Other possible benefit is to bring awareness to multicultural people that mixing behaviors may be happening without noticing it. I used mixing behaviors for self-protection, but I do not advise anybody to do it as a way of living, this disclosure may benefit someone.

Complicating Action

What do I think are the benefits of mixing behaviors?

I believe the benefits of mixing behaviors are to protect the inner self-peace, to self-empower, and to stop the negative vibes that may contaminate the self. Mixing behaviors could be a strategy to ignore those behaviors that may disturb my life in general. Mixing behaviors could also serve as a protective barrier when cultural interactions are difficult to manage, to comprehend, and confront, and when the intersection of cultures intersect with the already clashing cultural interactions. Mixing behaviors was a strategy I use to lead myself to be who I want to be and where I want to go.

What barriers did I overcome by mixing behaviors?

I can say that mixing behaviors helped me to overcome barriers built by people who, for some reason, have problems with people who look different to them. I have avoided more

240

tagging, aggressions, retaliation, disempowering, and so forth; mainly I have overcame suppression. I realized that cultural problems are extremely distracting, hurt deep inside, are confusing, and can lead the self to an unfamiliar territory where the self could get lost. Mixing behaviors helped me to reach the American dream, to reach some of the opportunities this land offers, but mainly, to keep my own faith and beliefs strong and intact.

I remember the first time I heard the word "token." I did not know what people meant when they talked about a "token." I knew a token as a coin or special coin. During my first permanent job, someone told me that I was the "token" of the office. I was somewhat proud when I heard her saying that because I thought I was special. How cool is that! The office's token! One day I told to another coworker about being proud to be the token of the office and laughing she explained to me what token meant. My multiple cultures or my social classifications made me a token for the organizations.

I was quiet because I was not sure how to respond to her explanation. I was wondering if she wanted me to cry, be upset, or be happy. Internally I was OK with it. If my social classifications as minority help me to get a well-paid job and to be known nationally, I was not certain how such tag would affect me. I was confused on what behavior adopt based on her description of the term as something very low, discriminatory label, and was even more confusing when she explained that my position was specially created for me because of my social classifications or my tokenism, and to do me a service.

I could get offended, hurt, discouraged, but mixing behaviors helped me to overcome the idea of being a token or that my position was developed based on pity. I had a job, I was making an income that paid for my expenses, and if the job was specially created for me, I thank God for letting me be the office's token and for letting the boss creating a job just for me. The pity part bothered me, but instead of upsetting me, I gained new skills and became a skillful employee to become an asset better than the token. I remember when I resigned that specific position the organization had to hire five people to replace me and my tokenism –I was unique.

How did I manage discrimination, stigmatization, or rejection by mixing behaviors?

I did not manage discrimination, stigmatization, or rejection I only ignore the behaviors. Mixing behaviors helped me to recognize and to ignore those behaviors, and empowered me to lead myself to an inner save place. I learned how to detect the behaviors that could affect my inner self as a multicultural person carrying many social classifications and by mixing behaviors I could move forward or move on safely.

I remember I wanted to open my own business. I wanted the freedom of working from home, planning my own time with my own deadlines. I wanted to be an independent worker, a free spirit. I was doing OK as a hired employee, with my own space, fair responsibilities, and doing the advocacy and activism that I love to do, but I was missing something –I needed a change.

I was invited to sell insurance for a large company, I struggled to pass the license test, but after trying a couple of times, I got my license on the mail and a mentor was assigned to me. I had a friend playing as my mentor, but I needed someone recognized and qualified by the company as my official mentor, and then one was assigned to me. I was told that I would be an asset for my new mentor because he was very successful and needed some help with the Latino community. He needed someone who spoke Spanish and understood the culture. The "token" me was the perfect match.

I could help my new mentor not only speaking Spanish to outreach the Latino or Hispanic communities, but also I could help him empathizing with some people because I had a physical disability. I agreed that I was an asset for my new mentor's group and for the company. I planned to make my label as a "token" to work benefiting my new group, my new mentor, and myself. I had the skills and the determination to make a fantastic income.

One evening, my new mentor called me requesting to meet next afternoon to talk about my new position and responsibilities. We agreed to meet in a coffee shop in a large local casino. I remember I was excited! Next day, I arrived to the casino's coffee shop a few minutes earlier to find a comfortable table where I could accommodate my wheelchair without moving people around asking them to make some space for me. Few minutes later, I saw a handsome White man, dressed with shorts and a t-shirt walking toward me. He looked like a movie star, the perfect profile of a Caucasian male.

He said hi, introduced himself, and placed much insurance material on the table. After explaining the material he said, "Cecilia, well, I hope you understand that I cannot take you with my clients. I do not know what they would think about me taking someone like you, you know, in a wheelchair with me. You are on your own. Good luck to you." I remember his words felt like ice cubes. I did not know what to say, I did not know how to react, I did not expect anything similar, and I responded, "Yes. I understand and I thank you for your honesty. Good luck to you too."

The experience illustrates how I was treated and how I responded by mixing behaviors. I could yell discrimination right there in front of the casino's clients, employees, and whoever else was there. I could not do anything because my social classifications against a White male would work against me. I could even get deportation if I step into a jail. Filing a lawsuit against him was not an option either because it was my word against his. I would win nothing but I would lose all. Mixing behaviors gave me the opportunity to be safe, calmed, and not to give up the best of me to the situation.

Yes, when I went back home, I cried and cried, I felt bad, and I questioned my own reaction, but I was in my home and nobody could see how much such action hurt me. I could not work with the group any longer, I could not motivate myself to sell their product, I lost faith and trust in them, I had to move on in peace. I knew that not only I could file a formal complaint against the entire company, but I also knew I could bring strong problems to my life in addition to lose the case.

Other experiences similar but less obvious include my interactions with some doctors or with other professionals from the medical sector. I have encountered some doctors patting my head like a kid, one doctor told me that he did not make miracles, and one doctor told me that I did not need to have sex that was not necessary in my case. Other doctors diagnosing assumed that my disability was the cause of my illnesses (diabetes), and some doctors assumed I have the same needs of a person who lost mobility in an accident –paraplegic or quadriplegic- because I use a wheelchair. One doctor did not allow me to go into his office, although I had an appointment to see him, he personally took my X-rays to the waiting room, handed them to me, and told me to find another doctor. Just to mention some.

Mixing behaviors helped me to recognize and to ignore wrong perceptions, assumptions, different treatment, and so forth because I was able to move forward or to move on without putting my peace and safety at risk. In many occasions, I am perceived, as I need to be fix or that I am unfixable. I am not a broken doll and cannot fix me, but letting people know about their wrongdoing or of my thoughts and feelings could mean to take a high risk for me.

How and why mixing behaviors play as a shield or bubble to protect achieving my dreams and goals.

Smiling and listening have been my best tools when mixing behaviors to encourage people to stop, to move on, or to change the behavior. Smiling influences my brain not to process the negative information and serves as a tool to disarm the person's behavior. The best way I can describe this process is like "me entra por un oído y me sale por el otro (the information goes in one ear and out the other)."

Listening and watching body language have also helped me to make sure I am not mistaking the situation. I learned to distinguish between administration and personal discriminatory behavior. I know some people do not know when they are discriminating because they are following some policy, like a job's policy, and they trust their employer. Some people are so good at discriminating that their behavior could be overlooked.

I remember that in my masters' graduation ceremony, I was among graduates, wearing my graduation gown like every graduated, and I "was parked" on the corridor next to the graduates' seats waiting to hear my name. I made sure to lock my wheelchair to avoid sliding down the corridor. Suddenly, I felt someone grabbing my wheelchair's back handles and felt like my wheelchair shook. I immediately smiled thinking it was a friend or someone who knew me and wanted to congratulate me for my achieving.

I turned my face to greed the person, but I did not know her. This woman kept trying to push or pull my chair saying, "Mom, you need to move, this is not your place. You do not belong here mom." She kept trying to push my wheelchair but it was locked. I told her that I was graduating and soon they would call my name. I could not leave the corridor and that specific space was designated to me by the university's administration. She kept telling me that I did not belong there and I needed to move at the same time she was forcing my wheelchair to move until the graduate next to me stood up and told the woman to leave because I was part of the group and I was not going to leave. The woman left and the graduate looked at me and said, "Aren't you shocked? How can you smile? I would be throwing a fit! That was horrible!" I told her that it was our graduation and I could not do an act or drama that day, that I would leave it for another day or week.

I wrote a letter and mailed it to the administration office telling what happened and I recommended sensitivity training for employees. The company did not answer to my letter, meaning they ignored my compliant and my request. I took the risk of mailing the written letter because I was "forced" by a friend to do it. She said to do it or she would do it, and knowing her, she could get me in trouble. I moved on and left the company alone hoping the letter raised some awareness because what the employee did was wrong and emotionally disturbed not only me but also the witness.

I cannot even image what could have happened if either the employee took me away or if I reacted and protested right there in the middle of the ceremony. My assumptions are that I would be arrested for some reason and the employee would be in the right arguing that in an emergency my wheelchair obstructed the pathway of some people. I would lose either way. Smiling took me to the end of my graduation without even recalling the woman I thought she wanted to congratulate me for my achievement.

I remember that in one place I worked, there was a fire drill and I requested to be except of the drill because of my disability. The office manager told me that I had to participate. I asked if presenting an ADA would help me not being part of the drill, but answered that the ADA did not exist in that office and if I wanted my job I had to participate. She was laughing and singing, I think even dancing, and I overlooked her behavior.

I was concerned because the office was in the third floor. I looked in eBay for something that could help me and I ordered a special chair. I learned to use the chair and brought it to the office. A week after I brought the chair, the office manager decided to have a fire drill. She had two of my coworkers helping me going down the stairs with the heavy special chair. Two months later she had them to do it again but this time she changed the "helpers." They struggled as much as I was embarrassed.

A few months after I resigned such position, I was hired to work for an office in the third floor also. In order to enter in the new job building I had to talk to security officers. When I talked to them, I offered to bring my "special" chair with me, and they looked at me with their eyes wide opened and said, "What are you talking about? A special chair? For what?" I told them about my experience with the fire drill in my previous employer and they were astonished. "No Cecilia. That is against the ADA! They put your life at risk and the life of your former coworkers helping you! Wow!"

I said and thought the same thing, "Wow!" I really missed that one, but I am not sure how mixing behaviors would change my situation there. I did not show my truth feelings about doing the fire drill, but I bought a special chair to comply with her demands. I think my only option would have been mixing my behaviors to sign, laugh, and dance as she was doing when perpetrated her discriminatory behavior.

I remember, there I could not mix behaviors even trying the hardest I could because the discrimination against a specific group was very strong. My behavior of smiling and listening to please others did not agree with my morals and values, I could not join their group and discriminate too. I could not become a quiet and docile follower because their behavior was against my morals and values. I moved on, but I remember I mixed behaviors when I left. I smiled and thanked them, but I was praying for them to go to hell and calling karma to the rescue of those women being victimized.

Evaluation

How would my life be today if I had not mixed behaviors?

If I had not adopted mixing behaviors I am not sure where my life would be today. Perhaps, I would be here in America suppressed by many cultures or I would be acculturated or molded as desired. Or I would be still dreaming about having my own place and a dog, driving, learning, and confirming the impossibility of my dreams. Or I would be back to Mexico City to continue begging money on the streets, depending on my relatives, and drinking. Perhaps I would be a multitude follower following others' pathways, without illusions, dreams, goals, personal influence, or self-leadership. I would be just one more person lost within the massive angriness made by many cultures and their intersection.

How did I manage my inner emotions when I noticed I needed to mix behaviors?

I managed my inner emotions when I noticed I had to mix behaviors by talking to my self and following its lead. I always told myself "It will be well!" or "It will be OK" to calm my inner emotions and to clear my mind in order to follow the leading of myself. At home, where nobody saw me, I talked to my dogs and I cried if necessary. I shared my emotions a few times with a couple of people who I called friends, but their response was negative, intense, and suggested fighting back without thinking of the reprisals against me, then I decided not to share but with my dogs.

Many times, after the cultural experience (or to stop the interaction) I went outdoors with the excuse of smoking. If I could not go anywhere else, I distracted myself singing in my head or counting in silence. Many times, in my mind, I made fun at the situation to make me laugh, but mainly I distracted myself and made me feel at peace.

How did I know I needed to mix behaviors?

I learned how to perceive or understand people's body language before or during my social interaction, their nonverbal communication toward me indicates the moment to mix behaviors and to remind myself of my purpose of being there. Words or behaviors do not mean much to me. I use people's body language as an indicator, which helps me to be aware of possible hidden feelings, and helps me to evaluate the expectations or the situation.

Many people think that not saying anything or pretending being "nice" to me would be enough to cover their negative perception. Their body language as staring or eye movement, facial gestures, hand movements, and the closeness or avoidance to me (or my wheelchair) most of the time, uncovers their truth thinking. Once again, I remind myself the reasons I am there or what I need from being at that specific place. If it is worth, I finish my business, but if not I move on. I do not find any reason to fight what is not fightable. I am not willing to educate the uneducable.

I remember in a Latino or Hispanic conference that I attended because of my job description, I was the only person in a wheelchair, as usual. I saw a table available close to the exit and with enough space for me to move around or leave the conference room if necessary. I saw people walking next to my table, peeked at me, and kept walking. First, I thought they believed that such table was assigned to people with wheelchairs only and they kept walking to find another table, but I was wrong.

There were no more tables available but mine, a large table that could fit many people, but people were grabbing the chairs from my table and making space within other already filled tables. I continued encouraging myself to think that my table looked like an assigned table until three people arriving late sat down, one left to talk with someone else at front, I thought. Actually she went to find available spaces or to make some, came back told the other two, grabbed their stuff, chairs, and left.

I attended the conference all myself in a large table, nobody sat with me. There was no hi, hello, hola, bye, adios, or so long, nothing, just absolute rejection. I sat there, ate, and talked to myself. I had two options leave the conference or forget about what happened. I could not leave because I needed to report to my boss about the conference. I had to stay and forget about what happened. I felt some tears in my eyes and I told myself to smile to help my brain not to let the experience in. When I reported to my boss, I also mixed behaviors and I reported what I have learned saying that it was very informative. I could not tell her what happened because I noticed she had some issues with multicultural people. She would blame the entire experience on me or she would make a statement remarking my experience next time I needed to attend a similar event.

I avoided attending Latino or Hispanic conferences or reunions or events or anything that could put me at risk of rejection, I preferred not going, but I had to attend a few more because of my jobs' requirements. The token me! Similar situation happened in one, but I already had the experience then it was not difficult to be there to get what I needed and ignore those damaging behaviors.

In another reunion or small conference, with just a few Latinas or Hispanic women and two or three White women, I gave up sharing my life and my experiences. That is what we supposed to do in that summit, sharing our experiences as women of color. I did not think I needed to mix behaviors there and I did not. I even encouraged myself to letting people (like me) know what I have encountered during my social interactions, but I did not disclose mixing identities or behaving as a cultural chameleon. Something told me to keep that strategy to myself. I was not sure about the reasons but I listened to my leader (self) and kept it for me.

At the end of the event, something told me to turn slowly my face around to see a group of the summit's attendees chatting away from me, and then I noticed the organizer's body language when she was looking at me, I smiled, but felt like cold water running from my head to toes. I realized that I was the "unique" of the reunion, I understood that I was there, invited to be part of the group, to find out how much of a menace I represented for the organizer. I think all people there were invited for a specific reason, and they did not seem to have more or less than the organizer, just me, my wheelchair. Realizing such low behavior gave me the goosebumps, I felt very vulnerable, and next day I was a very different person. I was quiet, I smiled, I avoided participating, I thanked the women for the invitation, I told them that it was an amazing summit, and I drove home.

How did I learn that mixing behaviors could be a strategy to overcome social barriers? After crying much and beginning to believe what some people told me I was and what I should do with my life, I confronted my inner self by asking if a man in a wheelchair could be advertised as an inspiration, why would I be taken as a misfortune. Something was wrong with me.

I went to the local libraries looking for information to answer my self-inquiry. I also bought several books for my personal use. The books were on self-development, none mentioned about hiding feelings or pretending to be who I was not to meet society's expectations, but many of those books' authors discussed the need to protect one's inner self of any negativity, disempowering, or any other behavior that may disturb one's own progress, existence, or identity. Some authors discussed the use of self-frequency, human aura manipulation to deal with challenges, praying to bring the "I" in hard situations, and so forth.

Some authors indicated to walk away from negativity and to join positive people who could influence one's progress, but to walk away, for me, meant to walk away from everybody, including some relatives, and that was not an option. I concluded that the best option for me was to walk away internally by building a bubble around me to protect myself against the angriness of many cultures that wanted to push their negativity into me affecting my inner self.

After learning about different concepts, ideas, and theories of self-development, including personal power, mental strength, self-empowering, self-leadership, determination, making decisions, leadership, self-frequency, self-pray, and many others concepts, I decided to implement my new learning by mixing behaviors to avoid bad and negative vibes, and to get what I needed and wanted. My strategy of mixing behaviors was not to manipulate or influence people's behaviors, but to make my life's trajectory easier than planned or expected by society's expectations and demands.

How and why did I keep my behavior of mixing identities as a sealed personal secret?
I am honest, authentic, and me when the person deserves interacting with me. I could be the best friend to have, the best resource, and I give my best to who deserves it. I kept my behavior of mixing identities as a secret because there is too much rage within society that disclosing would cause me to be judged and blamed for my inner defending strategy. People would question my behavior (natural or adopted) and I would have (or will) be tagged with more labels that I do not need, including a mental illness.

Mixing behaviors was not easy to learn, to use, and it is difficult to understand. Some people already had "diagnosed" me with low self-esteem, or as a pleaser, or coward, or loser, and so forth, without owning their part. I did not find any reason to share with nobody about my need of mixing behaviors to deal with them. It was my strategy and nobody else's business.

I never told them, nobody, and if they figured it out, nobody talked to me about it. Probably people thought I had some type of mental problem since I use a wheelchair, because for many people, being in a wheelchair means having a mental disorder too. I did not feel the need to disclose and to explain like "do not ask, do not tell."

How people acted or re-acted when noticed I mixed behaviors?

251

I am not sure people could tell when I mixed behaviors, but I can tell that many people got somewhat aggressive or desperate because I did not react the way they wanted me to react. I have encountered furious people demanding I confront them, or to respond to their aggressions. Some kept pushing the issue of ignoring them, others called me loser, hypocrite, coward, and on. I think that even if people could tell that I am mixing behaviors they would blame it on me. I am not saying that they should blame themselves for my own behavior, but I believe people should take responsibility and understand that if someone, in this case me, is changing identities is because the person feels threatened by his or her external environment.

How did I respond to people when they noticed I mixed behaviors?
I do not think people have noticed when I mix behaviors. I am very good at it and my change is subtle enough that people do not notice any intentional change. Mixing behaviors or not, I am respectful, nice, kind, sociable, cordial, helpful, and a good friend. I think that makes people to ignore or not to recognize that I needed to protect myself of their behaviors.

Result

Why do I continue mixing behaviors during social situations?
Although my interactions are less, hence my mixing behaviors, but I continue doing it because discrimination, stereotyping, rejecting, and so on will never end, or at least in my lifetime. I will be in a wheelchair for the rest of my life, and I will be Latina, woman, immigrant and else or multicultural until I died. I think that stopping now would let the outside angriness into my soul. If I do not continue mixing behaviors, I could be an easy target for those who need power to exist.

How is mixing behaviors easier now than before?
It never has been easy or pleasing, and it gets more difficult each day. I am physically tired and mentally exhausted. The intersection of cultures makes it even harder to the point that I do not want to mix anymore, but I do not want to confront it constantly either. The intersection of cultures is so hard to distinguish because I am not sure which culture or

intersection affects more than the other does. Sometimes I do not even try. I just move on or shut down. I feel that I do not care much anymore.

What did I gain by mixing behaviors?

By mixing behaviors, I gained to maintain my inner peace, to reach many of my goals, to strength my belief and faith on me, and to ignore what I do not have to own. Mixing behaviors gave me the opportunity to work, to have a house with a large backyard for my four dogs and a place for them. I also have traveled, and my name is known on national and international organizations. I became a strong advocate and an activist, although I had to protect myself within those movements.

What did I lose by mixing behaviors?

I lost energy and desire. I feel like "dejar que el mundo ruede (let the world roll)" and to continue my life's trajectory. It is hard to smile when, inside, I feel like speaking up, crying or saying, "I see you at court!" instead of saying "Good luck to you!"

What happened during mixing behaviors that I believe my feelings and emotions are vulnerable today?

I was defending myself constantly from the strong monster that lives within society and perpetrates unfair acts against people who look different. My feelings and emotions feel vulnerable today because I am worn-out and older. I know, sooner I will fall into other social classifications because of my age, and whatever else comes with it. I am not sure how I will ignore discrimination, stereotyping, and rejection adding more classifications to my existence.

How do I know that my feelings and emotions are stronger and not weaker?

I know that becoming a doctoral learner have changed my life in a very positive way, and I believe that some my feelings and emotions are stronger. I am still not sure how my doctorate degree could influence people to change their behaviors against my social classifications. What I can say is that my feelings and emotions are stronger because I belief on me, I trust myself, and I have faith on me stronger than I did when I immigrated to the U.S. and encountered the issues of being a person with multiple cultures.

How perceiving the need of mixing behaviors during social interactions has affected my trust on other people?

I trust people until I see their body language when interacting with me, if they communicate what they are not showing and I need to mix behaviors, the trust is gone. The woman who mentioned, "There is always something" with me, I trusted her for over ten years, I behave me with her, I shared many experiences with her, and she never gave me the need to mix behaviors interacting with her. Immediately after her comment, the trust vanished and now my interactions with her are through mixing behaviors. I feel vulnerable because I am not sure if she shared with someone else that, there is always something with me or if she thinks or tells that, I have a problem based on her perception. I feel sad because I thought she was my cultural competent friend.

Coda

Where do I perceive myself now compared to before mixing behaviors?

I perceive myself as following my life's pathway; continue trying, looking, achieving, and dreaming. I do not need to question my behavior or my existence wondering the reasons people would treat me differently even if I treated them with respect. I perceived myself as being where I wanted to be before mixing behaviors, but if I had not adopt such strategy I would be somewhere else dominated by the angriness of many cultures.

What could have happened if I did not mix behaviors?

If I did not mix behaviors, I would be lost and dominated. Dominated by the senselessness against people who look different, dominated by people who need power and make others vulnerable, dominated by violence, and dominated by dependency and control. I would be lost in an unknown sphere.

Why do I want to continue mixing behaviors during social interactions?

I do not what to continue mixing behaviors during social interactions, but I do not want to initiate what I have avoided or ignored by mixing behaviors for long time. If I want to continue is because I want to feel safe, secure, and in peace.

What does mixing behaviors represent for me now compared when I did not know about mixing behaviors as a strategy to continue my path in life?

Mixing behaviors, for me, represent a strategy for safety, to avoid problems, to stop negative vibes, and to allow myself to listen and follow my self-leadership. By mixing behaviors, I could stop any reaction to a negative or problematic interaction that could bring something bad or wrong to my life. This strategy helped me to get to a place that many people told me I could not get because it was too high for me to reach. It helped me taking or leaving a sense of an interaction. It assisted me to move on just in time to avoid the unexpected.

It helped me not to feel forced to explain my life to others and finding excuses for not doing what they told me I should do based on how I was. It helped me to take the positive of the negative. I became a happy token, with a wannabe tag, who does not belong here, there, or over there, but who knows how to build a pathway on her own.